The
Around
the World
Cookbook

*Over 350 authentic
recipes from the world's
best-loved cuisines*

HERMES
HOUSE

This edition published by Hermes House
27 West 20th Street, New York, NY 10011

HERMES HOUSE books are available for bulk purchase for sales promotion
and for premium use. For details, write or call the sales director,
Hermes House, 27 West 20th Street, New York, NY 10011;
(800) 354-9657

Hermes House is an imprint of
Anness Publishing Inc.

ISBN 1 84038 111 6

Publisher: Joanna Lorenz
Senior Cookery Editor: Linda Fraser
Editor: Sarah Ainley
Design: Siân Keogh and Ian Sandom
Jacket design: Simon Wilder
Photography: William Adams-Lingwood, Steve Baxter, James Duncan,
Amanda Heywood, Patrick McLeavey, Thomas Odulate and Juliet Piddington
Recipes: Carla Capalbo, Kit Chan, Carole Clements, Silvana Franco,
Rosamund Grant, Rebekah Hassan, Masaki Ko, Elizabeth Lambert Ortiz,
Ruby Le Bois, Sallie Morris, Laura Washburn and Elizabeth Wolf-Cohen
Illustrator: Madeleine David

*The material in this book was previously published
as part of the Creative Cooking Library series.*

Printed and bound in Germany

© Anness Publishing Limited 1998
Updated © 1999
1 3 5 7 9 10 8 6 4 2

CONTENTS

Introduction

*How often have you wished you could recreate in your own kitchen
a favorite take-away dish or one once enjoyed while travelling
abroad? Holidays in far flung places have increased our awareness of
different foods, and restaurants on every street corner now offer dishes
that not so long ago would have been unfamiliar. This cookbook takes
its inspiration from some of the world's most exciting cuisines and
brings together a collection which celebrates the diversity of traditional
cooking styles around the globe. Most of the recipes use accessible fresh
ingredients and store-cupboard staples, and even the more exotic foods
are now commonly available from supermarkets and delicatessens.
From Africa, India and the Orient, through Europe to the Americas,
the classic cuisines of the world are at your fingertips.*

AFRICA

Lamb and Pumpkin Soup

INGREDIENTS

Serves 4

4 ounces split black-eyed peas, soaked
  for 1–2 hours, or overnight
1½ pounds shoulder of lamb, cut into
  medium-size chunks
1 teaspoon chopped fresh thyme, or
  ½ teaspoon dried
2 bay leaves
5 cups stock or water
1 onion, sliced
8 ounces pumpkin, diced
2 black cardamom pods
1½ teaspoons ground turmeric
1 tablespoon chopped fresh cilantro
½ teaspoon caraway seeds
1 fresh green chili, seeded and chopped
2 green bananas
1 carrot
salt and freshly ground black pepper

1 Drain the black-eyed peas, place them in a saucepan and cover with fresh cold water.

2 Bring the peas to a boil, boil rapidly for 10 minutes and then reduce the heat and simmer, covered, for 40–50 minutes until tender, adding more water if necessary. Remove from the heat and set aside to cool.

3 Meanwhile, put the lamb in a large saucepan, add the thyme, bay leaves and stock or water and bring to a boil. Cover and simmer over a moderate heat for 1 hour or until tender.

4 Add the onion, pumpkin, cardamom, turmeric, cilantro, caraway, chili and seasoning and stir. Bring back to a simmer and then cook, uncovered, for 15 minutes or until the pumpkin is tender, stirring occasionally.

5 When the peas are cool, spoon into a blender or food processor with their liquid and blend to a smooth purée.

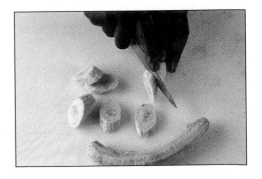

6 Cut the bananas into medium slices and the carrot into thin slices. Stir into the soup with the peas and cook for 10–12 minutes, until the vegetables are tender. Adjust seasoning and serve.

Assortment of Plantains

This melange of succulent sweet and savory plantains makes a delicious crunchy appetizer.

INGREDIENTS

Serves 4
2 green plantains
1 yellow plantain
½ onion
pinch of garlic powder
salt and cayenne pepper
vegetable oil, for shallow frying

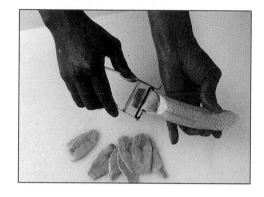

1 Heat the oil in a large frying pan over a moderate heat. While the oil is heating, peel one of the green plantains and cut into very thin rounds, using a vegetable peeler.

2 Fry the plantain rounds in the oil for about 3 minutes, turning, until golden brown. Drain on paper towels and keep warm.

3 Coarsely grate the other green plantain and put on a plate. Slice the onion into wafer-thin shreds and mix with the grated plantain.

4 Heat a little more oil in the frying pan and fry handfuls of the mixture for 2–3 minutes, until golden, turning once. Drain on paper towels and keep warm with the green plantain rounds.

5 Heat a little more oil in the frying pan and, while it is heating, peel the yellow plantain, cut in half lengthwise and dice. Sprinkle with garlic powder and cayenne pepper and then fry in the hot oil until golden brown, turning to brown evenly. Drain on paper towels and then arrange the three varieties of cooked plantains in shallow dishes. Sprinkle with salt and serve as a snack.

Cameroon Suya

INGREDIENTS

Serves 4

1 pound round or flank steak
½ teaspoon sugar
1 teaspoon garlic powder
1 teaspoon ground ginger
1 teaspoon paprika
1 teaspoon ground cinnamon
pinch of chili powder
2 teaspoons onion salt
½ cup peanuts, finely crushed
vegetable oil, for brushing

2 Mix the sugar, garlic powder, spices and onion salt together in a small bowl. Add the crushed peanuts, then add this mixture to the steak, mixing well so that the spices are worked into the meat.

1 Trim the steak of any fat and then cut into 1-inch wide strips. Place in a bowl or a shallow dish.

3 Thread the steak on to six satay sticks, pushing the meat close together. Place in a shallow dish, cover loosely with foil and let marinate in a cool place for a few hours.

4 Preheat a broiler or barbecue grill. Brush the meat with a little oil and then cook over a moderate heat for about 15 minutes, until evenly brown.

—— COOK'S TIP ——

If barbecueing the meat, try to avoid it cooking too quickly or burning.

Akkras

These tasty fritters, are almost always made from black-eyed peas. For a quicker version: after soaking the peas, drain and purée without removing the skins.

INGREDIENTS

Serves 4

1¼ cups dried black-eyed peas
1 onion, chopped
1 red chili, halved, with seeds removed
 (optional)
⅔ cup water
oil, for deep frying

1 Soak the black-eyed peas in plenty of cold water for 6–8 hours or overnight. Drain the beans and then, with a brisk action, rub the beans between the palms of your hands to remove the skins.

2 Return the beans to the bowl, cover with water and the skins will float to the surface. Discard the skins and soak the beans again for 2 hours.

3 Place the beans in a blender or food processor with the onion, chili, if using, and a little water. Blend to make a thick paste. Pour the mixture into a large bowl and whisk for a few minutes.

4 Heat the oil in a large heavy saucepan and fry spoonfuls of the mixture for 4 minutes until golden brown.

Nigerian Meat Stew

This recipe was adapted from a Nigerian stew, originally made with meats of different flavors, such as beef, liver and mutton, along with dried fish or snails, and served with yam or rice.

INGREDIENTS

Serves 4–6

1½ pounds oxtail, chopped
1 pound stewing beef, cubed
1 pound skinless, boneless chicken breasts, chopped
2 garlic cloves, crushed
1½ onions
2 tablespoons palm or vegetable oil
2 tablespoons tomato paste
14-ounce can plum tomatoes
2 bay leaves
1 teaspoon dried thyme
1 teaspoon allspice
salt and freshly ground black pepper

1 Place the oxtail in a large saucepan, cover with water and bring to a boil. Skim the surface of any froth, then cover and cook for 1½ hours, adding more water as necessary.

2 Add the beef and continue to cook for another hour or until tender.

3 Meanwhile, season the chicken with the crushed garlic and coarsely chop one of the onions.

4 Heat the oil in a large saucepan over a moderate heat and fry the chopped onion for about 5 minutes until soft. Stir in the tomato paste, cook briskly for a few minutes, then add the chicken. Stir well and cook gently for 5 minutes.

5 Meanwhile, place the plum tomatoes and the remaining half onion in a food processor and blend to a purée. Stir into the chicken mixture with the bay leaves, thyme, allspice and seasoning.

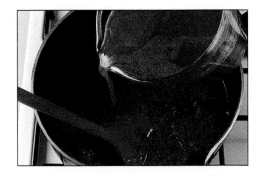

6 Add about 2½ cups of stock from the cooked oxtail and beef and simmer for 35 minutes.

7 Add the oxtail and beef to the chicken. Heat gently, adjust the seasoning and serve hot.

Lamb Tagine with Cilantro and Spices

This Moroccan-style stew can be made with chops or cutlets and either marinated for a few hours before cooking or cooked immediately after seasoning.

INGREDIENTS

Serves 4
4 lamb chops or cutlets
2 garlic cloves, crushed
pinch of saffron strands
½ teaspoon ground cinnamon, plus extra to garnish
½ teaspoon ground ginger
1 tablespoon chopped fresh cilantro
1 tablespoon chopped fresh parsley
1 onion, finely chopped
3 tablespoons olive oil
1¼ cups lamb stock
½ cup blanched almonds, to garnish
1 teaspoon sugar
salt and freshly ground black pepper

1 Season the lamb with the garlic, saffron, cinnamon, ginger and a little salt and black pepper. Place on a large plate and sprinkle with the cilantro, parsley and onion. Cover loosely and set aside in the fridge for a few hours to marinate.

2 Heat the oil in a large frying pan, over a moderate heat. Add the marinated lamb and all the herbs and onion from the dish.

3 Fry for 1–2 minutes, turning once, then add the stock, bring to a boil and simmer gently for 30 minutes, turning the chops once.

4 Meanwhile, heat a small frying pan over a moderate heat, add the almonds and dry fry until golden, shaking the pan occasionally to make sure they color evenly. Transfer to a bowl and set aside.

5 Transfer the chops to a serving plate and keep warm. Increase the heat under the pan and boil the sauce until reduced by about half. Stir in the sugar. Pour the sauce over the chops and sprinkle with the fried almonds and a little extra ground cinnamon.

COOK'S TIP

Lamb tagine is a fragrant dish, originating in North Africa. It is traditionally made in a cooking dish known as a tagine, from which it takes its name. This dish consists of a shallow pot with a conical lid. It has a narrow opening to let steam escape, while retaining the flavor.

Beef in Eggplant Sauce

When served with boiled yam or rice, this makes a hearty dish.

INGREDIENTS

Serves 4

1 pound stewing beef
1 teaspoon dried thyme
3 tablespoons palm or vegetable oil
1 large onion, finely chopped
2 garlic cloves, crushed
4 canned plum tomatoes, chopped, plus
    4 tablespoons of the juice
1 tablespoon tomato paste
½ teaspoon allspice
1 fresh red chili, seeded and chopped
3¾ cups stock or water
1 large eggplant, about 12 ounces
salt and freshly ground black pepper

1 Cut the beef into cubes and season with ½ teaspoon of the thyme and salt and pepper.

2 Heat 1 tablespoon of the oil in a large saucepan and fry the meat, in batches if necessary, for 8–10 minutes until well browned. Transfer to a bowl using a slotted spoon and set aside.

3 Heat the remaining oil in the saucepan and fry the onion and garlic for a few minutes, then add the tomatoes and tomato juice and simmer for 5–10 minutes, stirring occasionally.

4 Add the tomato paste, allspice, chili and remaining thyme, stir well, then add the reserved beef cubes and the stock or water. Bring to a boil, cover and let the beef mixture simmer gently for 30 minutes.

5 Cut the eggplant into ½-inch dice. Stir into the beef mixture and cook, covered, for another 30 minutes or until the beef is completely tender. Adjust the seasoning and serve hot.

Duck with Sherry and Pumpkin

INGREDIENTS

Serves 6

1 whole duck, about 4–4½ pounds
1 lemon
1 teaspoon garlic powder or 2 garlic
   cloves, crushed
1 teaspoon curry powder
½ teaspoon paprika
¾ teaspoon five-spice powder
2 tablespoons soy sauce
salt and freshly ground black pepper
vegetable oil, for frying

For the sauce

3 ounces pumpkin
1 onion, chopped
4 canned plum tomatoes
1¼ cups medium-dry sherry
1¼ cups water

1 Cut the duck into ten pieces and place in a large bowl. Halve the lemon and squeeze the juice all over the duck and set aside.

2 In a small bowl, mix together the garlic, curry powder, paprika, five-spice powder and salt and pepper and rub into each of the duck pieces.

3 Sprinkle the duck with the soy sauce, cover loosely with plastic wrap and let marinate overnight.

4 To make the sauce, cook the pumpkin in boiling water until tender, then blend to a purée with the onion and tomatoes.

COOK'S TIP

The back and wings of the duck are rather bony, so try and use just the fleshier parts or buy leg or breast portions.

---

5 Pat the duck pieces dry with paper towels, then heat a little oil in a wok or large frying pan and fry the duck for 15 minutes or until crisp and brown. Set aside on a plate.

6 Wipe off the excess oil from the wok or frying pan with paper towels and pour in the pumpkin purée. Add the sherry and a little of the water, then bring to a boil and add the fried duck. Simmer for about 1 hour or until the duck is cooked, adding more water if the sauce becomes too thick. Serve hot and pass soy sauce separately.

Joloff Chicken and Rice

Serve this well-known, colorful West African dish at a dinner party or other special occasion.

INGREDIENTS

Serves 4

2¼-pound chicken, cut into 4–6 pieces
2 garlic cloves, crushed
1 teaspoon dried thyme
2 tablespoons palm or vegetable oil
14-ounce can chopped tomatoes
1 tablespoon tomato paste
1 onion, chopped
1⅞ cups chicken stock or water
2 tablespoons dried shrimp or crayfish, ground
1 green chili, seeded and finely chopped
1½ cups long grain rice, washed

1 Rub the chicken with the garlic and thyme and set aside.

2 Heat the oil in a saucepan until hot but not smoking and then add the chopped tomatoes, tomato paste and onion. Cook over a moderately high heat for about 15 minutes, until the tomatoes are well reduced, stirring occasionally at first and then more frequently as the tomatoes thicken.

3 Reduce the heat a little, add the chicken pieces and stir well to coat with the sauce. Cook for 10 minutes, stirring, then add the stock or water, the dried shrimp or crayfish and the chili. Bring to a boil and simmer for 5 minutes, stirring occasionally.

4 Put the rice in a separate saucepan. Scoop 1¼ cups of the sauce into a 2-cup measure, add water to make up to 1⅞ cups and stir into the rice.

5 Cook, covered, until the liquid is absorbed, place a piece of foil on top of the rice, cover the pan with a lid and cook over a low heat for 20 minutes until the rice is cooked, adding a little more water if necessary.

6 Transfer the chicken pieces to a warmed serving plate. Simmer the sauce until reduced by half. Pour over the chicken and serve with the rice.

Chicken with Lentils

Kuku, this delicious tangy chicken stew, comes from Kenya. The amount of lemon juice can be reduced, if you would prefer a less sharp sauce.

INGREDIENTS

Serves 4–6
6 chicken thighs or pieces
½–¾ teaspoon ground ginger
2 ounces mung beans
4 tablespoons corn oil
2 onions, finely chopped
2 garlic cloves, crushed
5 tomatoes, peeled and chopped
1 green chili, seeded and finely
  chopped
2 tablespoons lemon juice
1¼ cups coconut milk
1¼ cups water
1 tablespoon chopped fresh cilantro
salt and freshly ground black pepper

1 Season the chicken pieces with the ginger and a little salt and pepper and set aside in a cool place to marinate. Meanwhile, boil the mung beans in plenty of water for 35 minutes until soft, drain, and then mash well.

2 Heat the oil in a large saucepan over a moderate heat and fry the chicken pieces, in batches if necessary, until evenly browned. Transfer to a plate and set aside, reserving the oil and chicken juices in the pan.

3 In the same pan, fry the onions and garlic for 5 minutes, then add the tomatoes and chili and cook for another 1–2 minutes, stirring well.

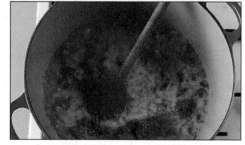

4 Add the mashed mung beans, lemon juice and coconut milk to the pan. Simmer for 5 minutes, then add the chicken pieces and a little water, if the sauce is too thick. Stir in the cilantro and simmer for about 35 minutes or until the chicken is cooked through. Serve with a green vegetable and rice or chappatis.

Fish and Shrimp with Spinach and Coconut

INGREDIENTS

Serves 4

1 pound white fish fillets (cod or
   haddock)
1 tablespoon lemon or lime juice
1/2 teaspoon garlic powder
1 teaspoon ground cinnamon
1/2 teaspoon dried thyme
1/2 teaspoon paprika
1/2 teaspoon freshly ground black pepper
seasoned flour, for dusting
vegetable oil, for shallow frying
salt

For the sauce

2 tablespoons butter or margarine
1 onion, finely chopped
1 garlic clove, crushed
1 1/4 cups coconut milk
4 ounces fresh spinach, finely sliced
8–10 ounces cooked, peeled and
   deveined shrimp
1 red chili, seeded and finely chopped

1 Place the fish fillets in a shallow
bowl and sprinkle with the lemon
or lime juice.

2 Blend together the garlic powder,
cinnamon, thyme, paprika, pepper
and salt and sprinkle over the fish.
Cover loosely with plastic wrap and let
marinate in a cool place or refrigerator
for a few hours.

3 Meanwhile, make the sauce. Melt
the butter or margarine in a large
saucepan and fry the onion and garlic
for 5–6 minutes, until the onion is soft,
stirring frequently.

4 Place the coconut milk and spinach
in a separate saucepan and bring to
the boil. Cook gently for a few minutes
until the spinach has wilted and the
coconut milk has reduced a little, then
set aside to cool slightly.

5 Blend the spinach mixture in a
blender or food processor for 30
seconds and add to the onion with the
shrimp and red chili. Stir well and
simmer gently for a few minutes, then
set aside while cooking the fish.

6 Cut the marinated fish into 2-inch
pieces and dip in the seasoned
flour. Heat a little oil in a large frying
pan and fry the fish pieces, in batches if
necessary, for 2–3 minutes each side
until golden brown. Drain on paper
towels.

7 Arrange the fish on a warmed
serving plate. Gently reheat the
sauce and serve separately in a sauce
boat or poured over the fish.

Tanzanian Fish Curry

INGREDIENTS

Serves 2–3

1 large snapper or red porgy, about
   1–1½ pounds
1 lemon
3 tablespoons vegetable oil
1 onion, finely chopped
2 garlic cloves, crushed
3 tablespoons curry powder
14-ounce can chopped tomatoes
1 heaping tablespoon smooth peanut
   butter, preferably sweet
½ green bell pepper, chopped
2 slices fresh ginger
1 green chili, seeded and chopped
about 2½ cups fish stock
1 tablespoon finely chopped fresh
   cilantro
salt and freshly ground black pepper

1 Season the fish, inside and out, with salt and pepper and place in a shallow bowl. Halve the lemon and squeeze the juice all over the fish. Cover loosely with plastic wrap and let marinate for at least 2 hours.

2 Heat the oil in a large saucepan and fry the onion and garlic for 5–6 minutes or until soft. Reduce the heat, add the curry powder and cook, stirring, for a further 5 minutes.

3 Stir in the tomatoes and then the peanut butter, mixing well, then add the green pepper, ginger, chili and stock. Stir well and simmer gently for 10 minutes.

COOK'S TIP

The fish can be fried before adding to the sauce, if preferred. Dip in seasoned flour and fry in oil in a pan or a wok for a few minutes before adding to the sauce.

4 Cut the fish into pieces and gently lower into the sauce. Simmer for a further 20 minutes or until the fish is cooked, then using a slotted spoon, transfer the fish pieces to a plate.

5 Stir the cilantro into the sauce and adjust the seasoning. If the sauce is very thick, add a little extra stock or water. Return the fish to the sauce, cook gently to heat through and then serve immediately.

Jumbo Shrimp in Almond Sauce

INGREDIENTS

Serves 4

1 pound raw jumbo shrimp
2½ cups water
3 thin slices fresh ginger
2 teaspoons curry powder
2 garlic cloves, crushed
1 tablespoon butter or margarine
4 tablespoons ground almonds
1 green chili, seeded and finely
    chopped
3 tablespoons light cream
salt and freshly ground black pepper

For the vegetables

1 tablespoon mustard oil
1 tablespoon vegetable oil
1 onion, sliced
½ red bell pepper, seeded and thinly
    sliced
½ green bell pepper, seeded and thinly
    sliced
1 chayote, peeled, pitted and cut into
    strips
salt and freshly ground black pepper

1 Shell the shrimp and place the shells in a saucepan with the water and ginger. Simmer, uncovered, for 15 minutes until reduced by half. Strain into a pitcher and discard the shells.

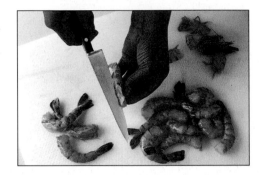

2 Devein the shrimp, place in a bowl and season with the curry powder, garlic and salt and pepper and set aside.

3 Heat the mustard and vegetable oils in a large frying pan, add all the vegetables and stir fry for 5 minutes. Season with salt and pepper, spoon into a serving dish and keep warm.

4 Wipe out the frying pan, then add and melt the butter or margarine and sauté the shrimp for about 5 minutes or until pink. Spoon over the bed of vegetables, cover and keep warm.

5 Add the ground almonds and chili to the pan, stir fry for a few seconds and then add the reserved stock and bring to a boil. Reduce the heat, stir in the cream and simmer for a few minutes, without boiling.

6 Pour the sauce over the vegetables and shrimp before serving.

Fried Porgy in Coconut Sauce

INGREDIENTS

Serves 4

4 medium porgy or butterfish
juice of 1 lemon
1 teaspoon garlic powder
salt and freshly ground black pepper
vegetable oil, for shallow frying

For the coconut sauce

1⅞ cups water
2 thin slices fresh ginger
1 cup coconut cream
2 tablespoons vegetable oil
1 red onion, sliced
2 garlic cloves, crushed
1 green chili, seeded and thinly sliced
1 tablespoon chopped fresh cilantro
salt and freshly ground black pepper

1 Cut the fish in half and sprinkle inside and out with the lemon juice. Season with the garlic powder and salt and pepper and set aside to marinate for a few hours.

2 Heat a little oil in a large frying pan. Pat off the excess lemon juice from the fish, fry in the oil for 10 minutes, turning once. Set aside.

3 To make the sauce, place the water in a saucepan with the slices of ginger, bring to a boil and simmer until the liquid is reduced to just over 1¼ cups. Take out the ginger and reserve, then add the coconut cream to the pan and stir until the coconut has been absorbed.

4 Heat the oil in a wok or large pan and fry the onion and garlic for 2–3 minutes. Add the reserved ginger and coconut stock, the chili and cilantro, stir well and then gently lower in the fish. Simmer for 10 minutes, until the fish is cooked through. Transfer the fish to a warmed serving plate, adjust the seasoning for the sauce and pour over the fish. Serve immediately.

Donu's Lobster Piri Piri

Lobster in its shell, in true Nigerian style, flavored with dried shrimp.

INGREDIENTS

Serves 2–4
2 cooked lobsters, halved
fresh cilantro sprigs, to garnish

For the piri piri sauce
4 tablespoons vegetable oil
2 onions, chopped
1 teaspoon chopped fresh ginger
1 pound fresh or canned tomatoes,
    chopped
1 tablespoon tomato paste
8 ounces cooked, peeled shrimp
2 teaspoons ground coriander
1 green chili, seeded and chopped
1 tablespoon ground dried shrimp or
    crayfish
2½ cups water
1 green bell pepper, seeded and sliced
salt and freshly ground black pepper

1 Heat the oil in a large flameproof casserole and fry the onions, ginger, tomatoes and tomato paste for 5 minutes or until the onions are soft.

2 Add the shrimp, ground coriander, chili and ground shrimp or crayfish and stir well to mix.

3 Stir in the water, green pepper and salt and pepper, bring to a boil and simmer, uncovered, over a moderate heat for about 20–30 minutes or until the sauce is reduced.

4 Add the lobsters to the sauce and cook for a few minutes to heat through. Arrange the lobster halves on warmed serving plates and pour the sauce over each one. Garnish with cilantro sprigs and serve with fluffy white rice.

Tilapia in Turmeric, Mango and Tomato Sauce

Tilapia is widely used in African cooking, but can be found in most fishmarkets. Yam or boiled yellow plantains are good accompaniments.

INGREDIENTS

Serves 4
4 tilapia
¹/₂ lemon
2 garlic cloves, crushed
¹/₂ teaspoon dried thyme
2 tablespoons chopped scallions
vegetable oil, for shallow frying
flour, for dusting
2 tablespoons peanut oil
1 tablespoon butter or margarine
1 onion, finely chopped
3 tomatoes, peeled and finely chopped
1 teaspoon ground turmeric
4 tablespoons white wine
1 green chili, seeded and finely chopped
2¹/₂ cups strong fish stock
1 teaspoon sugar
1 medium underripe mango, peeled and diced
1 tablespoon chopped fresh parsley
salt and freshly ground black pepper

2 Heat a little vegetable oil in a large frying pan, coat the fish with some flour, then fry the fish on both sides for a few minutes until golden brown. Remove with a slotted spoon to a plate and set aside.

4 Add the turmeric, white wine, chili, fish stock and sugar, stir well and bring to a boil, then simmer gently, covered, for 10 minutes.

5 Add the fish and cook over a gentle heat for about 15–20 minutes, until the fish is cooked through. Add the mango, arranging it around the fish, and cook briefly for 1–2 minutes to heat through.

1 Place the fish in a shallow bowl, squeeze the lemon juice all over the fish and gently rub in the garlic, thyme and some salt and pepper. Place some of the scallion in the cavity of each fish, cover loosely with plastic wrap and let marinate for a few hours or overnight in the fridge.

3 Heat the peanut oil and butter or margarine in a saucepan and fry the onion for 4–5 minutes, until soft. Stir in the tomatoes and cook briskly for a few minutes.

6 Arrange the fish on a warmed serving plate with the mango and tomato sauce poured over. Garnish with chopped parsley and serve immediately.

Egusi Spinach and Egg

This is a superbly balanced dish for those who don't eat meat. Egusi, or ground melon seed, is widely used in West African cooking, adding a creamy texture and a nutty flavor to many recipes. It is especially good with fresh spinach.

INGREDIENTS

Serves 4

2 pounds fresh spinach
4 ounces ground egusi
6 tablespoons peanut or vegetable oil
4 tomatoes, peeled and chopped
1 onion, chopped
2 garlic cloves, crushed
1 slice fresh ginger, finely chopped
⅔ cup vegetable stock
1 red chili, seeded and finely chopped
6 eggs
salt

1 Roll the spinach into bundles and cut into strips. Place in a bowl.

2 Cover with boiling water, then drain through a strainer. Press with your fingers to remove excess water.

3 Place the egusi in a bowl and gradually add enough water to form a paste, stirring all the time.

4 Heat the oil in a saucepan, add the tomatoes, onion, garlic and ginger and fry over a moderate heat for about 10 minutes, stirring frequently.

5 Add the egusi paste, stock, chili and salt, cook for 10 minutes, then add the spinach and stir into the sauce. Cook for 15 minutes, uncovered, stirring frequently.

6 Meanwhile hard-boil the eggs, let stand in cold water for a few minutes to cool and then shell and cut in half. Arrange in a shallow serving dish and pour the egusi spinach over the top. Serve hot.

— COOK'S TIP —

Instead of using boiled eggs, you could make an omelet flavored with herbs and garlic. Serve it either whole, or sliced, with the egusi sauce. If you can't find egusi, use ground almonds as a substitute.

Marinated Vegetables on Skewers

These kebabs are a delightful main dish for vegetarians, or can be served as a vegetable side dish.

INGREDIENTS

Serves 4

4 ounces pumpkin
1 red onion
1 small zucchini
1 ripe plantain
1 eggplant
½ red bell pepper, seeded
½ green bell pepper, seeded
12 button mushrooms
4 tablespoons lemon juice
4 tablespoons olive or sunflower oil
3–4 tablespoons soy sauce
⅔ cup tomato juice
1 green chili, seeded and chopped
½ onion, grated
3 garlic cloves, crushed
1½ teaspoons dried tarragon, crushed
¾ teaspoon dried basil
¾ teaspoon dried thyme
¾ teaspoon ground cinnamon
2 tablespoons butter or margarine
1¼ cups vegetable stock
freshly ground black pepper
fresh parsley sprigs, to garnish

1 Peel and cube the pumpkin, place in a small bowl and cover with boiling water. Blanch for 2–3 minutes, then drain and refresh under cold water.

2 Cut the onion into wedges, slice the zucchini and plantain and cut the eggplant and red and green peppers into chunks. Trim the mushrooms. Place the vegetables, including the pumpkin in a large bowl.

3 Mix together the lemon juice, oil, soy sauce, tomato juice, chili, grated onion, garlic, herbs, cinnamon and black pepper and pour over the vegetables. Toss together and then set aside in a cool place to marinate for a few hours.

4 Thread the vegetables on to eight skewers, using a variety of vegetables on each to make a colorful display. Preheat the broiler.

5 Broil the vegetables under a low heat, for about 15 minutes, turning frequently, until golden brown, basting with the marinade to keep the vegetables moist.

6 Place the remaining marinade, butter or margarine and stock in a pan and simmer for 10 minutes to cook the onion and reduce the sauce.

7 Pour the sauce into a serving pitcher and arrange the vegetable skewers on a plate. Garnish with parsley and serve with a rice dish or salad.

COOK'S TIP

You can use any vegetable that you prefer. Just first parboil any that may require longer cooking.

Vegetables in Peanut Sauce

INGREDIENTS

Serves 4

1 tablespoon palm or vegetable oil
1 onion, chopped
2 garlic cloves, crushed
14-ounce can tomatoes, puréed
3 tablespoons smooth peanut butter,
   preferably unsalted
3²⁄₃ cups water
1 teaspoon dried thyme
1 green chili, seeded and chopped
1 vegetable stock cube
¹⁄₂ teaspoon ground allspice
2 carrots
4 ounces white cabbage
6 ounces okra
¹⁄₂ red bell pepper, seeded
²⁄₃ cup vegetable stock
salt

1 Heat the oil in a large saucepan and fry the onion and garlic over a moderate heat for 5 minutes, stirring frequently. Add the tomatoes and peanut butter and stir well.

2 Stir in the water, thyme, chili, stock cube, allspice and a little salt. Bring to a boil and then simmer gently, uncovered, for about 35 minutes.

3 Cut the carrots into sticks, slice the cabbage, remove the ends of the okra, and seed and slice the red pepper.

4 Place the vegetables in a saucepan with the stock, bring to a boil and cook until they are just tender but still with a little "bite".

5 Drain the vegetables and place in a warmed serving dish. Pour the sauce over the top and serve.

Bean and Gari Loaf

This recipe is a newly created vegetarian dish using typically Ghanaian flavors and ingredients.

INGREDIENTS

Serves 4

1¼ cups red kidney beans, soaked overnight
1 tablespoon butter or margarine
1 onion, finely chopped
2 garlic cloves, crushed
½ red bell pepper, seeded and chopped
½ green bell pepper, seeded and chopped
1 green chili, seeded and finely chopped
1 teaspoon mixed chopped herbs
2 eggs
1 tablespoon lemon juice
5 tablespoons gari
salt and freshly ground black pepper

1 Drain the kidney beans, then place in a saucepan, cover with water and boil rapidly for 15 minutes. Reduce the heat and continue boiling for about 1 hour, until the beans are tender, adding more water if necessary. Drain, reserving the cooking liquid. Preheat the oven to 375°F and grease an 8½- x 4½-inch loaf pan.

2 Melt the butter or margarine in a large frying pan and fry the onion, garlic and peppers for 5 minutes, then add the chili, mixed herbs and a little salt and pepper.

3 Place the cooked kidney beans in a large bowl or in a food processor and mash or process to a pulp. Add the onion and pepper mixture and stir well to mix. Cool slightly, then stir in the eggs and lemon juice.

4 Place the gari in a separate bowl and sprinkle generously with warm water. The gari should become soft and fluffy after about 5 minutes.

5 Pour the gari into the bean and onion mixture and stir together thoroughly. If the consistency is too stiff, add a little of the bean liquid. Spoon the mixture into the prepared loaf pan and bake in the oven for 35–45 minutes, until firm to the touch.

6 Cool the loaf in the pan and then turn out on to a plate. Cut into thick slices and serve.

COOK'S TIP

Gari is a course-grained flour, used as a staple food, in a similar way to ground rice. Gari is made from a starchy root vegetable, cassava, which is first dried, then ground.

Efua's Ghanaian Salad

INGREDIENTS

Serves 4

4 ounces cooked, peeled shrimp
1 garlic clove, crushed
½ tablespoon vegetable oil
2 eggs
1 yellow plantain, halved
4 lettuce leaves
2 tomatoes
1 red bell pepper
1 avocado
juice of 1 lemon
1 carrot
7-ounce can tuna or sardines
1 green chili, finely chopped
2 tablespoons chopped scallion
salt and freshly ground black pepper

1 Put the shrimp in a small bowl, add the garlic and a little seasoning.

2 Heat the oil in a small saucepan, add the shrimp and cook over a low heat for a few minutes. Transfer to a plate to cool.

3 Hard-boil the eggs, place in cold water to cool, then shell and cut into slices.

4 Boil the plantain in a pan of water for 15 minutes, cool, then peel and slice thickly.

5 Shred the lettuce and arrange on a large serving plate. Slice the tomatoes and red pepper and peel and slice the avocado, sprinkling it with a little lemon juice. Arrange vegetables on the plate. Cut the carrot into matchstick-size pieces and arrange over the lettuce with the other vegetables.

6 Add the plantain, eggs, shrimp and tuna or sardines. Sprinkle with the remaining lemon juice, sprinkle the chili and scallion on top and season with salt and pepper to taste. Serve as a luncheon salad or as a side dish.

—— COOK'S TIP ——

To make a complete meal, serve this salad with a meat or fish dish. Vary the ingredients, use any canned fish and a mixture of attractive lettuce leaves.

Plantain and Green Banana Salad

The plantains and bananas may be cooked in their skins to retain their soft texture. They will then absorb all the flavor of the dressing.

INGREDIENTS

Serves 4
2 firm yellow plantains
3 green bananas
1 garlic clove, crushed
1 red onion
1–2 tablespoons chopped fresh cilantro
3 tablespoons sunflower oil
1½ tablespoons malt vinegar
salt and coarse-grain black pepper

1 Slit the plantains and bananas lengthwise along their natural ridges, then cut in half and place in a large saucepan.

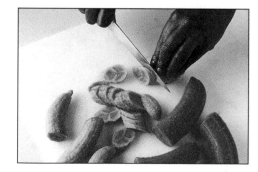

2 Cover the plantains and bananas with water, add a little salt and bring to a boil. Boil gently for 20 minutes until tender, then remove from the water. When they are cool enough to handle, peel and cut into medium-size slices.

3 Put the plantain and banana slices into a bowl and add the garlic, turning to mix.

4 Halve the onion and slice thinly. Add to the bowl with the cilantro, oil, vinegar and seasoning. Toss together to mix, then serve as an accompaniment to a main dish.

Cameroon Coconut Rice

This version of a favorite African dish, Coconut Joloff, can be left moist, like a risotto, or cooked longer for a drier result.

INGREDIENTS

Serves 4
2 tablespoons vegetable oil
1 onion, chopped
2 tablespoons tomato paste
2½ cups coconut milk
2 carrots
1 yellow bell pepper
1 teaspoon dried thyme
½ teaspoon ground allspice
1 fresh green chili, seeded and chopped
1½ cups long grain rice
salt

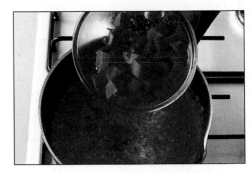

1 Heat the oil in a large saucepan and fry the onion for 2 minutes. Add the tomato paste and cook over a moderate heat for 5–6 minutes, stirring constantly. Add the coconut milk, stir well and bring to a boil.

2 Coarsely chop the carrots and chop the pepper, discarding the seeds.

3 Stir the carrots, pepper, thyme, allspice, chili and rice into the onion mixture, season with salt and bring to a boil. Cover and cook over a low heat until the rice has absorbed most of the liquid. Cover the rice with foil, secure with the lid and steam very gently until the rice is done. Serve hot.

Chick-pea and Okra Fry

Other vegetables can be added to this stir-fry to make a pleasing side dish. Mushrooms, cooked potatoes, zucchini or green beans would all be suitable additions.

INGREDIENTS

Serves 4
1 pound okra
1 tablespoon vegetable oil
1 tablespoon mustard oil
1 tablespoon butter or margarine
1 onion, finely chopped
1 garlic clove, crushed
2 tomatoes, finely chopped
1 green chili, seeded and finely
  chopped
2 slices fresh ginger
1 teaspoon ground cumin
1 tablespoon chopped fresh cilantro
15-ounce can chick-peas, drained
salt and freshly ground black pepper

1 Wash and dry the okra, remove the ends and chop coarsely.

2 Heat the vegetable and mustard oils and the butter or margarine in a large frying pan.

3 Fry the onion and garlic for 5 minutes until the onion is slightly softened. Add the chopped tomatoes, chili and ginger and stir well, then add the okra, cumin and cilantro. Simmer for 5 minutes, stirring frequently, then stir in the chick-peas and a little seasoning.

4 Cook gently for a few minutes for the chick-peas to heat through, then spoon into a serving bowl and serve at once.

Fresh Pineapple with Coconut

This refreshing dessert can also be made with canned pineapple. This makes a good substitute, but fresh is best.

INGREDIENTS

Serves 4

1 fresh pineapple, peeled
slivers of fresh coconut
1¼ cups pineapple juice
4 tablespoons coconut liqueur
1-inch piece preserved ginger, plus
   3 tablespoons of the syrup

1 Peel and slice the pineapple, arrange in a serving dish and sprinkle the coconut slivers on top.

2 Place the pineapple juice and coconut liqueur in a saucepan and heat gently.

3 Thinly slice the ginger and add to the pan along with the ginger syrup. Bring just to a boil and then simmer gently until the liquid is slightly reduced and the sauce is fairly thick.

4 Pour the sauce over the pineapple and coconut, let cool, then chill before serving.

COOK'S TIP

If fresh coconut is not available, then use dried coconut instead.

Papaya and Mango with Mango Cream

INGREDIENTS

Serves 4

2 large ripe mangoes
1¼ cups extra thick heavy cream
8 dried apricots, halved
⅔ cup orange juice or water
1 ripe papaya

1 Take one thick slice from one of the mangoes and, while still on the skin, slash the flesh with a sharp knife in a criss-cross pattern to make cubes.

2 Turn the piece of mango inside-out and cut away the cubed flesh from the skin. Place in a bowl, mash with a fork to a pulp, then add the cream and mix together well. Spoon into a freezer container and freeze for about 1–1½ hours until half frozen.

3 Meanwhile, put the apricots and orange juice or water in a small saucepan. Bring to a boil, then simmer gently until the apricots are soft, adding a little more juice or water if necessary, so that the apricots remain moist. Remove the pan from the heat and set aside to cool.

4 Chop or dice the remaining mangoes as above and place in a bowl. Cut the papaya in half, remove the seeds and peel. Dice the flesh and add to the mango.

5 Pour the apricot sauce over the fruit and gently toss together so the fruit is well coated.

6 Stir the half-frozen mango cream a few times until spoonable but not soft. Serve the fruit topped with the mango cream.

COOK'S TIP

Mangoes vary tremendously in size. If you can only find small ones, buy three instead of two to use in this dessert.

Tropical Fruit Pancakes

INGREDIENTS

Serves 4

1 cup self-rising flour
pinch of grated nutmeg
1 tablespoon superfine sugar
1 egg
1¼ cups milk
1 tablespoon melted butter or
    margarine, plus extra for frying
1 tablespoon fine dried coconut
    (optional)
fresh cream, to serve

For the filling

8 ounces ripe, firm mango
2 bananas
2 kiwi fruit
1 large orange
1 tablespoon lemon juice
2 tablespoons orange juice
1 tablespoon honey
2–3 tablespoons orange liqueur
    (optional)

1 Sift the flour, nutmeg and superfine sugar into a large bowl. In a separate bowl, beat the egg lightly, then beat in most of the milk. Add to the flour mixture and beat with a wooden spoon to mix to a thick, smooth batter.

2 Add the remaining milk, butter and coconut, if using, and continue beating until the batter is smooth and of a fairly thin, pourable consistency.

3 Melt a little butter or margarine in a large nonstick frying pan. Swirl to cover the pan, then pour in a little batter to cover the bottom of the pan. Fry until golden brown, then toss or turn with a spatula. Repeat with the remaining mixture to make about eight pancakes.

4 Dice the mango, coarsely chop the bananas and slice the kiwi fruit. Cut away the peel and pith from the orange and cut into segments.

5 Place the fruit in a bowl. Mix the lemon and orange juices, honey and orange liqueur, if using, then pour over the fruit.

6 Spoon a little fruit down the center of a pancake and fold over each side. Repeat with the remaining pancakes, then serve with fresh cream.

Spiced Nutty Bananas

Cinnamon and nutmeg are spices which perfectly complement bananas in this delectable dessert.

INGREDIENTS

Serves 3

6 ripe, but firm, bananas
2 tablespoons chopped unsalted cashew nuts
2 tablespoons chopped unsalted peanuts
2 tablespoons dried coconut
½–1 tablespoon raw sugar
1 teaspoon ground cinnamon
½ teaspoon freshly grated nutmeg
⅔ cup orange juice
4 tablespoons rum
1 tablespoon butter or margarine
heavy cream, to serve

1 Preheat the oven to 400°F. Slice the bananas and place in a greased, shallow ovenproof dish.

2 Mix together the cashew nuts, peanuts, coconut, sugar, cinnamon and nutmeg in a small bowl.

3 Pour the orange juice and rum over the bananas, then sprinkle with the nut and sugar mixture.

4 Dot the top with butter or margarine, then bake in the oven for 15–20 minutes or until the bananas are golden and the sauce is bubbly. Serve with heavy cream.

COOK'S TIP

Freshly grated nutmeg makes all the difference to this dish. More rum can be added if preferred. Chopped mixed nuts can be used instead of peanuts.

Banana and Melon in Orange Vanilla Sauce

Most large supermarkets and health food stores sell vanilla beans. If vanilla beans are hard to find, use a few drops of natural vanilla extract instead.

INGREDIENTS

Serves 4

1¼ cups orange juice
1 vanilla bean or a few drops vanilla extract
1 teaspoon grated orange rind
1 tablespoon sugar
4 bananas
1 honeydew melon
2 tablespoons lemon juice

1 Place the orange juice in a small saucepan with the vanilla bean, orange rind and sugar and gently bring to a boil.

2 Reduce the heat and simmer gently for 15 minutes or until the sauce is syrupy. Remove from the heat and set aside to cool. If using vanilla extract, stir into the sauce once it has cooled.

3 Coarsely chop the bananas and melon, place in a large serving bowl and toss with the lemon juice.

4 Pour the cooled sauce over the fruit and chill before serving.

Banana Mandazi

INGREDIENTS

Serves 4

1 egg
2 ripe bananas, coarsely chopped
⅔ cup milk
½ teaspoon vanilla extract
2 cups self-rising flour
1 teaspoon baking powder
3 tablespoons sugar
vegetable oil, for deep frying

1 Place the egg, bananas, milk, vanilla extract, flour, baking powder and sugar in a blender or food processor.

2 Process to make a smooth batter. It should have a creamy pourable consistency. If it is too thick, add a little extra milk. Set aside for 10 minutes.

3 Heat the oil in a heavy saucepan or deep-fat fryer. When hot, carefully place spoonfuls of the mixture in the oil and fry for 3–4 minutes until golden. Remove with a slotted spoon and drain on paper towels. Keep warm while cooking the remaining mandazis, then serve at once.

CHINA

Wonton Soup

In China, wonton soup is served as a snack or dim sum rather than as a soup course during a large meal.

INGREDIENTS

Serves 4
6 ounces pork, not too lean,
  roughly chopped
8 medium shrimp, shelled and ground
1 teaspoon light brown sugar
1 tablespoon Chinese rice wine or
  dry sherry
2 tablespoons light soy sauce
1 teaspoon finely chopped scallion
1 teaspoon finely chopped fresh
  ginger
24 wonton wrappers
3 cups chicken stock
finely chopped scallions, to garnish

1 In a bowl, mix the chopped pork and ground shrimp with the sugar, rice wine or sherry, 1 tablespoon of the soy sauce, the scallions and chopped ginger. Blend well and set aside for 25–30 minutes for the flavors to blend.

2 Place 1 teaspoon of the filling in the center of each wonton wrapper.

3 Wet the edges of each wonton with a little water and press them together with your fingers to seal, then fold each wonton over.

4 To cook, bring the stock to a rolling boil in a wok, add the wontons and cook for 4–5 minutes. Add the remaining soy sauce and scallions, transfer to individual soup bowls and serve.

Hot-and-sour Soup

This surely must be the best-known and all-time favorite soup in Chinese restaurants throughout the world. It is fairly simple to make once you have all the necessary ingredients together.

INGREDIENTS

Serves 4

4–6 dried Chinese mushrooms, soaked in warm water for 30 minutes
4 ounces pork or chicken
8-ounce package fresh tofu
⅓ cup sliced bamboo shoots, drained
2½ cups chicken stock
1 tablespoon Chinese rice wine or dry sherry
1 tablespoon light soy sauce
1 tablespoon rice vinegar
salt and ground white pepper
1 tablespoon cornstarch paste

1 Squeeze the soaked mushrooms dry, then discard the hard stalks. Thinly shred the mushrooms, meat, tofu and bamboo shoots.

2 Bring the stock to a rolling boil in a wok and add the shredded ingredients. Bring back to a boil and simmer for about 1 minute.

3 Add the wine or sherry, soy sauce and vinegar and season. Bring back to a boil, then add the cornstarch paste, stir until thickened and serve.

Crab Spring Rolls and Dipping Sauce

Chili and grated ginger add a hint of heat to these sensational treats. Serve them as an appetizer or with other Chinese dishes as part of a main course.

INGREDIENTS

Serves 4–6
1 tablespoon peanut oil
1 teaspoon sesame oil
1 garlic clove, crushed
1 fresh red chili, seeded and finely
    sliced
1 pound fresh stir-fry vegetables, such
    as bean sprouts and shredded carrots,
    bell peppers and snow peas
2 tablespoons chopped cilantro
1-inch piece fresh ginger, grated
1 tablespoon Chinese rice wine or
    dry sherry
1 tablespoon soy sauce
12 ounces fresh dressed crabmeat
    (brown and white meat)
12 spring roll wrappers
1 small egg, beaten
oil, for deep-frying
salt and freshly ground black pepper
lime wedges and fresh cilantro, to
    garnish

For the dipping sauce
1 onion, thinly sliced
oil, for deep-frying
1 fresh red chili, seeded and finely
    chopped
2 garlic cloves, crushed
4 tablespoons dark soy sauce
4 teaspoons lemon juice or
    1–1½ tablespoons prepared tamarind
    juice
2 tablespoons hot water

1 First make the sauce. Spread the onion out on paper towels and let dry for 30 minutes. Then half-fill a wok with oil and heat to 375°F. Fry the onion in batches until crisp and golden, turning all the time. Drain on paper towels.

2 Combine the chili, garlic, soy sauce, lemon or tamarind juice and hot water in a bowl.

3 Stir in the onion and let stand for 30 minutes.

4 To make the spring rolls, heat the peanut and sesame oils in a clean, preheated wok. When hot, stir-fry the crushed garlic and chili for 1 minute. Add the vegetables, cilantro and ginger and stir-fry for 1 minute more. Drizzle with the rice wine or dry sherry and soy sauce. Allow the mixture to bubble up for 1 minute.

5 Using a slotted spoon, transfer the vegetables to a bowl. Set aside until cool, then stir in the crabmeat and season with salt and pepper.

6 Soften the spring roll wrappers, following the directions on the package. Place some of the filling on a wrapper, fold over the front edge and the sides, and roll up neatly, sealing the edges with a little beaten egg. Repeat with the remaining wrappers and filling.

7 Heat the oil for deep-frying in the wok and fry the spring rolls in batches, turning several times, until brown and crisp. Remove with a slotted spoon, drain on paper towels and keep hot while frying the remainder. Serve at once, garnished with lime wedges and cilantro, with the dipping sauce.

Dim Sum

Popular as a snack in China, these tiny dumplings are fast becoming fashionable in many restaurants in the West.

INGREDIENTS

Serves 4
For the dough
1¼ cups all–purpose flour
¼ cup boiling water
1½ tablespoons cold water
½ tablespoon vegetable oil

For the filling
3 ounces ground pork
3 tablespoons canned chopped
   bamboo shoots
½ tablespoon light soy sauce
1 teaspoon dry sherry
1 teaspoon light brown sugar
½ teaspoon sesame oil
1 teaspoon cornstarch
lettuce leaves such as iceberg or frisée,
   soy sauce, scallion curls, sliced fresh
   red chili and shrimp crackers,
   to serve

2 Divide the mixture into 16 equal pieces and shape into circles.

3 For the filling, mix together the pork, bamboo shoots, soy sauce, dry sherry, sugar and oil.

1 To make the dough, sift the flour into a bowl. Stir in the boiling water, then the cold water together with the oil. Mix to form a dough, turn out onto a lightly floured surface, and knead until smooth.

4 Add the cornstarch and stir well until thoroughly combined.

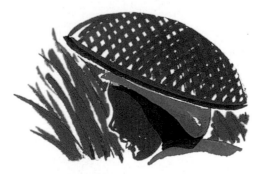

5 Place a little of the filling in the center of each dim sum circle. Pinch the edges of the dough together to form little "purses."

6 Line a steamer with a damp kitchen towel. Place the dim sum in the steamer and steam for 5–10 minutes. Arrange the lettuce leaves on four individual serving plates, top with the dim sum and serve with soy sauce, scallion curls, sliced red chili and shrimp crackers.

VARIATION

You can replace the pork with cooked, peeled shrimp. Sprinkle 1 tablespoon sesame seeds over the dim sum before cooking, if desired.

Pork Dumplings

These dumplings, when shallow-fried, make a good first course to a multicourse meal. They can also be steamed and served as a snack or poached in large quantities for a complete meal.

INGREDIENTS

Makes about 80–90
2½ cups all-purpose flour, plus extra
   for dusting
2 cups water
salt

For the filling
1 pound bok choy leaves or white
   cabbage
1 pound ground pork
1 tablespoon finely chopped scallions
1 teaspoon finely chopped fresh ginger
2 teaspoons salt
1 teaspoon light brown sugar
2 tablespoons light soy sauce
1 tablespoon Chinese rice wine or
   dry sherry
2 teaspoons sesame oil

For the dipping sauce
2 tablespoons red chili oil
1 tablespoon light soy sauce
1 teaspoon finely chopped garlic
1 tablespoon finely chopped scallions

2 For the filling, blanch the bok choy until soft. Drain and chop finely. Mix the bok choy with the pork, scallions, ginger, salt, sugar, soy sauce, wine or sherry and sesame oil.

3 Lightly dust a work surface with flour. Knead and roll the dough into a long sausage about 1 inch in diameter. Cut the sausage into 80–90 small pieces and flatten each piece with the palm of your hand.

4 Using a rolling pin, roll out each piece into a thin pancake about 2½ inches in diameter.

5 Place about 1½ tablespoons of the filling in the center of each pancake and fold into a half-moon pouch.

6 Pinch the edges firmly so that the dumpling is tightly sealed.

7 Bring ⅔ cup salted water to a boil in a wok. Add the dumplings and poach for 2 minutes. Remove the wok from the heat and leave the dumplings in the water for another 15 minutes.

8 Make the dipping sauce by combining all the sauce ingredients in a bowl and mixing well. Serve in a small bowl with the dumplings.

1 Sift the flour into a bowl, then pour in the water and mix to a firm dough. Knead until smooth on a lightly floured surface, then cover with a damp cloth and set aside for 25–30 minutes.

Deep-fried Ribs with Spicy Salt and Pepper

INGREDIENTS

Serves 4–6
10–12 pork spareribs (about 1¹/₂ pounds),
  excess fat trimmed
2–3 tablespoons flour
vegetable oil, for deep-frying
scallion tassels, to garnish (optional)

For the marinade
1 clove garlic, crushed
1 tablespoon light brown sugar
1 tablespoon light soy sauce
1 tablespoon dark soy sauce
2 tablespoons Chinese rice wine or
  dry sherry
¹/₂ teaspoon chili sauce
few drops of sesame oil

For the spicy salt and pepper
1 tablespoon salt
2 teaspoons ground Szechuan
  peppercorns
1 teaspoon five-spice powder

1 Chop each rib into three or four pieces, then mix with all the marinade ingredients and marinate for at least 2–3 hours.

— COOK'S TIP —

Ideally, each sparerib should be chopped into three or four bite-size pieces before or after deep-frying in a wok. If this is not possible, serve the ribs whole.

2 Coat the ribs with flour and deep-fry in medium-hot oil for 4–5 minutes, stirring to separate. Remove from the oil and drain.

3 Heat the oil to high and deep-fry the ribs again for about 1 minute or until the color is an even dark brown. Remove and drain.

4 To make the spicy salt and pepper, heat all the ingredients in a preheated dry wok for about 2 minutes over low heat, stirring constantly. Serve with the ribs. Garnish the dish with scallion tassels, if desired.

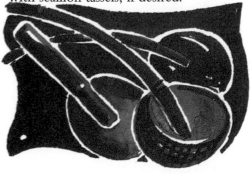

Deep-fried Squid with Spicy Salt and Pepper

This recipe is one of the specialities of the Cantonese school of cuisine. Southern China is famous for its seafood, often flavored with ginger.

INGREDIENTS

Serves 4

1 pound squid
1 teaspoon ginger juice (see
  Cook's Tip)
1 tablespoon Chinese rice wine or
  dry sherry
about 2½ cups boiling water
vegetable oil, for deep-frying
spicy salt and pepper (see index)
fresh cilantro leaves, to garnish

1 Clean the squid by discarding the head and the transparent backbone as well as the ink bag; peel off and discard the thin skin, then wash the squid and dry well on paper towels. Open up the squid and, using a sharp knife, score the inside of the flesh in a crisscross pattern.

2 Cut the squid into pieces, each about the size of a postage stamp. Marinate in a bowl with the ginger juice and rice wine or sherry for 25–30 minutes.

3 Blanch the squid in boiling water for a few seconds—each piece will curl up and the crisscross pattern will open out to resemble ears of corn. Remove and drain. Dry well.

--- COOK'S TIP ---

To make ginger juice, mix finely chopped or grated fresh ginger with an equal quantity of cold water and place in a piece of damp cheesecloth. Twist tightly to extract the juice. Alternatively, crush the ginger in a garlic press.

4 Heat sufficient oil for deep-frying in a wok. Deep-fry the squid for 15–20 seconds, remove quickly and drain. Sprinkle with the spicy salt and pepper and serve garnished with fresh cilantro leaves.

Crispy "Seaweed"

Surprisingly, the very popular and rather exotic-sounding "seaweed" served in Chinese restaurants is, in fact, just ordinary spring greens.

INGREDIENTS

Serves 4
1 pound collards or spring greens
vegetable oil, for deep-frying
$1/2$ teaspoon salt
1 teaspoon superfine sugar
1 tablespoon ground fried fish, to garnish (optional)

1 Cut out the hard stalks in the center of each spring green leaf. Pile the leaves on top of each other, and roll into a tight sausage shape. Thinly cut the leaves into fine shreds. Spread them out to dry.

2 Heat the oil in a wok until hot. Deep-fry the shredded greens in batches, stirring to separate them.

3 Remove the greens with a slotted spoon as soon as they are crispy, but before they turn brown. Drain. Sprinkle the salt and sugar evenly all over the "seaweed," mix well, garnish with ground fish, if desired, and serve.

Sesame Seed Shrimp Toasts

Use uncooked shrimp for this dish, as cooked ones will tend to separate from the bread during cooking.

INGREDIENTS

Serves 4
8 ounces uncooked shrimp, shelled
1 tablespoon vegetable shortening
1 egg white, lightly beaten
1 teaspoon finely chopped scallions
$1/2$ teaspoon finely chopped fresh ginger
1 tablespoon Chinese rice wine or dry sherry
1 tablespoon cornstarch paste
1 cup white sesame seeds
6 large slices white bread
vegetable oil, for deep-frying
salt and ground black pepper

1 Chop the shrimp with the shortening to form a smooth paste. In a bowl, mix with all the other ingredients except the sesame seeds and bread.

2 Spread the sesame seeds evenly on a large plate or baking sheet; spread the shrimp paste thickly on one side of each slice of bread, then press, spread side down, onto the seeds.

3 Heat the oil in a wok until medium-hot; fry 2–3 slices of the sesame bread at a time, spread side down, for 2–3 minutes. Remove and drain. Cut each slice into six or eight fingers (without crusts).

Chinese Sweet-and-Sour Pork

Sweet-and-sour pork must be one of the most popular dishes served in Chinese restaurants throughout the Western world. Unfortunately, it is often spoiled by cooks who use too much ketchup in the sauce. Here is a classic recipe from Canton, the city of its origin.

INGREDIENTS

Serves 4

12 ounces lean pork
¼ teaspoon salt
½ teaspoon ground Szechuan
  peppercorns
1 tablespoon Chinese rice wine or
  dry sherry
1 can (4 ounces) bamboo shoots
2 tablespoons all-purpose flour
1 egg, lightly beaten
vegetable oil, for deep-frying

For the sauce

1 tablespoon vegetable oil
1 garlic clove, finely chopped
1 scallion, cut into short sections
1 green bell pepper, seeded and diced
1 fresh red chili, seeded and cut into
  fine strips
1 tablespoon light soy sauce
2 tablespoons light brown sugar
2–3 tablespoons rice vinegar
1 tablespoon tomato paste
about ½ cup Basic Broth or water

1 Cut the pork into small bite-sized cubes and place in a shallow dish. Add the salt, peppercorns and rice wine or dry sherry and marinate for 15–20 minutes.

2 Drain the bamboo shoots and cut them into small cubes the same size as the pork.

3 Dust the pork with flour, dip in the beaten egg and coat with more flour. Heat the oil in a preheated wok and deep-fry the pork in moderately hot oil for 3–4 minutes, stirring to separate the pieces. Remove and drain.

4 Reheat the oil until hot, return the pork to the wok and add the bamboo shoots. Fry for about 1 minute, or until the pork is golden. Remove and drain well.

5 To make the sauce, heat the oil in a clean wok or frying pan and add the garlic, scallion, green bell pepper and red chili. Stir-fry for 30–40 seconds, then add the soy sauce, sugar, rice vinegar, tomato paste and broth or water. Bring to a boil, then add the pork and bamboo shoots. Heat through and stir to mix, then serve.

Pork Chow Mein

A perfect speedy meal, this family favorite is flavored with sesame oil for an authentic Asian taste.

INGREDIENTS

Serves 4

6 ounces medium egg noodles
12 ounces pork fillet
2 tablespoons sunflower oil
1 tablespoon sesame oil
2 garlic cloves, crushed
8 scallions, sliced
1 red bell pepper, seeded and roughly chopped
1 green bell pepper, seeded and roughly chopped
2 tablespoons dark soy sauce
3 tablespoons Chinese rice wine or dry sherry
6 ounces bean sprouts
3 tablespoons chopped flat-leaf parsley
1 tablespoon toasted sesame seeds

1 Soak the noodles according to the package instructions. Drain well.

2 Thinly slice the pork fillet. Heat the sunflower oil in a preheated wok or large frying pan and cook the pork over high heat until golden brown and cooked through.

3 Add the sesame oil to the wok or frying pan, with the garlic, scallions and bell peppers. Cook over high heat for 3–4 minutes, or until the vegetables are beginning to soften.

4 Reduce the heat slightly and stir in the noodles, with the soy sauce and rice wine or dry sherry. Stir-fry for 2 minutes. Add the bean sprouts and cook for another 1–2 minutes. If the noodles begin to stick, add a splash of water. Stir in the parsley and serve sprinkled with the sesame seeds.

Stir-fried Lamb with Scallions

This is a classic Beijing "meat and vegetables" recipe, in which the lamb can be replaced with either beef or pork, and the scallions by other strongly flavored vegetables, such as leeks or onions.

INGREDIENTS

Serves 4
12–14 ounces leg of lamb fillet
1 teaspoon light brown sugar
1 tablespoon light soy sauce
1 tablespoon Chinese rice wine or
 dry sherry
2 teaspoons cornstarch paste
½ ounce dried wood ears
6–8 scallions
1¼ cups vegetable oil
few small pieces of fresh ginger
2 tablespoons yellow bean sauce
few drops of sesame oil

2 Heat the oil in a preheated wok and stir-fry the lamb for about 1 minute, or until the color changes. Remove with a slotted spoon, drain and set aside.

3 Pour off all but about 1 tablespoon of the oil from the wok, then add the scallions, ginger, wood ears and yellow bean sauce. Blend well, then add the meat and stir for about 1 minute. Sprinkle with the sesame oil and serve.

1 Slice the lamb thinly and place in a shallow dish. Combine the sugar, soy sauce, rice wine or dry sherry and cornstarch paste, pour over the lamb and marinate for 30–45 minutes. Soak the wood ears in water for 25–30 minutes, then drain and cut into small pieces. Finely chop the scallions.

Szechuan Chicken

A wok is the ideal cooking pot for this stir-fried chicken dish. The flavors emerge wonderfully and the chicken is fresh and crisp.

INGREDIENTS

Serves 4

2 chicken thighs (about 12 ounces total), boned and skinned
$1/4$ teaspoon salt
$1/2$ egg white, lightly beaten
2 teaspoons cornstarch paste
1 green bell pepper
$1/4$ cup vegetable oil
3–4 dried red chilies, soaked in water for 10 minutes
1 scallion, cut into short sections
few small pieces of fresh ginger, peeled
1 tablespoon sweet bean paste or hoisin sauce
1 teaspoon chili bean paste
1 tablespoon Chinese rice wine or dry sherry
$2/3$ cup roasted cashews
few drops of sesame oil

1 Cut the chicken meat into small cubes, each about the size of a sugar cube. Combine the chicken, salt, egg white and cornstarch paste in a bowl.

2 Seed the bell pepper and cut it into cubes about the same size as the chicken.

3 Heat the oil in a preheated wok. Stir-fry the chicken cubes for about 1 minute or until the color changes. Remove from the wok with a slotted spoon and keep warm.

4 Add the bell pepper, chilies, scallion and ginger and stir-fry for about 1 minute. Then add the chicken, sweet bean paste, chili bean paste and wine or sherry. Blend well and cook for 1 more minute. Add the cashews and sesame oil. Serve hot.

Special Chow Mein

Lap cheong is a special air-dried Chinese sausage. It is available from most Chinese markets. If you cannot buy it, substitute with either diced ham, chorizo sausage or salami.

INGREDIENTS

Serves 4–6
3 tablespoons vegetable oil
2 garlic cloves, sliced
1 teaspoon chopped fresh ginger
2 red chilies, chopped
2 lap cheong, about 3 ounces, rinsed
    and sliced (optional)
1 boneless chicken breast, thinly sliced
16 uncooked jumbo shrimp, peeled,
    tails left intact, and deveined
1 cup green beans
1 cup bean sprouts
2 ounces garlic chives
1 pound egg noodles, cooked in
    boiling water until tender
2 tablespoons soy sauce
1 tablespoon oyster sauce
1 tablespoon sesame oil
salt and freshly ground black pepper
2 scallions, shredded, to garnish
1 tablespoon cilantro leaves,
    to garnish

2 Heat the rest of the oil in the same wok. Add the bean sprouts and garlic chives. Stir-fry for 1–2 minutes.

4 Return the shrimp mixture to the wok. Reheat and mix well with the noodles. Stir in the sesame oil. Serve garnished with scallions and cilantro leaves.

1 Heat 1 tablespoon of the oil in a wok or large frying pan and fry the garlic, ginger and chilies. Add the lap cheong, chicken, shrimp and beans. Stir-fry for about 2 minutes over high heat or until the chicken and shrimp are cooked. Transfer the mixture to a bowl and set aside.

3 Add the noodles and toss and stir to mix. Season with soy sauce, oyster sauce, salt and pepper.

Egg Foo Yung

A great way of turning a bowl of leftover cooked rice into a meal for four, this dish is tasty and full of texture.

INGREDIENTS

Serves 4
3 eggs, beaten
pinch of Chinese five-spice
  powder (optional)
3 tablespoons peanut or
  sunflower oil
4 scallions, sliced
1 garlic clove, crushed
1 small green bell pepper, seeded and
  chopped
4 ounces bean sprouts
generous 1 cup white rice, cooked
3 tablespoons light soy sauce
1 tablespoon sesame oil
salt and freshly ground black pepper

1 Season the eggs with salt and pepper to taste and beat in the five-spice powder, if using.

2 Heat 1 tablespoon of the oil in a preheated wok or large frying pan and, when quite hot, pour in the eggs. Cook rather like an omelet, pulling the mixture away from the sides and allowing the rest to slip underneath.

3 Cook the egg until firm, then slide out. Chop the omelet into small strips and set aside.

4 Heat the remaining oil and stir-fry the scallions, garlic, green bell pepper and bean sprouts for about 2 minutes, stirring and tossing continuously.

5 Combine the cooked rice and heat thoroughly, stirring well. Add the soy sauce and sesame oil, then return the egg strips to the pan and mix in well. Serve immediately, piping hot.

Noodles in Soup

In China, noodles in soup are far more popular than fried noodles. This is a basic recipe, which you can adapt by using different ingredients.

INGREDIENTS

Serves 4

8 ounces skinless, boneless chicken or
    pork loins
3–4 dried Chinese mushrooms, soaked
1 can (4 ounces) bamboo shoots, drained
4 ounces spinach leaves, lettuce hearts
    or Chinese cabbage
2 scallions
12 ounces dried egg noodles
2½ cups Basic Broth
2 tablespoons vegetable oil
1 teaspoon salt
½ teaspoon light brown sugar
1 tablespoon light soy sauce
2 teaspoons Chinese rice wine or
    dry sherry
few drops of sesame oil

1 Thinly slice the meat. Squeeze the mushrooms dry and discard any hard stalks. Thinly slice the mushroom caps, bamboo shoots, spinach, lettuce hearts or Chinese cabbage and the scallions. Keep the meat, the scallions and the other ingredients in three heaps.

2 Cook the noodles in boiling water according to the instructions on the package, then drain and rinse in cold water. Place in a serving bowl.

3 Bring the broth to a boil and pour over the noodles. Keep warm.

4 Heat the oil in a preheated wok, add the scallions and the meat and stir-fry for about 1 minute.

5 Add the mushrooms, bamboo shoots and spinach, lettuce or Chinese cabbage and stir-fry for 1 minute, or until the meat is cooked through. Add the salt, sugar, soy sauce, rice wine or dry sherry and sesame oil and blend well.

6 Pour the "dressing" over the noodles and serve.

Red-cooked Tofu with Chinese Mushrooms

"Red-cooked" is a term applied to Chinese dishes cooked with a dark soy sauce. This tasty dish can be served as either a side dish or a main course.

INGREDIENTS

Serves 4
8-ounce package fresh firm tofu
3 tablespoons dark soy sauce
2 tablespoons Chinese rice wine or
    dry sherry
2 teaspoons dark brown sugar
1 garlic clove, crushed
1 tablespoon grated fresh ginger
½ teaspoon five-spice powder
pinch of ground roasted Szechuan
    peppercorns
6 dried black Chinese mushrooms
1 teaspoon cornstarch
2 tablespoons peanut oil
5–6 scallions, sliced into 1-inch lengths,
    white and green parts separated
small fresh basil leaves, to garnish
rice noodles, to serve

2 Meanwhile, soak the dried black mushrooms in warm water for 30 minutes, until soft. Drain, reserving 6 tablespoons of the soaking liquid. Squeeze out any excess liquid from the mushrooms, remove the tough stalks and slice the caps. In a small bowl, blend the cornstarch with the reserved marinade and mushroom soaking liquid.

4 Add the mushrooms and white parts of the scallions to the wok and stir-fry for 2 minutes. Pour in the reserved marinade and stir for 1 minute, until thickened.

5 Return the tofu to the wok with the green parts of the scallions. Simmer gently for 1–2 minutes. Scatter the basil leaves on top and serve immediately with rice noodles.

1 Drain the tofu, pat dry with paper towels and cut into 1-inch cubes. Place in a shallow dish. In a small bowl, combine the soy sauce, rice wine or sherry, sugar, garlic, ginger, five-spice powder and Szechuan peppercorns. Pour the marinade over the tofu, toss well and let marinate for about 30 minutes. Drain, reserving the marinade.

3 Heat a wok until hot, add the oil and swirl it around. Add the tofu and stir-fry for 2–3 minutes, until evenly golden. Remove from the wok and set aside.

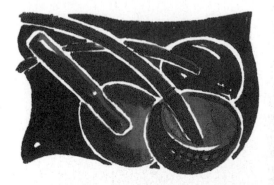

Thin Pancakes

Thin pancakes are not too difficult to make, but quite a lot of practice and patience are needed to achieve the perfect result. Nowadays, even restaurants buy frozen, ready-made ones from Chinese supermarkets. If you decide to use ready-made pancakes, or are reheating home-made ones, steam them for about five minutes, or microwave on high for one to two minutes.

INGREDIENTS

Makes 24–30
4 cups all-purpose flour, plus extra for dusting
about 1¼ cups boiling water
1 teaspoon vegetable oil

1 Sift the flour into a mixing bowl, then pour in the boiling water very gently, stirring as you pour. Mix with the oil and knead the mixture into a firm dough. Cover with a damp cloth and let stand for about 30 minutes.

2 Lightly dust a work surface with flour. Knead the dough for 5–8 minutes, or until smooth, then divide it into three equal portions. Roll out each portion into a long "sausage," cut each into eight to ten pieces and roll each into a ball. Using the palm of your hand, press each piece into a flat pancake. With a rolling pin, gently roll each into a 6-inch circle.

3 Heat an ungreased frying pan until hot, then reduce the heat to low and place the pancakes, one at a time, in the pan. Remove the pancakes when small brown spots appear on the underside. Keep under a damp cloth until all the pancakes are cooked.

Red Bean Paste Pancakes

If you are unable to find red bean paste, sweetened chestnut purée or mashed dates are possible substitutes.

INGREDIENTS

Serves 4
about 8 tablespoons sweetened red bean paste
8 Thin Pancakes
2–3 tablespoons vegetable oil
granulated or superfine sugar, to serve

1 Spread about 1 tablespoon of the red bean paste over about three-quarters of each pancake, then roll the pancake over three or four times.

2 Heat the oil in a preheated wok or frying pan and fry the pancake rolls until golden brown, turning once.

3 Cut each pancake roll into three or four pieces and sprinkle with sugar to serve.

Almond Curd Junket

Also known as almond float, this dessert is usually made with agar or isinglass, although gelatin can also be used.

INGREDIENTS

Serves 4–6

¼ ounce agar or 1 ounce gelatin
   powder
about 2½ cups water
4 tablespoons superfine sugar
1¼ cups milk
1 teaspoon almond extract
fresh or canned mixed fruit salad with
   syrup, to serve

1 In a saucepan, dissolve the agar in about half the water over gentle heat. This will take at least 10 minutes. (If using gelatin, follow the package instructions.)

2 In a separate saucepan, dissolve the sugar in the remaining water over medium heat. Add the milk and the almond extract, blending well. Do not allow the mixture to boil.

3 Mix the milk and sugar with the agar or gelatin mixture in a serving bowl. When cool, place in the refrigerator for 2–3 hours to set.

4 To serve, cut the junket into small cubes and spoon into a serving dish or into individual bowls. Pour the fruit salad, with the syrup, over the junket and serve.

Toffee Apples

A variety of fruits, such as bananas and pineapple, can be prepared and cooked in this way.

INGREDIENTS

Serves 4
4 firm apples
1 cup all-purpose flour
about $^1/_2$ cup water
1 egg, beaten
vegetable oil, for deep-frying, plus
  2 tablespoons for the toffee
$^3/_4$ cup sugar

1 Peel and core each apple and cut into eight pieces. Dust each piece of apple with a little of the flour.

2 Sift the remaining flour into a mixing bowl, then slowly add the cold water and stir well to make a smooth batter. Add the beaten egg and blend well.

3 Heat the oil for deep-frying in a wok. Dip the apple pieces in the batter and deep-fry for about 3 minutes, or until golden. Remove and drain. Drain off the oil.

4 Heat the remaining oil in the wok, add the sugar and stir constantly until the sugar has caramelized. Quickly add the apple pieces and blend well so that each piece of apple is thoroughly coated with the toffee. Dip the apple pieces in cold water to harden before serving.

JAPAN

Pork and Vegetable Soup

INGREDIENTS

Serves 4

2 ounces gobo (optional)
1 teaspoon rice vinegar
½ black konnyaku (about 4 ounces)
2 teaspoons oil
1 pork belly (7 ounces), cut into thin
 1–inch long strips
4 ounces daikon, peeled and
 thinly sliced
2 ounces carrot, thinly sliced
1 medium potato, thinly sliced
4 shiitake mushrooms, stems removed
 and thinly sliced
3½ cups kombu and bonito stock or
 instant dashi
1 tablespoon sake or dry white wine
3 tablespoons red or white miso paste

For the garnish

2 scallions, thinly sliced
seven-spice flavoring (*shichimi*)

1 Scrub the skin off the gobo, if using, with a vegetable brush. Slice the vegetable into fine shavings. Soak the prepared gobo for 5 minutes in plenty of water with the vinegar added to remove any bitter taste, then drain.

2 Put the piece of konnyaku in a small pan and add enough water just to cover it. Bring to a boil over medium heat, then drain and let cool. This removes any bitter taste.

3 Using your hands, tear the konnyaku into 1-inch lumps. Do not use a knife, as a smooth cut surface will not absorb any flavor.

4 Heat the oil in a deep saucepan and quickly stir-fry the pork. Add all the gobo, konnyaku, daikon, carrot, potato and shiitake mushrooms, then stir-fry for one minute. Pour in the stock and sake or wine.

5 Bring the soup to a boil, then skim it and simmer for 10 minutes, until the vegetables have softened.

6 Ladle a little of the soup into a small bowl and dissolve the miso paste in it. Pour the mixture back into the saucepan and bring to a boil once more. Do not continue to boil or the flavor will be lost. Remove from the heat, then pour into serving bowls. Sprinkle with the scallions and seven-spice flavoring, and serve immediately.

Fish Ball Soup

Tsumire means, quite literally, sardine balls, and these are added to this delicious *Tsumire-jiru* soup to impart their robust fish flavor. This is a warming and nutritious dish for winter.

INGREDIENTS

Serves 4

1 ounce fresh ginger
fresh sardines (1¾ pounds), gutted and
  heads removed
2 tablespoons white miso paste
1 tablespoon sake or dry white wine
½ tablespoon sugar
1 egg
2 tablespoons cornstarch
5 ounces shimeji mushrooms or
  6 shiitake mushrooms
1 leek or large scallion

For the soup

generous ⅓ cup sake or dry white wine
5 cups instant dashi (stock)
¼ cup white miso paste

1 First make the fish balls. Grate the ginger and squeeze it well to yield 1 teaspoon ginger juice.

2 Rinse the sardines under cold running water, then cut in half along the backbone. Remove all the bones. To skin a boned sardine, lay it skin side down on a board, then run a sharp knife slowly along the skin from tail to head.

3 Coarsely chop the sardines and process with the ginger juice, miso, sake or wine, sugar and egg to a thick paste in a food processor or blender. Transfer to a bowl and mix in the cornstarch well.

4 Trim the shimeji mushrooms and separate each stem, or remove the stems from the shiitake mushrooms and shred them. Cut the leek into 2–inch long strips.

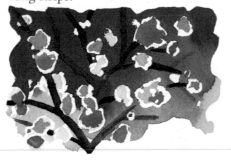

5 Bring the ingredients for the soup to a boil. Use two wet spoons to shape small portions of the sardine mixture into bite-sized balls and drop them into the soup. Add the mushrooms and leeks.

6 Simmer until the sardine balls float to the surface. Serve immediately, in four deep bowls.

Yakitori Chicken

Yakitori are Japanese-style chicken kebabs. They are easy to eat and ideal for barbecues or parties.

INGREDIENTS

Serves 4
6 boneless chicken thighs (skin on)
1 bunch scallions
seven-spice flavoring (*shichimi*), to serve
(optional)

For the yakitori sauce
⅔ cup soy sauce
½ cup sugar
5 teaspoons sake or dry white wine
1 tablespoon flour

1 To make the sauce, stir the soy sauce, sugar and sake or wine into the flour in a small saucepan and bring to a boil, stirring. Reduce the heat and simmer for 10 minutes, until the sauce is reduced by one-third. Then set aside.

2 Cut each chicken thigh into six chunks and cut the scallions into 1¼-inch-long pieces.

3 Thread the chicken and scallions alternately onto 12 bamboo skewers. Broil under medium heat or on the barbecue, brushing generously several times with the sauce. Allow 5–10 minutes, until the chicken is cooked but still moist.

4 Serve with a little extra yakitori sauce, offering seven-spice flavoring with the kebabs if possible.

Chicken Cakes with Teriyaki Sauce

These small chicken cakes, about the size of small meatballs, are known as *Tsukune.* Here, they are cooked with a glaze and garnished with scallions.

INGREDIENTS

Serves 4
For the chicken cakes
1 pound ground chicken
1 large egg
¼ cup grated onion
1½ teaspoons sugar
1½ teaspoons soy sauce
cornstarch, for coating
½ bunch scallions, finely
   shredded, to garnish
1 tablespoon oil

For the teriyaki sauce
2 tablespoons sake or dry white wine
2 tablespoons sugar
2 tablespoons mirin
2 tablespoons soy sauce

1 Mix the ground chicken with the egg, grated onion, sugar and soy sauce until the ingredients are thoroughly combined and well bound. This process takes about 3 minutes, until the mixture is quite sticky, which makes for a good texture. Shape the mixture into 12 small, flat, round cakes and dust them lightly all over with cornstarch.

2 Soak the scallions in cold water for 5 minutes and drain well.

3 Heat the oil in a frying pan. Place the chicken cakes in the pan in a single layer, and cook over medium heat for 3 minutes. Turn the cakes and cook for 3 minutes longer.

4 Mix the ingredients for the sauce and pour it into the pan. Turn the chicken cakes occasionally until they are evenly glazed. Move or gently shake the pan constantly to prevent the sauce from burning.

5 Arrange the chicken cakes on a plate and top with the scallions. Serve immediately.

> — COOK'S TIP —
>
> To make *Tsukune Yakitori*, make smaller chicken cakes, then thread them onto four bamboo skewers. Cook them under the broiler, brushing with the sauce given for Yakitori Chicken.

Simmered Beef with Potatoes

Another typical example of Japanese home cooking, known as *Nikujaga*, this would be thought of as a very special dish.

INGREDIENTS

Serves 4
4 medium potatoes, peeled
1 pound beef, thinly sliced
2 tablespoons frozen peas
1 tablespoon oil
1 large mild onion, cut into wedges
scant 1 cup instant dashi (stock)
   or water
2 tablespoons sugar
4 teaspoons sake or dry white wine
4 teaspoons mirin
4 teaspoons soy sauce

1 Cut each potato into thirds or quarters and soak them in cold water for 5 minutes. Drain well.

2 Cut the beef into 1–2-inch strips. Pour hot water over the frozen peas and leave until thawed, then drain.

3 Heat the oil in a deep-frying pan or saucepan. Remove from the heat and add the beef. Replace the pan on the heat and fry the beef for 1 minute. Add the onion and potatoes, and fry for 2 more minutes.

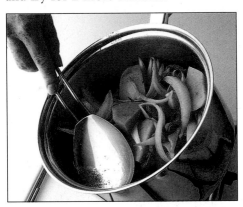

4 Fold a sheet of foil in half so it is just smaller than the diameter of the frying pan. Pour in the stock and bring to a boil. Skim the broth carefully. When the soup clears, cover the pan with the foil and simmer for 3–4 minutes. Stir in the sugar and sake or wine, cover and simmer for 4–5 more minutes.

5 Add the mirin and 3 teaspoons soy sauce, cover the pan and simmer for 6–7 minutes.

6 Finally, stir in the remaining soy sauce and simmer, uncovered, until only a little soup remains. Shake the pan gently, occasionally, to prevent the ingredients from burning. Serve the beef and potatoes in a large bowl, sprinkled with the peas.

Japanese-style Hamburgers

This recipe makes soft and moist hamburgers that are delicious with rice, especially with the daikon topping, which adds its own refreshing flavor.

INGREDIENTS

Serves 4

2 tablespoons oil, plus extra for
    greasing hands
1 small onion, finely chopped
1 pound ground beef
1 cup fresh white bread crumbs
1 egg
1 teaspoon salt
black pepper
4 ounces shiitake mushrooms, stems
    discarded and sliced
7 ounces daikon, finely grated and
    drained in a sieve
4 shiso leaves, finely shredded
    (optional)
4 teaspoons soy sauce

1 Heat 1 tablespoon oil in a frying pan and fry the onion gently until soft but not browned. Let cool.

2 Put the ground beef in a large bowl with the fried onion, bread crumbs and egg. Season with the salt and pepper. Knead well by hand until the ingredients are thoroughly combined and the mixture becomes sticky. It is important to keep the meat soft and juicy for this recipe. Divide the mixture into fourths.

3 Put a little oil on your hands. Take a portion of the mixture and throw it from one hand to the other five or six times to remove any air. Then shape the mixture into a thick burger. Repeat with the remaining mixture.

4 Heat the remaining oil in a frying pan and add the burgers. Fry over high heat until browned on one side, then turn over. Place the shiitake mushrooms in the pan, next to the burgers, cover and cook over low heat for 3–4 minutes or until cooked through, stirring the mushrooms occasionally.

5 Serve the burgers topped with the daikon, shiitake mushrooms and shiso leaves (if used). Pour 1 teaspoon soy sauce over each burger just before it is served.

Teriyaki Trout

Teriyaki sauce is very useful, not only for fish but also for meat.

INGREDIENTS

Serves 4
4 trout fillets

For the marinade
5 tablespoons soy sauce
5 tablespoons sake or dry white wine
5 tablespoons mirin

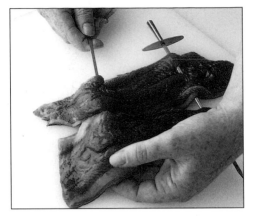

COOK'S TIP

To make a teriyaki barbecue sauce, heat the marinade until boiling, then reduce it until it thickens. When you grill the fish or meat, brush it with the sauce several times.

1 Lay the trout fillets in a shallow dish in a single layer. Mix the ingredients for the marinade and pour the marinade over the fish. Cover and marinate in the fridge for 5–6 hours, turning occasionally.

2 Thread two trout fillets neatly together on two metal skewers. Repeat with the remaining fillets. You can cut the fillets in half if they are too big.

3 Grill the trout on a barbecue, over high heat. Keep the fish about 4 inches away from the flame and brush it with the marinade several times. Grill each side until shiny and the trout is cooked through. Alternatively, cook the trout under the broiler for a few minutes on each side.

4 Slide the trout off the skewers while it is hot. Serve hot or cold with any remaining marinade.

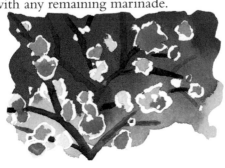

Grilled Tuna Kebabs

It is difficult to buy tuna fresh enough for *sashimi*, so try this recipe. Choose a fatty portion of tuna steak. This oily, pinkish part of the tuna is better for grilling and has a good texture.

INGREDIENTS

Serves 4

1 tuna steak (about 8 ounces)
1 bunch scallions
1 lime, quartered

For the marinade
2 teaspoons mirin
3 tablespoons soy sauce

1 Cut the tuna into 24 cubes, each about 1 inch. Mix the mirin and soy sauce, pour it over the tuna and let marinate for 30 minutes. Cut the scallions into 1–inch lengths.

COOK'S TIP

Soaking bamboo skewers in water for at least 30 minutes before using them helps to prevent them from catching fire under a hot broiler or on the barbecue. Drain the skewers just before threading the food on them and cook the kebabs immediately after threading them.

2 Thread the tuna and the scallions alternately onto eight bamboo skewers.

3 Preheat the broiler to the hottest setting and broil the tuna, turning the skewers frequently to avoid burning them. Brush the tuna with the marinade several times during cooking. Grill until the tuna is lightly cooked but still moist inside.

4 Serve the kebabs immediately, with lime wedges.

Fried Swordfish

This is a light and tasty cold dish that is suitable for serving on a hot summer's day.

INGREDIENTS

Serves 4
4 swordfish steaks (about 5 ounces), boned, skin left on
1 tablespoon soy sauce
1½ teaspoons rice vinegar
1 bunch scallions
4 asparagus spears, trimmed
2 tablespoons oil, for cooking

For the marinade
3 tablespoons soy sauce
3 tablespoons rice vinegar
2 tablespoons sake or dry white wine
1 tablespoon sugar
1 tablespoon instant dashi (stock) or water
1½ teaspoons sesame oil

1 Cut the swordfish steaks into 1½-inch chunks and place in a dish. Pour 1 tablespoon soy sauce and 1½ teaspoons rice vinegar over the fish, then let sit for 5 minutes. Meanwhile, cut the scallions into 1¼-inch lengths and the asparagus into 1½-inch lengths.

2 Mix the ingredients for the marinade in a dish. Heat three-quarters of the oil in a frying pan. Wipe the swordfish with paper towels, and fry over medium heat for about 1–2 minutes per side, or until cooked. Remove the fish from the frying pan and place it in the marinade.

3 Clean the frying pan and heat the remaining oil in it. Fry the scallions over medium heat until browned, then add them to the fish. Fry the asparagus in the oil remaining in the pan over low heat for 3–4 minutes, then add to the fish.

4 Let the fish and vegetables marinate for 10–20 minutes, turning the pieces occasionally. Serve the cold fish with the marinade on a large, deep plate.

Shrimp and Avocado with Wasabi

This dish is a perfect appetizer for entertaining, as it can be made easily; however, the whole dish must be made just before serving to prevent the avocado from discoloring and to preserve the flavor of the wasabi, which will be lost if allowed to stand for any length of time.

INGREDIENTS

Serves 4
2 avocados, halved, pitted and skinned
8 ounces cooked jumpo shrimp, shelled, or 8 raw tiger shrimp, heads removed

For the wasabi dressing
4 teaspoons usukuchi soy sauce
2 tablespoons rice vinegar
2 teaspoons wasabi paste

1 Mix the ingredients for the wasabi dressing.

2 Cut each avocado half into ¾-inch cubes.

3 If using raw shrimp, remove the black intestinal vein from the back. Cook them in salted simmering water for 1 minute, until they turn pink. Remove their shells and tails. Cut the shrimp into pieces measuring about 1 inch long.

4 Put the shrimp and the avocados in a bowl, toss well with the dressing, then serve promptly.

Daikon with Sesame Miso Sauce

This simple vegetable dish makes a good appetizer for a dinner party.

INGREDIENTS

Serves 4
1 medium daikon (about 2 pounds)
1 tablespoon rice, washed
1 sheet kombu seaweed (8 x 4 inches)
small bunch watercress, to garnish
salt

For the sesame miso sauce
generous ⅓ cup red miso paste
generous ⅓ cup white miso paste
¼ cup mirin
2 tablespoons sugar
4 teaspoons ground white sesame seeds

1 Slice the daikon into 1-inch-thick slices, then peel off the skin. Wrap the rice in a piece of muslin or cheesecloth and tie it with string, leaving room for the rice to expand during cooking. The bundle of rice should look like a commercial dried bouquet garni.

2 Place the daikon in a saucepan and fill with water. Add the rice bag and a little salt, bring to a boil, then simmer for 15 minutes. Gently drain the daikon and discard the rice.

—— COOK'S TIP ——

The small bag of uncooked rice is added to the cooking water to keep the daikon white during cooking and remove any bitterness from the vegetable.

3 Place the seaweed in a large, shallow pan, lay the daikon on top and fill with water. Bring to a boil, then simmer for 20 minutes.

4 Meanwhile, make the sauce. Mix the red and white miso pastes well in a saucepan. Add the mirin and sugar, then simmer for 6 minutes, stirring continuously. Remove from the heat, and add the sesame seeds.

5 Arrange the daikon and seaweed in a large dish with their hot cooking stock. Sprinkle watercress over the top. Serve the daikon on small plates with the sesame miso sauce poured over and garnished with some of the watercress. The seaweed is used only to flavor the daikon, it is not eaten.

Rice Omelette

Rice omelettes are a great
favorite with Japanese children,
who usually top them
with ketchup.

INGREDIENTS

Serves 4
1 skinned boneless chicken thigh
    (about 4 ounces), cut into small cubes
8 teaspoons butter
1 small onion, chopped
¼ cup carrot, chopped
2 shiitake mushrooms, stems
    removed and chopped
1 tablespoon finely chopped parsley
2 cups freshly boiled rice
2 tablespoons ketchup
6 eggs
¼ cup milk
1 teaspoon salt, plus extra to season and
    black or white pepper

For the garnish
ketchup
parsley sprigs

1 Season the chicken with salt and
pepper. Melt 2 teaspoons butter in
a frying pan. Fry the onion for
1 minute, then add the chicken and fry
until the chicken is white and cooked.
Add the carrot and mushrooms,
stir-fry until soft over medium heat,
then add the parsley. Set this mixture
aside and clean the frying pan.

2 Melt 2 teaspoons butter in the
frying pan, add the rice and stir
well. Mix in the fried ingredients,
ketchup and pepper. Stir well, adding
salt to taste if necessary. Keep the
mixture warm.

3 Beat the eggs lightly, add the milk,
1 teaspoon salt and pepper.

4 Melt 1 teaspoon butter in an
omelette pan over medium heat.
Pour in a quarter of the egg mixture
and stir it briefly with a fork, then let
set for 1 minute. Top with a quarter of
the rice mixture.

5 Fold the omelette over the rice and
slide it to the edge of the pan to
shape it into a curve. Do not cook the
omelette too much.

6 Invert the omelette onto a
warmed plate, cover with a
paper towel and press neatly into a
rectangular shape. Cook three more
omelettes from the remaining
ingredients. Serve immediately
with ketchup on top, garnished
with parsley.

Salmon Sealed with Egg

Tamago-toji, meaning egg cover, is the Japanese title for this type of dish, which can be made from various ingredients. Canned pink salmon is used here for a very delicate flavor. Fried bean curd can be used instead of salmon.

INGREDIENTS

Serves 4

1 can (14 ounces) pink salmon, drained, bones and skin removed
10 snow peas, trimmed
2 large mild onions, sliced
8 teaspoons sugar
2 tablespoons soy sauce
4 eggs, beaten

1 Flake the salmon. Boil the snow peas for 2–3 minutes, drain and slice finely.

2 Put the onion in a frying pan, add a scant 1 cup water and bring to a boil. Cook for 5 minutes over medium heat, then add the sugar and soy sauce. Cook for 5 more minutes.

3 Add the salmon and cook for 2–3 minutes or until the soup has virtually evaporated. Pour the egg over it to cover the surface. Sprinkle in the snow peas and cover the pan. Cook for 1 minute over medium heat, until just set. Do not overcook or the eggs will curdle and separate. Spoon onto a plate from the pan and serve immediately.

Japanese Savory Custard

INGREDIENTS

Serves 4

3 eggs
1 teaspoon salt
1 teaspoon usukuchi soy sauce
1 teaspoon sugar
2 cups kombu and bonito stock
1 chicken breast fillet (2 ounces), thinly sliced
4 shiitake mushrooms, stems removed and sliced
4 medium shrimp, shelled and thawed if frozen
2 teaspoons sake or dry white wine
2 teaspoons soy sauce
mitsuba leaves or watercress to garnish

1 Break the eggs into a bowl. To avoid introducing too much air, do not beat the eggs, but stir them using a pair of chopsticks and a cutting action.

2 Stir the salt, usukuchi soy sauce and sugar into the cold stock, then add the egg. Strain the mixture through a fine sieve into another bowl.

3 Season the chicken, shiitake mushrooms and shrimp with the sake or wine and soy sauce, then divide them equally between four custard cups or individual soufflé dishes. Pour the egg mixture on top.

4 Place in a steamer over a saucepan or wok of boiling water and cover. Steam over medium-high heat for 3 minutes, then remove the lid from the steamer and lay a dish towel over the top. Replace the lid and cook over low heat for 18–20 minutes, or until set.

5 Insert a bamboo skewer to check if the mixture is cooked; if a little clear liquid comes out, it is ready. Garnish with mitsuba leaves or watercress. If you have lids for the cups, put them on and serve immediately. Provide spoons with which to eat the custard.

Individual Noodle Casseroles

Traditionally, these individual casseroles are cooked in earthenware pots. *Nabe* means pot and *yaki* means to heat, providing the Japanese title of *Nabeyaki Udon* for this recipe.

INGREDIENTS

Serves 4

1 boneless chicken thigh (4 ounces)
1 teaspoon salt
1 teaspoon sake or dry white wine
1 teaspoon soy sauce
1 leek
4 ounces whole spinach, trimmed
12 ounces dried udon noodles or
  1 pound fresh
4 shiitake mushrooms, stems removed
4 eggs
seven-spice flavoring (*shichimi*), to serve
  (optional)

For the soup

6 cups kombu and bonito stock or
  instant dashi
4 teaspoons soy sauce
1 teaspoon salt
1 tablespoon mirin

1 Cut the chicken into small chunks and sprinkle with the salt, sake or wine and soy sauce. Cut the leek diagonally into 2-inch slices.

2 Boil the spinach for 1–2 minutes, then drain and soak in cold water for 1 minute. Drain, squeeze lightly, then cut into 2-inch lengths.

3 Boil dried udon according to the package instructions, allowing 3 minutes less than the suggested cooking time. If using fresh udon, place them in boiling water, disentangle the noodles well and then drain them.

4 Bring the ingredients for the soup to a boil in a saucepan and add the chicken and leeks. Skim the broth, then cook for 5 minutes. Divide the udon noodles between four individual flameproof casseroles. Pour the soup, chicken and leeks into the casseroles. Place over medium heat, then add the shiitake mushrooms.

5 Gently break an egg into each casserole. Cover and simmer for 2 minutes. Divide the spinach between the casseroles and simmer for 1 minute.

6 Serve immediately, standing the hot casseroles on plates or hot pads. Sprinkle seven-spice flavoring over the casseroles if desired.

COOK'S TIP

Assorted tempura could be served in these casseroles instead of chicken and egg.

Chilled Noodles

This classic Japanese dish of cold noodles is known as *somen*. The noodles are surprisingly refreshing when eaten with the accompanying ingredients and a delicately flavored dip. The noodles are served with ice to ensure they remain chilled until they are eaten.

INGREDIENTS

Serves 4
oil, for cooking
2 eggs, beaten with a pinch of salt
1 sheet yaki-nori seaweed, finely
   shredded
½ bunch scallions, thinly sliced
wasabi paste
1 pound dried somen noodles
ice cubes, for serving

For the dip
4 cups kombu and bonito stock or
   instant dashi
scant 1 cup soy sauce
1 tablespoon mirin

1 Prepare the dip in advance so it has time to cool and chill. Bring the ingredients to a boil, then let cool and chill thoroughly.

2 Heat a little oil in a frying pan. Pour in half the egg, tilting the pan to coat the base evenly. Let the egg set, then turn it over and cook the second side briefly. Turn the omelette out onto a board. Cook the remaining egg in the same way.

3 Let the omelettes cool and then shred them finely. Place the shredded omelette, nori, scallions and wasabi in four small bowls.

4 Boil the somen noodles according to the package instructions and drain. Rinse the noodles in or under cold running water, stirring with chopsticks, then drain well.

5 Place the noodles on a large plate and add some ice cubes on top to keep them cool.

6 Pour the cold dip into four small bowls. Noodles and selected accompaniments are dipped into the chilled dip before they are eaten.

COOK'S TIP

Use scissors to finely shred the nori. Stir the noodles gently with chopsticks when rinsing them, as they are tender once cooked and easily damaged.

Chicken and Egg with Rice

Oyako-don, the Japanese title for this dish, means parent (*oya*), child (*ko*) and bowl (*don*); it is so called because it uses both chicken meat and egg.

INGREDIENTS

Serves 4
2–3 boneless chicken thighs
  (a total of 12 ounces)
1 large mild onion, thinly sliced
scant 1 cup kombu and bonito
  stock or instant dashi
4 teaspoons sugar
¼ cup soy sauce
2 tablespoons mirin
7 cups freshly boiled rice
4–6 eggs, beaten
¼ cup frozen peas, thawed
½ sheet yaki-nori seaweed, shredded,
  to garnish

1 Slice the chicken diagonally, then cut it into 1-inch lengths.

2 Place the onion, stock, sugar, soy sauce and mirin in a saucepan and bring to a boil. Add the chicken and cook over medium heat for about 5 minutes, or until the chicken is cooked. Skim any scum off the sauce.

3 Ladle a quarter of the mixture into a frying pan and bring to a boil.

4 Spoon a quarter of the rice into an individual serving bowl.

5 Pour a quarter of the egg over the mixture in the frying pan and sprinkle with a quarter of the peas. Cover and cook over medium heat until the egg is set to your taste.

6 Slide the cooked mixture onto the rice. Prepare the remaining three portions in the same way. Serve hot, sprinkled with the yaki-nori seaweed.

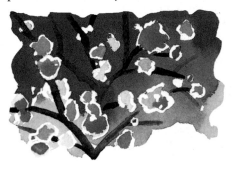

Steak Bowl

This appetizing dish looks very good at a dinner party and is also very easy to prepare, leaving the cook time to relax.

INGREDIENTS

Serves 4
1 large mild onion
1 red bell pepper, seeded
2 tablespoons oil
2 tablespoons butter
1 sirloin steak (about 1 pound),
  trimmed of excess fat
¼ cup ketchup
2 tablespoons Worcestershire sauce
2 tablespoons chopped parsley
7 cups freshly boiled rice
salt and black pepper

For the garnish
bunch of watercress
a few red peppercorns (optional)

1 Thinly slice the onion and red bell pepper.

2 Heat 1 tablespoon oil in a frying pan and cook the onion until golden on both sides, adding salt and pepper, then set aside.

3 Heat 1 tablespoon oil and 1 tablespoon butter. Cook the steak over a high heat until browned on both sides, then cut it into bite-sized pieces and set aside. For well-done steak, cook it on medium heat for 1–2 minutes each side.

4 For the sauce, mix the ketchup, Worcestershire sauce and 2 tablespoons water in the pan in which the steak was cooked. Stir over medium heat for 1 minute, mixing in the pan drippings.

5 Mix the remaining butter and the chopped parsley into the hot rice. Divide between four serving bowls. Top the rice with the red bell pepper, onion and steak, and pour on the sauce. Garnish with watercress and red peppercorns (if using) and serve.

INDONESIA

Spiced Vegetable Soup with Chicken and Shrimp

INGREDIENTS

Serves 6–8

1 onion, ½ cut in two, ½ sliced
2 garlic cloves, crushed
1 fresh red or green chili, seeded
    and sliced
½ teaspoon shrimp paste
3 macadamia nuts or 6 almonds
½ inch *laos*, peeled and sliced, or 1
    teaspoon *laos* powder
1 teaspoon sugar
oil for frying
8 ounces boned, skinned chicken
    breast, cut in ½-inch cubes
1¼ cups coconut milk
5 cups chicken broth
1 eggplant, diced
8 ounces green beans, chopped
small wedge of crisp white
    cabbage, shredded
1 red bell pepper, seeded and sliced
4 ounces cooked, peeled shrimp
salt and freshly ground black pepper

1 Grind the onion quarters, garlic, chili, shrimp paste, nuts, *laos* and sugar to a paste in a food processor or with a mortar and pestle.

2 Heat a wok, add the oil and then fry the paste, without browning, until it gives off a rich aroma. Add the sliced onion and chicken cubes and cook for 3–4 minutes. Stir in the coconut milk and broth. Bring to a boil and simmer for a few minutes.

3 Add the diced eggplant to the soup, with the beans, and cook for only a few minutes, until the beans are almost cooked.

4 A few minutes before serving, stir the cabbage, bell pepper and shrimp into the soup. The vegetables should be cooked so that they are still crunchy and the shrimp merely heated through. Taste the soup and adjust the seasoning if necessary.

Spiced Beef Satés

INGREDIENTS

Makes 18 skewers

1 pound rump steak, cut in ½-inch
    slices or strips
1 teaspoon coriander seeds, dry-fried
    and ground
½ teaspoon cumin seeds, dry-fried
    and ground
1 teaspoon tamarind pulp
1 small onion
2 garlic cloves
1 tablespoon brown sugar
1 tablespoon dark soy sauce
salt

To serve

cucumber chunks
lemon or lime wedges
Sambal Kecap

1 Mix the meat and spices in a non-metallic bowl. Soak the tamarind pulp in ⅓ cup water.

2 Strain the tamarind and reserve the juice. Put the onion, garlic, tamarind juice, sugar and soy sauce in a food processor and blend well. Alternatively, pound the onion and garlic in a mortar with a pestle, and add the remaining ingredients.

3 Pour the marinade over the meat and spices in the bowl and toss well together. Set aside for at least 1 hour. Meanwhile, soak some bamboo skewers in water to prevent them from burning while cooking.

4 Preheat the broiler. Thread 5 or 6 pieces of meat onto each of the skewers and sprinkle the meat with salt. Place under the hot broiler, or even better, over a charcoal barbecue, and cook, turning frequently, until tender. Baste with the marinade throughout the cooking, turning the skewers over from time to time.

5 Serve on a platter garnished with cucumber chunks and wedges of lemon or lime to squeeze over the *satés*. Put the *Sambal Kecap* in a small bowl and serve alongside.

Vegetable Broth with Ground Beef

INGREDIENTS

Serves 6

2 tablespoons peanut oil
4 ounces finely ground beef
1 large onion, grated or finely chopped
1 garlic clove, crushed
1–2 fresh chilies, seeded and chopped
½ teaspoon shrimp paste
3 macadamia nuts or 6 almonds,
   finely ground
1 carrot, finely grated
1 teaspoon brown sugar
4 cups chicken broth
2 ounces dried shrimp, soaked in warm
   water for 10 minutes
8 ounces spinach, cooked, drained and
   finely chopped
8 baby corn, sliced, or 7 ounces canned
   corn kernels
1 large tomato, chopped
juice of ½ lemon
salt

1 Heat the oil in a saucepan. Add the beef, onion and garlic and cook, stirring, until the meat changes color.

2 Add the chilies, shrimp paste, nuts, carrot, sugar and salt to taste.

COOK'S TIP

To make this broth, *Sayur Menir,* very hot and spicy, add the seeds from the chilies.

---

3 Add the broth and bring gently to a boil. Reduce the heat to a simmer and then add the soaked shrimp, with their soaking liquid. Simmer for about 10 minutes.

4 A few minutes before serving, add the spinach, corn, tomato and lemon juice. Simmer for a minute or two, to heat through. Do not overcook at this stage because this will spoil the appearance and the taste of the *sayur.*

Omelets with Spicy Meat Filling

INGREDIENTS

Serves 4

For the filling
½-inch cube *terasi*
3 garlic cloves, crushed
4 macadamia nuts or 8 almonds
½ inch fresh *laos*, peeled and sliced, or
   1 teaspoon *laos* powder (optional)
1 teaspoon ground coriander
½ teaspoon ground turmeric
1 teaspoon salt
2 tablespoons oil
8 ounces ground beef
2 scallions, chopped
½ celery stalk, finely chopped
2–3 tablespoons coconut milk

For the omelets
oil for frying
4 eggs, beaten with 4 tablespoons
   water
salt and freshly ground black pepper
salad and celery leaves, to serve

1 Grind the *terasi* to a paste, in a food processor or with a mortar and pestle, with the garlic, nuts and fresh *laos*, if using. Add the coriander, turmeric, *laos* powder, (if using), and the salt.

2 Heat the oil and fry the mixture for 1–2 minutes. Stir in the ground beef and cook until it changes color. Cook for 2–3 minutes. Stir in the scallions, celery and coconut milk. Cover and cook gently for 5 minutes.

3 Meanwhile, prepare the omelets. Heat a little oil in an omelet or frying pan. Season the eggs and use to make four thin omelets in the usual way. When each omelet is almost cooked, spoon a quarter of the filling on top and roll up. Keep warm while making the remaining omelets.

4 Cut the rolled omelets in half and arrange on a serving dish. Serve garnished with a few salad and celery leaves.

Peanut Fritters

You can buy rice powder and rice flour in any Asian shop. For this recipe, *Rempeyak Kacang*, it is best to use the rice flour which is ideal as it has a slightly more grainy texture. Peanut fritters are easy and quick to prepare. They go well with Festive Rice and make a good addition to a buffet.

INGREDIENTS

Makes 15–20

½ cup rice flour
½ teaspoon baking powder
1 garlic clove, crushed
½ teaspoon ground coriander
2 pinches ground cumin
½ teaspoon ground turmeric
⅜ cup peanuts, lightly crushed
⅝ cup water, or coconut milk or a mixture of both
oil for shallow-frying
salt
cilantro leaves, to garnish

1 Put the rice flour, salt to taste and baking powder in a bowl. Add the garlic, coriander, cumin, turmeric and peanuts. Gradually stir in the water or coconut milk, to make a smooth, slightly runny batter.

2 Heat a little oil in a frying pan. Use a dessertspoon to spoon the batter into the pan and cook several fritters at a time. When the tops are no longer runny and the undersides are lacy and golden brown, turn them over with a spatula and cook the other sides until crisp and brown.

3 Lift out and drain on paper towels. Either use immediately or cool and store in an airtight tin.

4 To reheat the fritters, place in a single layer on a large baking sheet. Bake at 350°F for about 10 minutes. Garnish with cilantro.

COOK'S TIP

You can use either salted or unsalted peanuts in this recipe, but remember to adjust the seasoning accordingly.

Shrimp Crackers

In Indonesia one can find a wide range of *kroepoek* (the "oe" spelling betrays the Dutch influence). They can be made from rice, wheat, corn or cassava and so have differing flavors – rather like our crisps. You may use the tiny Chinese-style shrimp crackers which are more readily available from Asian stores and some large supermarkets.

INGREDIENTS

oil for deep-frying
8-ounce package shrimp crackers, or ½ x 1¼-pound package large Indonesian shrimp crackers

1 Heat the oil in a deep-frying pan to 375°F, or when a cube of day-old bread browns in 30 seconds.

2 Fry just one of the large *kroepoek* at a time, especially if they are being cooked whole. Cook 8–10 small crackers at a time.

3 As soon as they have expanded and become very puffy, remove them immediately from the oil with a slotted spoon. Do not allow them to color. Drain the crackers on paper towels. They can be cooked a few hours in advance and any leftovers can be kept in an airtight container.

Spicy Meat Fritters

INGREDIENTS

Makes 30

1 pound potatoes, boiled and drained
1 pound lean ground beef
1 onion, quartered
1 bunch scallions, chopped
3 garlic cloves, crushed
1 teaspoon ground nutmeg
1 tablespoon coriander seeds, dry-fried
    and ground
2 teaspoons cumin seeds, dry-fried
    and ground
4 eggs, beaten
oil for shallow-frying
salt and freshly ground black pepper

1 While the potatoes are still warm, mash them in the pan until they are well broken up. Add to the ground beef and mix well together.

2 Finely chop the onion, scallions and garlic. Add to the meat with the ground nutmeg, coriander and cumin. Stir in enough beaten egg to give a soft consistency which can be formed into fritters. Season to taste.

3 Heat the oil in a large frying pan. Using a dessertspoon, scoop out 6–8 oval-shaped fritters and drop them into the hot oil. Allow to set, so that they keep their shape (this will take about 3 minutes) and then turn over and cook for another minute.

4 Drain well on paper towels and keep warm while cooking the remaining fritters.

Barbecued Pork Spareribs

INGREDIENTS

Serves 4

2¼ pounds pork spareribs
1 onion
2 garlic cloves
1 inch fresh ginger root
⅓ cup dark soy sauce
1–2 fresh red chilies, seeded
    and chopped
1 teaspoon tamarind pulp, soaked in
    ⅓ cup water
1–2 tablespoons dark brown sugar
2 tablespoons peanut oil
salt and freshly ground black pepper

1 Wipe the pork ribs and place them in a wok, wide frying pan or large flameproof casserole.

2 Finely chop the onion, crush the garlic and peel and slice the ginger. Blend the soy sauce, onion, garlic, ginger and chopped chilies together to a paste in a food processor or with a mortar and pestle. Strain the tamarind and reserve the juice. Add the tamarind juice, brown sugar, oil and seasoning to taste to the onion mixture and mix well together.

3 Pour the sauce over the ribs and toss well to coat. Bring to a boil and then simmer, uncovered and stirring frequently, for 30 minutes. Add extra water if necessary.

4 Put the ribs on a rack in a roasting pan, place under a preheated broiler, on a barbecue grill or in the oven at 400°F. Continue cooking until the ribs are tender, about 20 minutes, depending on the thickness of the ribs. Baste the ribs with the sauce and turn them over from time to time.

Rendang

INGREDIENTS

Serves 6–8

2¼ pounds prime beef in one piece
2 onions or 5–6 shallots, sliced
4 garlic cloves, crushed
1 inch fresh *laos*, peeled and sliced, or
   1 teaspoon *laos* powder
1 inch fresh ginger root, peeled
   and sliced
4–6 fresh red chilies, seeded and sliced
1 lemon grass stem, lower part, sliced
1 inch fresh turmeric, peeled and
   sliced, or 1 teaspoon ground turmeric
1 teaspoon coriander seeds, dry-fried
   and ground
1 teaspoon cumin seeds, dry-fried
   and ground
2 lime leaves
1 teaspoon tamarind pulp, soaked in
   4 tablespoons warm water
2 x 14-fluid ounce cans coconut milk
1¼ cups water
2 tablespoons dark soy sauce
8 small new potatoes, scrubbed
salt
Deep-fried Onions, to garnish

1 Cut the meat in long strips and then into pieces of even size and place in a bowl.

2 Grind the onions or shallots, garlic, *laos* or *laos* powder, ginger, chilies, sliced lemon grass and turmeric to a fine paste in a food processor or with a mortar and pestle.

3 Add the paste to the meat with the coriander and cumin and mix well. Tear the lime leaves and add them to the mixture. Cover and leave in a cool place to marinate while you prepare the other ingredients.

4 Strain the tamarind and reserve the juice. Pour the coconut milk, water and the tamarind juice into a wok or flameproof casserole and stir in the spiced meat and soy sauce. Add seasoning as desired.

5 Stir until the liquid comes to a boil and then reduce the heat and simmer gently, half-covered, for about 1½–2 hours or until the meat is tender and the liquid reduced.

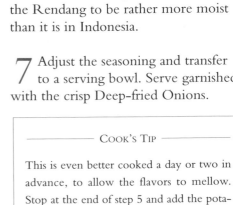

6 Add the new potatoes about 20–25 minutes before the end of the cooking time. The potatoes will absorb some of the sauce, so add a little more water to compensate if you prefer the Rendang to be rather more moist than it is in Indonesia.

7 Adjust the seasoning and transfer to a serving bowl. Serve garnished with the crisp Deep-fried Onions.

— COOK'S TIP —

This is even better cooked a day or two in advance, to allow the flavors to mellow. Stop at the end of step 5 and add the potatoes when you reheat.

Beef and Eggplant Curry

INGREDIENTS

Serves 6

½ cup sunflower oil
2 onions, thinly sliced
1 inch fresh ginger root, sliced and
  cut in matchsticks
1 garlic clove, crushed
2 fresh red chilies, seeded and very
  finely sliced
1 inch fresh turmeric, peeled and
  crushed, or 1 teaspoon
  ground turmeric
1 lemon grass stem, lower part finely
  sliced, top bruised
1½ pounds braising steak, cut in even-
  size strips
14 fluid-ounce can coconut milk
1¼ cups water
1 eggplant, sliced and patted dry
1 teaspoon tamarind pulp, soaked in
  4 tablespoons warm water
salt and freshly ground black pepper
finely sliced chili, (optional) and
  Deep-fried Onions, to garnish
boiled rice, to serve

1 Heat half the oil and fry the
onions, ginger and garlic until they
give off a rich aroma. Add the chilies,
turmeric and the lower part of the
lemon grass. Push to one side and then
turn up the heat and add the steak,
stirring until the meat changes color.

—— COOK'S TIP ——

If you want to make this curry, *Gulai
Terung Dengan Daging,* ahead, prepare to
the end of step 2 and finish later.

2 Add the coconut milk, water,
lemon grass top and seasoning to
taste. Cover and simmer gently for
1½ hours, or until the meat is tender.

3 Towards the end of the cooking
time heat the remaining oil in a
frying pan. Fry the eggplant slices until
brown on both sides.

4 Add the browned eggplant slices to
the beef curry and cook for
another 15 minutes. Stir gently from
time to time. Strain the tamarind and
stir the juice into the curry. Taste and
adjust the seasoning. Put into a warm
serving dish. Garnish with the sliced
chili, if using, and Deep-fried Onions,
and serve with boiled rice.

Balinese Spiced Duck

There is a delightful hotel on the beach at Sanur which cooks this delicious duck dish perfectly.

INGREDIENTS

Serves 4
8 duck portions, fat trimmed
  and reserved
¹/₄ cup dried coconut
³/₄ cup coconut milk
salt and freshly ground black pepper
Deep-fried Onions and salad leaves or
  fresh herb sprigs, to garnish

For the spice paste
1 small onion or 4–6 shallots, sliced
2 garlic cloves, sliced
¹/₂ inch fresh ginger root, peeled
  and sliced
¹/₂ inch fresh *laos*, peeled and sliced
1 inch fresh turmeric or
  ¹/₂ teaspoon ground turmeric
1–2 red chilies, seeded and sliced
4 macadamia nuts or 8 almonds
1 teaspoon coriander seeds, dry-fried

1 Place the duck fat trimmings in a heated frying pan, and render the fat over a low heat. Reserve the fat.

2 Dry-fry the dried coconut in a preheated pan until crisp and brown in color.

3 To make the spice paste, blend the onion or shallots, garlic, ginger, *laos*, fresh or ground turmeric, chilies, nuts and coriander seeds to a paste in a food processor or with a mortar and pestle.

4 Spread the spice paste over the duck portions and let marinate in a cool place for 3–4 hours. Preheat the oven to 325°F. Shake off and reserve the spice paste, then transfer the duck breasts to an oiled roasting pan. Cover with a double layer of foil and cook the duck breasts in the preheated oven for 2 hours.

5 Turn the oven temperature up to 375°F. Heat the reserved duck fat in a pan, add the spice paste and fry for 1–2 minutes. Stir in the coconut milk and simmer for 2 minutes. Discard the duck juices then cover the duck with the spice mixture and sprinkle with the toasted coconut. Cook in the oven for 20–30 minutes.

6 Arrange the duck on a warm serving platter and sprinkle with the Deep-fried Onions. Season to taste and serve with the salad leaves or fresh herb sprigs of your choice.

Duck with Chinese Mushrooms and Ginger

Ducks are often seen, comically herded in single file, along the water channels between the rice paddies throughout the country. The substantial Chinese population in Indonesia is particularly fond of duck and the delicious ingredients in this recipe give it an oriental flavor.

INGREDIENTS

Serves 4

5½-pound duck
1 teaspoon sugar
¼ cup light soy sauce
2 garlic cloves, crushed
8 dried Chinese mushrooms, soaked in 1½ cups warm water for 15 minutes
1 onion, sliced
2 inches fresh ginger root, sliced and cut in matchsticks
7 ounces baby corn
3–4 scallions, white bulbs left whole, green tops sliced
1–2 tablespoons cornstarch, mixed to a paste with 4 tablespoons water
salt and freshly ground black pepper
boiled rice, to serve

2 Strain the mushrooms, reserving the soaking liquid. Trim and discard the stalks.

1 Cut the duck along the breast, open it up and cut along each side of the backbone. Use the backbone, wings and giblets to make a stock, to use later in the recipe. Any trimmings of fat can be rendered in a frying pan, to use later in the recipe. Cut each leg and each breast in half. Place in a bowl, rub with the sugar and then pour over the soy sauce and garlic.

3 Fry the onion and ginger in the duck fat, in a frying pan, until they give off a good aroma. Push to one side. Lift the duck pieces out of the soy sauce and fry them until browned. Add the mushrooms and reserved liquid.

4 Add 2½ cups of the duck stock or water to the browned duck pieces. Season, cover and cook over a gentle heat for about 1 hour, or until the duck is tender.

5 Add the corn and the white part of the scallions and cook for another 10 minutes. Remove from the heat and add the corn paste. Return to the heat and bring to a boil, stirring. Cook for about 1 minute until glossy. Sprinkle with the sliced scallion tops and serve with boiled rice.

VARIATION

Replace the corn with chopped celery and slices of drained, canned water chestnuts.

Aromatic Chicken from Madura

Magadip is best cooked ahead so that the flavors permeate the chicken flesh making it even more delicious. A cool cucumber salad is a good accompaniment.

INGREDIENTS

Serves 4

3–3½-pound chicken, cut in quarters, or 4 chicken quarters
1 teaspoon sugar
2 tablespoons coriander seeds
2 teaspoons cumin seeds
6 whole cloves
½ teaspoon ground nutmeg
½ teaspoon ground turmeric
1 small onion
1 inch fresh ginger root, peeled and sliced
1¼ cups chicken broth or water
salt and freshly ground black pepper
boiled rice and Deep-fried Onions, to serve

1 Cut each chicken quarter in half to obtain eight pieces. Place in a flameproof casserole, sprinkle with sugar and salt and toss together. This helps release the juices in the chicken. Use the backbone and any remaining carcass to make chicken stock for use later in the recipe, if you like.

2 Dry-fry the coriander, cumin and whole cloves until the spices give off a good aroma. Add the nutmeg and turmeric and heat briefly. Grind in a processor or with a mortar and pestle.

--- COOK'S TIP ---

Add a large piece of bruised ginger and a small onion to the chicken stock to ensure a good flavor.

3 If using a processor, put in the onion and ginger until finely chopped. Otherwise, finely chop the onion and ginger and pound to a paste with a mortar and pestle. Add the spices and broth or water and mix well.

4 Pour over the chicken in the flameproof casserole. Cover with a lid and cook over a gentle heat until the chicken pieces are really tender, about 45–50 minutes.

5 Serve portions of the chicken, with the sauce, on boiled rice, sprinkled with crisp Deep-fried Onions.

Chicken Cooked in Coconut Milk

Traditionally, the chicken pieces would be part-cooked by frying, but roasting in the oven is a better option. *Ayam Opor* is an unusual recipe in that the sauce is white as it does not contain chilies or turmeric, unlike many other Indonesian dishes. The dish is usually served with crisp Deep-fried Onions.

INGREDIENTS

Serves 4

3–3½-pound chicken or
    4 chicken quarters
4 garlic cloves
1 onion, sliced
4 macadamia nuts or 8 almonds
1 tablespoon coriander seeds, dry-fried,
    or 1 teaspoon ground coriander
3 tablespoons oil
1 inch fresh *laos*, peeled
    and bruised
2 lemon grass stems, fleshy part bruised
3 lime leaves
2 bay leaves
1 teaspoon sugar
2½ cups coconut milk
salt
boiled rice and Deep-fried Onions,
    to serve

1 Preheat the oven to 375°F. Cut the chicken into four or eight pieces. Season with salt. Put in an oiled roasting pan and cook in the oven for 25–30 minutes. Meanwhile, prepare the sauce.

2 Grind the garlic, onion, nuts and coriander to a fine paste in a food processor or with a mortar and pestle. Heat the oil and fry the paste to bring out the flavor. Do not allow it to brown.

3 Add the part-cooked chicken pieces to a wok together with the *laos*, lemon grass, lime and bay leaves, sugar, coconut milk and salt to taste. Mix well to coat in the sauce.

4 Bring to a boil and then reduce the heat and simmer gently for 30–40 minutes, uncovered, until the chicken is tender and the coconut sauce is reduced and thickened. Stir the mixture occasionally during cooking.

5 Just before serving remove the bruised *laos* and lemon grass. Serve with boiled rice and sprinkle with Deep-fried Onions.

Shrimp with Chayote in Turmeric Sauce

This delicious, attractively colored dish is called *Gule Udang Dengan Labu Kuning*.

INGREDIENTS

Serves 4

1–2 chayotes or 2–3 zucchini
2 fresh red chilies, seeded
1 onion, quartered
¼ inch fresh *laos,* peeled
1 lemon grass stem, lower 2 inches
   sliced, top bruised
1 inch fresh turmeric, peeled
⅞ cup water
lemon juice
14-ounce can coconut milk
1 pound cooked, peeled shrimp
salt
red chili shreds, to garnish (optional)
boiled rice, to serve

1 Peel the chayotes, remove the seeds and cut into strips. If using zucchini, cut into 2-inch strips.

2 Grind the fresh red chilies, onion, sliced *laos*, sliced lemon grass and the fresh turmeric to a paste in a food processor or with a mortar and pestle. Add the water to the paste mixture, with a squeeze of lemon juice and salt to taste.

3 Pour into a pan. Add the top of the lemon grass stem. Bring to the boil and cook for 1–2 minutes. Add the chayote or zucchini pieces and cook for 2 minutes. Stir in the coconut milk. Taste and adjust the seasoning.

4 Stir in the shrimp and cook gently for 2–3 minutes. Remove the lemon grass stem. Garnish with shreds of chili, if using, and serve with rice.

Doedoeh of Fish

Haddock or cod fillet may be substituted in this recipe.

INGREDIENTS

Serves 6–8

2¼ pounds fresh mackerel
   fillets, skinned
2 tablespoons tamarind pulp, soaked in
   ⅞ cup water
1 onion
½ inch fresh *laos*
2 garlic cloves
1–2 fresh red chilies, seeded, or
   1 teaspoon chili powder
1 teaspoon ground coriander
1 teaspoon ground turmeric
½ teaspoon ground fennel seeds
1 tablespoon dark brown sugar
6–7 tablespoons oil
⅞ cup coconut cream
salt and freshly ground black pepper
fresh chili shreds, to garnish

1 Rinse the fish fillets in cold water and dry them well on paper towels. Put into a shallow dish and sprinkle with a little salt. Strain the tamarind and pour the juice over the fish fillets. Set aside for 30 minutes.

2 Quarter the onion, peel and slice the *laos* and peel the garlic. Grind the onion, *laos*, garlic and chilies or chili powder to a paste in a food processor or with a mortar and pestle. Add the ground coriander, turmeric, fennel seeds and sugar.

3 Heat half of the oil in a frying pan. Drain the fish fillets and fry for 5 minutes, or until cooked. Set aside.

4 Wipe out the pan and heat the remaining oil. Fry the spice paste, stirring constantly, until it gives off a spicy aroma. Do not let it brown. Add the coconut cream and simmer gently for a few minutes. Add the fish fillets and gently heat through.

5 Taste for seasoning and serve sprinkled with shredded chili.

Spicy Fish

If you make *Ikan Kecap* a day ahead, put it straight onto a serving dish after cooking and then pour over the sauce, cover and chill until required.

INGREDIENTS

Serves 3–4
1 pound fish fillets, such as mackerel, cod or haddock
2 tablespoons flour
peanut oil for frying
1 onion, coarsely chopped
1 small garlic clove, crushed
1½ inches fresh ginger root, peeled and grated
1–2 fresh red chilies, seeded and sliced
½ teaspoon shrimp paste
4 tablespoons water
juice of ½ lemon
1 tablespoon brown sugar
2 tablespoons dark soy sauce
salt
roughly torn lettuce leaves, to serve

1 Rinse the fish fillets under cold water and dry well on absorbent paper towels. Cut into serving portions and remove any bones.

2 Season the flour with salt and use it to dust the fish. Heat the oil in a frying pan and fry the fish on both sides for 3–4 minutes, or until cooked. Lift onto a plate and set aside.

3 Rinse out and dry the pan. Heat a little more oil and fry the onion, garlic, ginger and chilies just to bring out the flavor. Do not brown.

4 Blend the shrimp paste with a little water, to make a paste. Add it to the onion mixture, with a little extra water if necessary. Cook for 2 minutes and then stir in the lemon juice, brown sugar and soy sauce.

5 Pour over the fish and serve, hot or cold, with roughly torn lettuce.

--- COOK'S TIP ---

For a buffet dish cut the fish into bite-size pieces or serving portions.

Squid from Madura

This squid dish, *Cumi Cumi Madura*, is popular in Indonesia. It is quite usual to be invited into the restaurant kitchen and given a warm welcome.

INGREDIENTS

Serves 2–3
1 pound cleaned and drained squid, body cut in strips, tentacles left whole
3 garlic cloves
¼ teaspoon ground nutmeg
1 bunch of scallions
4 tablespoons sunflower oil
1 cup water
1 tablespoon dark soy sauce
salt and freshly ground black pepper
1 lime, cut in wedges (optional)
boiled rice, to serve

1 Squeeze out and discard the little central "bone" from each tentacle. Heat a wok, toss in the squid and stir-fry for 1 minute. Remove the squid.

2 Crush the garlic with the nutmeg and some salt and pepper. Trim the roots from the scallions, cut the white part into small pieces, slice the green part and then set aside.

3 Heat the wok, add the oil and fry the white part of the scallions. Stir in the garlic paste and the squid.

4 Rinse out the garlic paste container with the water and soy sauce and add to the pan. Half-cover and simmer for 4–5 minutes. Add the scallion tops, toss lightly and serve at once, with lime, if using, and rice.

Sambal Kecap

This can be served as a dip for *satés* instead of the usual peanut sauce and is particularly good with beef and chicken *satés* and deep-fried chicken.

INGREDIENTS

Makes about ⅝ cup
1 fresh red chili, seeded and finely chopped
2 garlic cloves, crushed
4 tablespoons dark soy sauce
4 teaspoons lemon juice, or 1–1½ tablespoons prepared tamarind juice
2 tablespoons hot water
2 tablespoons Deep-fried Onions (optional)

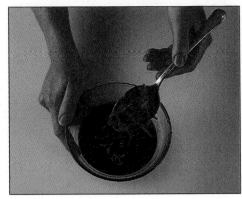

1 Mix the chili, garlic, soy sauce, lemon or tamarind juice and hot water together in a bowl.

2 Stir in the Deep-fried Onions, if using, and leave to stand for 30 minutes before serving.

Deep-fried Onions

Known as *Bawang Goreng,* these are a traditional garnish and accompaniment to many Indonesian dishes. Asian stores sell them ready-made, but it is simple to make them at home, using fresh onions, or for an even faster way, use an 2–3-ounce package of freeze-dried onions, which you can fry in about 1 cup of sunflower oil. This gives you 4 ounces of fried onion flakes. The small red onions that can be bought in Asian shops are excellent when deep-fried as they contain less water than most European varieties.

INGREDIENTS

Makes 1 pound
1 pound onions
oil for deep-frying

1 Peel and slice the onions as evenly and finely as possible.

2 Spread out thinly on paper towels, in an airy place, and leave to dry for 30 minutes to 2 hours.

3 Heat the oil in deep-fryer or wok to 375°F. Fry the onions in batches, until crisp and golden, turning all the time. Drain well on paper towels and cool. Deep-fried Onions may be stored in an airtight container.

> ——— COOK'S TIP ———
>
> Garlic can be prepared and cooked in the same way, or some can be fried with the last batch of onions. Deep-fried Garlic gives an added dimension in flavor as a garnish for many dishes.

Spiced Cauliflower Braise

A delicious vegetable stew, known as *Sambal Kol Kembang,* which combines coconut milk with spices and is perfect as a vegetarian main course or as part of a buffet.

INGREDIENTS

Serves 4

1 cauliflower
2 medium or 1 large tomato(es)
1 onion, chopped
2 garlic cloves, crushed
1 fresh green chili, seeded
½ tablespoon ground turmeric
½ teaspoon shrimp paste
2 tablespoons sunflower oil
14-fluid ounce can coconut milk
1 cup water
1 teaspoon sugar
1 teaspoon tamarind pulp, soaked in
 3 tablespoons warm water
salt

1 Trim the stalk from the cauliflower and divide into tiny florets. Skin the tomato(es) if liked. Chop the flesh into ½–1-inch pieces.

2 Grind the chopped onion, garlic, green chili, ground turmeric and shrimp paste together to a paste in a food processor or with a mortar and pestle. Heat the sunflower oil in a wok or large frying pan and fry the spice paste to bring out the aromatic flavors, without allowing it to brown.

3 Add the cauliflower florets and toss well to coat in the spices. Stir in the coconut milk, water, sugar and salt to taste. Simmer for 5 minutes. Strain the tamarind and reserve the juice.

4 Add the tamarind juice and chopped tomatoes to the pan then cook for 2–3 minutes only. Taste for check the seasoning and serve.

Spicy Scrambled Eggs

This is a lovely way to liven up scrambled eggs. When making *Orak Arik,* prepare all the ingredients ahead so that the vegetables retain all their crunch and color.

INGREDIENTS

Serves 4

2 tablespoons sunflower oil
1 onion, finely sliced
8 ounces Chinese cabbage, finely sliced
 or cut in diamonds
7-ounce can corn kernels
1 small fresh red chili, seeded and finely
 sliced (optional)
2 tablespoons water
2 eggs, beaten
salt and freshly ground black pepper
Deep-fried Onions, to garnish

1 Heat a wok, add the oil and fry the onion, until soft but not browned.

2 Add the Chinese cabbage and toss well together. Add the corn, chili and water. Cover with a lid and cook for 2 minutes.

3 Remove the lid and stir in the beaten eggs and the seasoning. Stir constantly until the eggs are creamy and just set. Serve on warmed plates, sprinkled with crisp Deep-fried Onions.

Cooked Vegetable Gado-Gado

Instead of putting everything on a large platter, you can serve individual servings of this salad. It is a perfect recipe for lunchtime or informal gatherings.

INGREDIENTS

Serves 6

8 ounces waxy potatoes, cooked
1 pound mixed cabbage, spinach and
   bean sprouts, in equal proportions,
   rinsed and shredded
½ cucumber, cut in wedges, salted and
   set aside for 15 minutes
2–3 eggs, hard-boiled and shelled
4 ounces fresh bean curd
oil for frying
6–8 large Shrimp Crackers
lemon juice
Deep-fried Onions, to garnish
Peanut Sauce, to serve

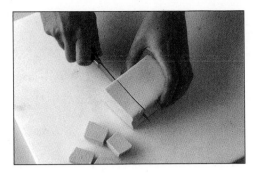

1 Cube the potatoes and set aside. Bring a large pan of salted water to a boil. Plunge one type of raw vegetable at a time into the pan for just a few seconds to blanch. Lift out the vegetables with a large slotted spoon or sieve and run under very cold water, or plunge them into iced water and set aside 2 minutes. Drain thoroughly. Blanch all the vegetables, except the cucumber, in this way.

2 Rinse the cucumber pieces and drain them well. Cut the eggs in quarters. Cut the bean curd into cubes.

3 Fry the bean curd in hot oil in a wok until crisp on both sides. Lift out and drain on paper towels.

4 Add more oil to the pan and then deep-fry the Shrimp Crackers one or two at a time. Reserve them on a tray lined with paper towels.

5 Arrange all the cooked vegetables attractively on a platter, with the cucumber, hard-boiled eggs and bean curd. Scatter with the lemon juice and Deep-fried Onions at the last minute.

6 Serve with the prepared Peanut Sauce and hand round the fried Shrimp Crackers separately.

Stir-fried Greens

Quail's eggs look very attractive in *Chah Kang Kung*, but you can substitute some baby corn, halved at an angle.

INGREDIENTS

Serves 4

2 bunches spinach or chard or 1 head Chinese cabbage
3 garlic cloves, crushed
2 inches fresh ginger root, peeled and cut in matchsticks
3–4 tablespoons peanut oil
14 ounces boneless, skinless chicken breast, or pork loin, or a mixture of both, very finely sliced
12 quail's eggs, hard-boiled and shelled
1 fresh red chili, seeded and shredded
2–3 tablespoons oyster sauce
1 tablespoon brown sugar
2 teaspoons cornstarch, mixed with ¼ cup cold water
salt

COOK'S TIP

As with all stir-fries, don't start cooking until you have prepared all the ingredients and arranged them to hand. Cut everything into small, even-size pieces so the food can be cooked very quickly and all the colors and flavors preserved.

1 Wash the chosen leaves well and shake them dry. Strip the tender leaves from the stems and tear them into pieces. Discard the lower, tougher part of the stems and slice the remainder evenly.

2 Fry the garlic and ginger in the hot oil, without browning, for a minute. Add the chicken and/or pork and keep stirring it in the wok until the meat changes color. When the meat looks cooked, add the sliced stems first and cook them quickly; then add the torn leaves, quail's eggs and chili. Spoon in the oyster sauce and a little boiling water, if necessary. Cover and cook for 1–2 minutes only.

3 Remove the lid, stir and add sugar and salt to taste. Stir in the cornstarch and water mixture and toss thoroughly. Cook until the mixture is well coated in a glossy sauce.

4 Serve immediately, while still very hot and the colors are bright and glowingly jewel-like.

Black Glutinous Rice Pudding

This very unusual rice pudding, *Bubor Pulot Hitam,* which uses bruised fresh ginger root, is quite delicious. When cooked, black rice still retains its husk and has a nutty texture. Serve in small bowls, with a little coconut cream poured over each helping.

INGREDIENTS

Serves 6
4 ounces black glutinous rice
2 cups water
½ inch fresh ginger root, peeled
   and bruised
⅜ cup dark brown sugar
¼ cup superfine sugar
1¼ cups coconut milk
   or cream, to serve

1 Put the rice in a strainer and rinse well under cold running water. Drain and put in a large pan, with the water. Bring to a boil and stir to prevent the rice from settling on the bottom of the pan. Cover and cook for about 30 minutes.

2 Add the ginger and the brown and superfine sugars. Cook for about 15 minutes more, adding a little more water if necessary, until the rice is cooked and like porridge. Remove the ginger and serve warm, in bowls, topped with coconut milk or cream.

Deep-fried Bananas

Known as *Pisang Goreng*, these delicious deep-fried bananas should be cooked at the last minute, so that the outer crust of batter is crisp in texture and the banana is soft and warm inside.

INGREDIENTS

Serves 8
4 ounces self-rising flour
⅜ cup rice flour
½ teaspoon salt
1 cup water
finely grated lime rind (optional)
8 small bananas
oil for deep-frying
sugar and 1 lime, cut in wedges,
   to serve

1 Sift both the flours and the salt together into a bowl. Add just enough water to make a smooth, coating batter. Mix well, then add the lime rind, if using.

2 Peel the bananas and dip them into the batter two or three times.

3 Heat the oil to 375°F or when a cube of day-old bread browns in 30 seconds. Deep-fry the batter-coated bananas until crisp and golden. Drain and serve hot, dredged with sugar and with the lime wedges to squeeze over the bananas.

Pancakes Filled with Sweet Coconut

Traditionally, the pale green color in the batter for *Dadar Gulung* was obtained from the juice squeezed from *pandan* leaves – a real labor of love. Green food coloring can be used as the modern alternative to this lengthy process.

INGREDIENTS

Makes 12–15 pancakes
¾ cup dark brown sugar
2 cups water
1 *pandan* leaf, stripped through with a
  fork and tied into a knot
6 ounces dried coconut
oil for frying
salt

For the pancake batter
8 ounces flour, sifted
2 eggs, beaten
2 drops edible green food coloring
few drops vanilla extract
scant 2 cups water
3 tablespoons peanut oil

1 Dissolve the sugar in the water with the *pandan* leaf, in a pan over gentle heat, stirring constantly. Increase the heat and allow to boil gently for 3–4 minutes, until the mixture just becomes syrupy. Do not let it caramelize.

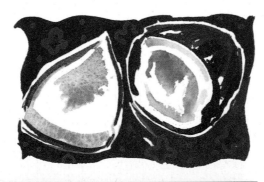

2 Put the coconut into a wok with a pinch of salt. Pour over the prepared sugar syrup and cook over a very gentle heat, stirring from time to time, until the mixture becomes almost dry; this will take 5–10 minutes. Set aside until required.

3 To make the batter, blend together the flour, eggs, food coloring, vanilla extract, water and oil either by hand or in a food processor.

4 Brush a 7-inch frying pan with oil and cook 12–15 pancakes. Keep the pancakes warm. Fill each pancake with a generous spoonful of the coconut mixture, roll up and serve them immediately.

Steamed Coconut Custard

Srikaya is a very popular dessert that turns up all over South-east Asia, rather as crème caramel is found all over Europe and the Americas.

INGREDIENTS

Serves 8
14-fluid ounce can coconut milk
5 tablespoons water
1 ounce sugar
3 eggs, beaten
1 ounce cellophane noodles, soaked in warm water for 5 minutes
4 ripe bananas or plantains, peeled and cut in small pieces
salt
vanilla ice cream, to serve (optional)

1 Stir the coconut milk, water and sugar into the beaten eggs and whisk well together.

2 Strain into a 7½-cup heatproof soufflé dish.

3 Drain the noodles well and cut them into small pieces with scissors. Stir the noodles into the coconut milk mixture, together with the chopped bananas or plantains. Stir in a pinch of salt.

4 Cover the dish with foil and place in a steamer for about 1 hour, or until set. Test by inserting a thin, small knife or skewer into the center. Serve hot or cold, on its own or topped with vanilla ice cream.

THAILAND

Ginger, Chicken and Coconut Soup

This aromatic soup is rich with coconut milk and intensely flavored with galangal, lemongrass and kaffir lime leaves.

INGREDIENTS

Serves 4–6

3 cups unsweetened coconut milk
2 cups chicken stock
4 lemongrass stalks, bruised
 and chopped
1-inch piece galangal, thinly sliced
10 black peppercorns, crushed
10 kaffir lime leaves, torn
11 ounces boneless chicken, cut
 into thin strips
1½ cups button mushrooms
5 tablespoons canned baby corn
4 tablespoons lime juice
3 tablespoons fish sauce
2 red chilies, chopped, to garnish
chopped scallions, to garnish
cilantro leaves, to garnish

1 Bring the coconut milk and chicken stock to a boil. Add the lemongrass, galangal, peppercorns and half the kaffir lime leaves, reduce the heat and simmer gently for 10 minutes.

3 Stir in the lime juice, fish sauce to taste and the rest of the lime leaves. Serve hot, garnished with red chilies, scallions and cilantro.

2 Strain the stock into a clean pan. Return to the heat, then add the chicken, button mushrooms and baby corn. Cook for about 5–7 minutes or until the chicken is cooked.

Hot and Sour Shrimp Soup with Lemongrass

This classic Thai seafood soup – *Tom Yam Goong* – is probably the most popular and well-known soup from Thailand.

INGREDIENTS

Serves 4–6

1 pound jumbo shrimp
4 cups chicken stock or water
3 lemongrass stalks
10 kaffir lime leaves, torn in half
8-ounce can straw mushrooms, drained
3 tablespoons fish sauce
¼ cup lime juice
2 tablespoons chopped scallion
1 tablespoon cilantro leaves
4 red chilies, seeded and chopped
2 scallions, finely chopped

1 Shell and devein the shrimp and set aside. Rinse the shrimp shells and place in a large saucepan with the stock or water and bring to a boil.

3 Strain the stock and return to the saucepan and reheat. Add the mushrooms and shrimp, then cook until the shrimp turn pink.

2 Bruise the lemongrass stalks with the blunt edge of a chopping knife and add them to the stock, together with half the lime leaves. Simmer gently for 5–6 minutes, until the stalks change color and the stock is fragrant.

4 Stir in the fish sauce, lime juice, scallions, cilantro, red chilies and the rest of the lime leaves. Taste and adjust the seasoning. It should be sour, salty, spicy and hot.

Rice Cakes with Spicy Dipping Sauce

Rice cakes are a classic Thai appetizer. They are easy to make and can be kept in an airtight box almost indefinitely.

INGREDIENTS

Serves 4–6
1 cup jasmine rice
1½ cups water
oil for frying and greasing

For the spicy dipping sauce
6–8 dried chilies
½ teaspoon salt
2 shallots, chopped
2 garlic cloves, chopped
4 cilantro roots
10 white peppercorns
1 cup unsweetened coconut milk
1 teaspoon shrimp paste
4 ounces ground pork
4 ounces cherry tomatoes, chopped
1 tablespoon fish sauce
1 tablespoon palm sugar
2 tablespoons tamarind juice
2 tablespoons coarsely chopped
  roasted peanuts
2 scallions, finely chopped

1 Stem the chilies and remove most of the seeds. Soak the chilies in warm water for 20 minutes. Drain and transfer to a mortar.

2 Add the salt and grind with a pestle until the chilies are crushed. Add the shallots, garlic, cilantro roots and peppercorns. Pound together until you have a coarse paste.

3 Pour the coconut milk into a saucepan and boil until it begins to separate. Add the pounded chili paste. Cook for 2–3 minutes, until it is fragrant. Stir in the shrimp paste. Cook for another minute.

4 Add the pork, stirring to break up any lumps. Cook for about 5–10 minutes. Add the tomatoes, fish sauce, palm sugar and tamarind juice. Simmer until the sauce thickens.

5 Stir in the chopped peanuts and scallions. Remove from the heat and set aside to cool.

6 Wash the rice in several changes of water. Put in a saucepan, add the water and cover with a tight-fitting lid. Bring to a boil, reduce the heat and simmer gently for about 15 minutes.

7 Remove the lid and fluff up the rice. Turn out on to a lightly greased tray and press down with the back of a large spoon. Set aside to dry out overnight in a very low oven, until it is completely dry and firm.

8 Remove the rice from the tray and break into bite-size pieces. Heat the oil in a wok or deep-fat fryer.

9 Deep-fry the rice cakes in batches for about 1 minute, until they puff up, taking care not to brown them too much. Remove and drain. Serve accompanied with the dipping sauce.

Fish Cakes with Cucumber Relish

These wonderful small fish cakes are a very familiar and popular appetizer. They are usually accompanied by Thai beer.

INGREDIENTS

Makes about 12

11 ounces white fish fillet, such as cod, cut into chunks
2 tablespoons red curry paste
1 egg
2 tablespoons fish sauce
1 teaspoon sugar
2 tablespoons cornstarch
3 kaffir lime leaves, shredded
1 tablespoon chopped cilantro
2 ounces green beans, finely sliced
oil for frying
Chinese mustard cress, to garnish

For the cucumber relish

4 tablespoons Thai coconut or rice vinegar
4 tablespoons water
4 tablespoons sugar
1 head pickled garlic
1 cucumber, quartered and sliced
4 shallots, finely sliced
1 tablespoon finely chopped ginger
2 red chilies, seeded and finely sliced

1 For the cucumber relish, bring the vinegar, water and sugar to a boil. Stir until the sugar dissolves, remove from the heat and cool.

2 Combine the rest of the relish ingredients together in a bowl and pour over the vinegar mixture.

3 Combine the fish, curry paste and egg in a food processor and process well. Transfer the mixture to a bowl, add the rest of the ingredients, except for the oil and garnish, and mix well.

4 Mold and shape the mixture into cakes about 2 inches in diameter and ¼ inch thick.

5 Heat the oil in a wok or deep-fat fryer. Fry the fish cakes, a few at a time, for about 4–5 minutes or until golden brown. Remove and drain on paper towels. Garnish with Chinese mustard cress and serve with the cucumber relish.

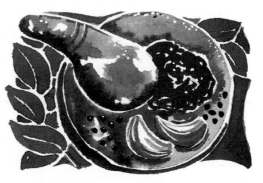

Pogo Satay

Originating in Indonesia, satay are skewers of meat marinated with spices and grilled quickly over charcoal. It's street food at its best, prepared by vendors with portable grills who set up stalls at every street corner and market place. As well as pork, you can also make satay with chicken, beef or lamb. Serve with satay sauce and cucumber relish.

INGREDIENTS

Makes about 20
1 pound lean pork
1 teaspoon grated ginger
1 lemongrass stalk, finely chopped
3 garlic cloves, finely chopped
1 tablespoon medium curry paste
1 teaspoon ground cumin
1 teaspoon ground turmeric
4 tablespoons coconut cream
2 tablespoons fish sauce
1 teaspoon sugar
20 wooden satay skewers
oil for cooking

For the satay sauce
1 cup unsweetened coconut milk
2 tablespoons red curry paste
½ cup crunchy peanut butter
½ cup chicken stock
3 tablespoons brown sugar
2 tablespoons tamarind juice
1 tablespoon fish sauce
1 teaspoon salt

1 Cut the pork thinly into 2-inch strips. Mix together the ginger, lemongrass, garlic, medium curry paste, cumin, turmeric, coconut cream, fish sauce and sugar.

3 Meanwhile, make the sauce. Heat the coconut milk over a medium heat, then add the red curry paste, peanut butter, chicken stock and sugar.

4 Cook and stir until smooth, about 5–6 minutes. Add the tamarind juice, fish sauce and salt to taste.

5 Thread the meat onto skewers. Brush with oil and grill over charcoal or under a preheated broiler for 3–4 minutes on each side, turning occasionally, until cooked and golden brown. Serve with the satay sauce.

2 Pour over the pork and set aside to marinate for about 2 hours.

Chicken and Sticky Rice Balls

These balls can either be steamed or deep-fried. The fried versions are crunchy and are excellent for serving at cocktail parties.

INGREDIENTS

Makes about 30
1 pound ground chicken
1 egg
1 teaspoon tapioca flour
4 scallions, finely chopped
2 tablespoons chopped cilantro
2 tablespoons fish sauce
pinch of sugar
8 ounces cooked sticky rice
banana leaves
oil for brushing
freshly ground black pepper
1 small carrot, shredded, to garnish
1 red bell pepper, to garnish
chopped chives, to garnish
sweet chili sauce, to serve

1 In a mixing bowl, combine the ground chicken, egg, tapioca flour, scallions and cilantro. Mix well and season with fish sauce, sugar and freshly ground black pepper.

2 Spread the cooked sticky rice on a plate or flat tray.

3 Place a teaspoonful of the chicken mixture on the bed of rice. With damp hands, roll and shape the mixture in the rice to make a ball about the size of a walnut. Repeat with the rest of the chicken mixture.

COOK'S TIP

Sticky rice, also known as glutinous rice, has a very high gluten content. It is so called because the grains stick together when cooked. It can be eaten both as a savory and as a sweet dish.

4 Line a bamboo steamer with banana leaves and lightly brush them with oil. Place the chicken balls on the leaves, spacing well apart to prevent them sticking together. Steam over high heat for about 10 minutes or until cooked.

5 Remove and arrange on serving plates. Garnish with shredded carrots, strips of red pepper and chives. Serve with sweet chili sauce.

Green Beef Curry with Thai Eggplant

This is a very quick curry so be sure to use good quality meat.

INGREDIENTS

Serves 4–6
3 tablespoons vegetable oil
3 tablespoons green curry paste
2½ cups unsweetened coconut milk
1 pound boneless sirloin steak
4 kaffir lime leaves, torn
1–2 tablespoons fish sauce
1 teaspoon palm sugar
5 ounces small Thai eggplant, halved
a small handful of Thai basil
2 green chilies, to garnish

For the green curry paste
15 hot green chilies
2 lemongrass stalks, chopped
3 shallots, sliced
2 garlic cloves
1 tablespoon chopped galangal
4 kaffir lime leaves, chopped
½ teaspoon grated kaffir lime rind
1 teaspoon chopped cilantro root
6 black peppercorns
1 teaspoon coriander seeds, roasted
1 teaspoon cumin seeds, roasted
1 tablespoon sugar
1 teaspoon salt
1 teaspoon shrimp paste (optional)

1 To make the green curry paste, combine all the ingredients except the oil. Pound using a mortar and pestle or process in a food processor until smooth. Add about 2 tablespoons of the oil, a little at a time, blending well. Keep in a jar in the fridge until required.

2 Heat the remaining oil in a large pan. Add 3 tablespoons of the curry paste and fry until fragrant.

3 Stir in half the coconut milk, a little at a time. Cook for about 5–6 minutes, until an oily sheen appears.

4 Cut the beef into long thin slices and add to the saucepan with the kaffir lime leaves, fish sauce, sugar and eggplant. Cook for 2–3 minutes, then stir in the remaining coconut milk.

5 Bring back to a simmer and cook until the meat and eggplant are tender. Stir in the Thai basil just before serving. Finely shred the green chilies and use as a garnish.

Steamed Eggs with Beef and Scallions

This is a very delicate dish. You can add less liquid for a firmer custard, but cooked this way it is soft and silky. Other types of meat or seafood can be used instead of the beef.

INGREDIENTS

Serves 4–6

4 ounces sirloin or round steak
1 teaspoon grated fresh ginger
1 tablespoon fish sauce
3 eggs
½ cup chicken stock or water
2 tablespoons finely chopped
   scallions
1 tablespoon vegetable oil
2 garlic cloves, finely sliced
freshly ground black pepper

1 Finely chop the beef and place in a large bowl. Add the ginger, fish sauce and freshly ground black pepper.

2 Beat the eggs together with the stock. Stir the mixture into the beef, add the scallions and beat together until well-blended. Try to avoid making too many bubbles.

3 Pour the mixture into a heatproof dish or individual ramekins.

4 Place in a steamer and steam over gentle heat for 10–15 minutes, or until the custard is set.

5 Meanwhile, heat the oil in a frying pan. Add the garlic, and stir to break up any lumps and fry for about 2 minutes, until golden.

6 To serve, pour the garlic and oil over the egg custards. Allow to cool slightly before serving.

--- COOK'S TIP ---

The Japanese make a similar version of this recipe called *Chewan Mushi,* using spinach, shrimp and shiitake mushrooms.

Sweet and Sour Pork, Thai-style

Sweet and sour is traditionally a Chinese creation, but the Thais do it very well. This version has an altogether fresher and cleaner flavor and it makes a good one-dish meal with rice.

INGREDIENTS

Serves 4

12 ounces lean pork
2 tablespoons vegetable oil
4 garlic cloves, finely sliced
1 small red onion, sliced
2 tablespoons fish sauce
1 tablespoon sugar
1 red bell pepper, seeded and diced
½ cucumber, seeded and sliced
2 plum tomatoes, cut into wedges
4 ounces pineapple, cut into
  small chunks
freshly ground black pepper
2 scallions, cut into short lengths
cilantro leaves and shredded scallions,
  to garnish

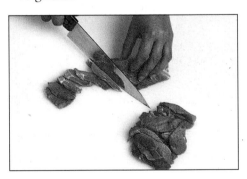

1 Slice the pork into thin strips. Heat the oil in a wok or large frying pan.

2 Add the garlic and fry until golden, then add the pork and stir-fry for about 4–5 minutes. Add the onion.

3 Season with fish sauce, sugar and freshly ground black pepper. Stir and cook for 3–4 minutes, or until the pork is cooked.

4 Add the rest of the vegetables, the pineapple and scallions. You may need to add a few tablespoons of water. Continue to stir-fry for about another 3–4 minutes. Serve hot, garnished with cilantro leaves and scallions.

Burmese-style Pork Curry

Burmese-style curries use pork instead of chicken or beef and water rather than coconut milk. The flavors of this delicious dish improve when it is reheated.

INGREDIENTS

Serves 4–6

1-inch piece fresh ginger, crushed
8 dried red chilies, soaked in warm water for 20 minutes
2 lemongrass stalks, finely chopped
1 tablespoon chopped galangal
1 tablespoon shrimp paste
2 tablespoons brown sugar
1 pound pork, with some of its fat
2½ cups water
2 teaspoons ground turmeric
1 teaspoon dark soy sauce
4 shallots, finely chopped
1 tablespoon chopped garlic
3 tablespoons tamarind juice
1 teaspoon sugar
1 tablespoon fish sauce
green beans, to serve
red chilies, to garnish

1 In a mortar, pound the ginger, chilies, lemongrass and galangal into a coarse paste with a pestle, then add the shrimp paste and brown sugar to produce a dark, grainy purée.

2 Cut the pork into large chunks and place in a large heavy-bottomed pan. Add the curry purée and stir to coat the meat thoroughly.

3 Cook over low heat, stirring occasionally, until the meat has changed color and rendered some of its fat and the curry paste is fragrant.

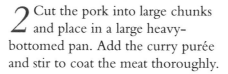

4 Stir in the water, turmeric and soy sauce. Simmer until the meat is tender, for about 40 minutes.

5 Add the shallots, garlic, tamarind juice, sugar and fish sauce. Serve with freshly cooked green beans, and garnish with chilies.

Savory Pork Ribs with Snake Beans

This is a rich and pungent dish. If snake beans are hard to find, you can substitute fine green beans or wax beans.

INGREDIENTS

Serves 4–6

1½ pounds pork spare ribs or boneless
  pork loin
2 tablespoons vegetable oil
½ cup water
1 tablespoon palm sugar
1 tablespoon fish sauce
5 ounces snake beans, cut into
  2-inch lengths
2 kaffir lime leaves, finely sliced
2 red chilies, finely sliced, to garnish

For the chili paste

3 dried red chilies, seeded and soaked
4 shallots, chopped
4 garlic cloves, chopped
1 teaspoon chopped galangal
1 lemongrass stalk, chopped
6 black peppercorns
1 teaspoon shrimp paste
2 tablespoons dried shrimp, rinsed

1 Put all the ingredients for the chili paste in a mortar and grind together with a pestle until it forms a thick paste.

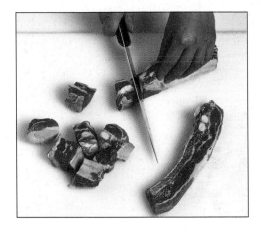

2 Slice and chop the spare ribs (or pork loin) into 1½-inch lengths.

3 Heat the oil in a wok or frying pan. Add the pork and fry for about 5 minutes, until lightly browned.

4 Stir in the chili paste and continue to cook for another 5 minutes, stirring constantly to keep the paste from sticking to the pan.

5 Add the water, cover and simmer for 7–10 minutes, or until the spare ribs are tender. Season with palm sugar and fish sauce.

6 Mix in the snake beans and kaffir lime leaves and fry until the beans are cooked. Serve garnished with sliced red chilies.

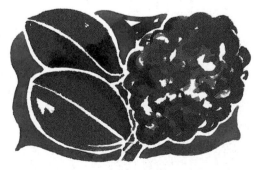

Chicken Livers, Thai-style

Chicken liver is a good source of iron and is a popular meat, especially in the north-east. Serve this dish as an appetizer with salad, or as part of a main course with jasmine rice.

INGREDIENTS

Serves 4–6

3 tablespoons vegetable oil
1 pound chicken livers, trimmed
4 shallots, chopped
2 garlic cloves, chopped
1 tablespoon roasted ground rice
3 tablespoons fish sauce
3 tablespoons lime juice
1 teaspoon sugar
2 lemongrass stalks, bruised
  and finely chopped
2 tablespoons chopped cilantro
10–12 mint leaves, to garnish

1 Heat the oil in a wok or large frying pan. Add the livers and fry over medium-high heat for about 4 minutes, until the liver is golden brown and cooked, but still pink inside.

2 Move the liver to one side of the pan and add the shallots and garlic. Fry for about 1–2 minutes.

3 Add the roasted ground rice, fish sauce, lime juice, sugar, lemongrass and cilantro. Stir to combine. Remove from the heat and serve garnished with mint leaves.

Barbecued Chicken

Barbecued chicken is served almost everywhere in Thailand, from roadside stalls to sports stadiums and beaches.

INGREDIENTS

Serves 4–6

1 chicken, about 3–3½ pounds, cut
  into 8–10 pieces
2 limes, cut into wedges and 2 red
  chilies, finely sliced, to garnish

For the marinade

2 lemongrass stalks, chopped
1-inch piece fresh ginger
6 garlic cloves
4 shallots
½ bunch cilantro roots
1 tablespoon palm sugar
½ cup unsweetened coconut milk
2 tablespoons fish sauce
2 tablespoons soy sauce

1 To make the marinade, put all the ingredients into a food processor and process until smooth.

2 Put the chicken pieces in a dish and pour over the marinade. Set aside in a cool place to marinate for at least 4 hours or overnight.

3 Barbecue the chicken over glowing coals, or place on a rack over a baking pan and bake at 400°F for about 20–30 minutes, or until the chicken is cooked and golden brown. Turn the pieces occasionally and brush them with the marinade.

4 Garnish with lime wedges and finely sliced red chilies.

Cashew Chicken

In this Chinese-inspired dish, tender pieces of chicken are stir-fried with cashews, red chilies and a touch of garlic for a delicious combination.

INGREDIENTS

Serves 4–6

1 pound boneless chicken breasts
2 tablespoons vegetable oil
2 garlic cloves, sliced
4 dried red chilies, chopped
1 red bell pepper, seeded and cut
  into ¾-inch dice
2 tablespoons oyster sauce
1 tablespoon soy sauce
pinch of sugar
1 bunch scallions, cut into
  2-inch lengths
1½ cups cashews, roasted
cilantro leaves, to garnish

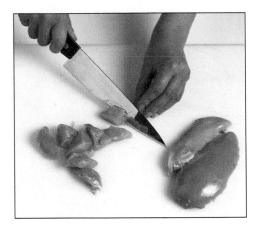

1 Remove and discard the skin from the chicken breasts. With a sharp knife, cut the chicken into bite-size pieces and set aside.

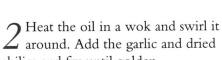

2 Heat the oil in a wok and swirl it around. Add the garlic and dried chilies and fry until golden.

3 Add the chicken and stir-fry until it changes color, then add the red pepper. If necessary, add a little water.

4 Stir in the oyster sauce, soy sauce and sugar. Add the scallions and cashews. Stir-fry for about another 1–2 minutes. Serve garnished with cilantro leaves.

Stir-fried Chicken with Basil and Chilies

This quick and easy chicken dish is an excellent introduction to Thai cuisine. Deep-frying the basil adds another dimension to this dish. Thai basil, which is sometimes known as Holy basil, has a unique, pungent flavor that is both spicy and sharp. The dull leaves have serrated edges.

INGREDIENTS

Serves 4–6

3 tablespoons vegetable oil
4 garlic cloves, sliced
2–4 red chilies, seeded
    and chopped
1 pound chicken, cut into
    bite-size pieces
2–3 tablespoons fish sauce
2 teaspoons dark soy sauce
1 teaspoon sugar
10–12 Thai basil leaves
2 red chilies, finely sliced and 20 Thai
    basil leaves, deep-fried (optional),
    to garnish

1 Heat the oil in a wok or large frying pan and swirl it around.

COOK'S TIP

To deep-fry Thai basil leaves, make sure that the leaves are completely dry. Deep-fry in hot oil for about 30–40 seconds, lift out and drain on paper towels.

2 Add the garlic and chilies and stir-fry until golden.

3 Add the chicken and stir-fry until it changes color.

4 Season with fish sauce, soy sauce and sugar. Continue to stir-fry for 3–4 minutes, or until the chicken is cooked. Stir in the fresh Thai basil leaves. Garnish with sliced chilies and the deep-fried basil, if using.

Baked Fish in Banana Leaves

Fish that is prepared in this way is particularly succulent and flavorful. Fillets are used here rather than whole fish – easier for those who don't like to mess around with bones. It is a great dish for outdoor barbecues.

INGREDIENTS

Serves 4

1 cup unsweetened coconut milk
2 tablespoons red curry paste
3 tablespoons fish sauce
2 tablespoons superfine sugar
5 kaffir lime leaves, torn
4 x 6-ounce fish fillets, such as snapper
6 ounces mixed vegetables, such as carrots or leeks, finely shredded
4 banana leaves, or aluminum foil
2 tablespoons shredded scallions and 2 red chilies, finely sliced, to garnish

1 Combine the coconut milk, curry paste, fish sauce, sugar and kaffir lime leaves in a shallow dish.

2 Marinate the fish in this mixture for about 15–30 minutes. Preheat the oven to 400°F.

3 Mix the vegetables together and lay a portion on top of a banana leaf or piece of foil. Place a piece of fish on top with a little of its marinade.

4 Wrap the fish up by turning in the sides and ends of the leaf and secure with toothpicks. Repeat with the rest of the leaves and the fish.

5 Bake in the hot oven for 20–25 minutes or until the fish is cooked. Alternatively, cook under the broiler or on the barbecue. Just before serving, garnish the fish with a sprinkling of scallions and sliced red chilies.

Stir-fried Scallops with Asparagus

Asparagus is extremely popular among the Chinese Thai. The combination of garlic and black pepper gives this dish its spiciness. You can substitute the scallops with shrimp or other firm fish.

INGREDIENTS

Serves 4–6

4 tablespoons vegetable oil
1 bunch asparagus, cut into 2-inch lengths
4 garlic cloves, finely chopped
2 shallots, finely chopped
1 pound scallops, cleaned
2 tablespoons fish sauce
½ teaspoon coarsely ground black pepper
½ cup unsweetened coconut milk
cilantro leaves, to garnish

1 Heat half the oil in a wok or large frying pan. Add the asparagus and stir-fry for about 2 minutes. Transfer the asparagus to a plate and set aside.

2 Add the rest of the oil, garlic and shallots to the same wok and fry until fragrant. Add the scallops and cook for another 1–2 minutes.

3 Return the asparagus to the wok. Add the fish sauce, black pepper and coconut milk.

4 Stir and cook for about another 3–4 minutes or until the scallops and asparagus are cooked. Garnish with the cilantro leaves.

Shrimp Satay

Serve this enticing and tasty dish with greens and jasmine rice.

INGREDIENTS

Serves 4–6

1 pound jumbo shrimp, shelled, tail
   ends left intact and deveined
½ bunch cilantro leaves, to garnish
4 red chilies, finely sliced and scallions,
   cut diagonally, to garnish

For the peanut sauce

3 tablespoons vegetable oil
1 tablespoon chopped garlic
1 small onion, chopped
3–4 red chilies, crushed and chopped
3 kaffir lime leaves, torn
1 lemongrass stalk, bruised
   and chopped
1 teaspoon medium curry paste
1 cup unsweetened coconut milk
½-inch cinnamon stick
⅓ cup crunchy peanut butter
3 tablespoons tamarind juice
2 tablespoons fish sauce
2 tablespoons palm sugar
juice of ½ lemon

1 To make the sauce, heat half the oil in a wok or large frying pan and add the garlic and onion. Cook for about 3–4 minutes, until it softens.

2 Add the chilies, kaffir lime leaves, lemongrass and curry paste. Cook for a further 2–3 minutes.

COOK'S TIP

Curry paste has a far superior, authentic flavor to powdered varieties. Once opened, it should be kept in the fridge and used within two months.

3 Stir in the coconut milk, cinnamon stick, peanut butter, tamarind juice, fish sauce, palm sugar and lemon juice.

4 Reduce the heat and simmer gently for 15–20 minutes until the sauce thickens, stirring occasionally to make sure that the sauce doesn't stick to the bottom of the pan.

5 Heat the rest of the oil in a wok or large frying pan. Add the shrimp and stir-fry for about 3–4 minutes, or until the shrimp turn pink and are slightly firm to the touch.

6 Mix the shrimp with the sauce. Serve garnished with cilantro leaves, red chilies and scallions.

Sweet and Sour Fish

When fish is cooked in this way the skin becomes crispy on the outside, while the flesh remains moist and juicy inside. The sweet and sour sauce, with its colorful cherry tomatoes, complements the fish beautifully.

INGREDIENTS

Serves 4–6

1 large or 2 medium-size fish such as
   snapper or mullet, heads removed
2 tablespoons cornstarch
½ cup vegetable oil
1 tablespoon chopped garlic
1 tablespoon chopped fresh ginger
2 tablespoons chopped shallots
8 ounces cherry tomatoes
2 tablespoons red wine vinegar
2 tablespoons sugar
2 tablespoons tomato ketchup
1 tablespoon fish sauce
3 tablespoons water
salt and freshly ground black pepper
cilantro leaves and shredded scallions,
   to garnish

1 Thoroughly rinse and clean the fish. Score the skin diagonally on both sides of the fish.

2 Coat the fish lightly on both sides with 1 tablespoon cornstarch. Shake off any excess.

3 Heat the oil in a wok or large frying pan and slide the fish into the wok. Reduce the heat to medium and fry the fish for about 6–7 minutes, until crisp and brown on both sides.

4 Remove the fish with a spatula and place on a large platter.

5 Pour off all but 2 tablespoons of the oil and add the garlic, ginger and shallots. Fry until golden.

6 Add the cherry tomatoes and cook until they burst open. Stir in the vinegar, sugar, tomato ketchup and fish sauce. Simmer gently for 1–2 minutes and adjust the seasoning to taste.

7 Blend the remaining 1 tablespoon cornstarch with the water. Stir into the sauce and heat until it thickens. Pour the sauce over the fish and garnish with cilantro leaves and shredded scallions.

Pineapple Curry with Shrimp and Mussels

The delicate sweet-and-sour flavor of this curry comes from the pineapple and, although it seems an odd combination, it is rather delicious. Use the freshest shellfish that you can find.

INGREDIENTS

Serves 4–6

2½ cups unsweetened coconut milk
2 tablespoons red curry paste
2 tablespoons fish sauce
1 tablespoon sugar
8 ounces jumbo shrimp, shelled
  and deveined
1 pound mussels, cleaned and
  beards removed
6 ounces fresh pineapple, finely crushed
  or chopped
5 kaffir lime leaves, torn
2 red chilies, chopped, and cilantro
  leaves, to garnish

1 In a large saucepan, bring half the coconut milk to a boil and heat, stirring, until it separates.

2 Add the red curry paste and cook until fragrant. Add the fish sauce and sugar and continue to cook for a few moments.

3 Stir in the rest of the coconut milk and bring back to a boil. Add the jumbo shrimp, mussels, pineapple and kaffir lime leaves.

4 Reheat until boiling and then simmer for 3–5 minutes, until the shrimp are cooked and the mussels have opened. Remove any mussels that have not opened and discard. Serve garnished with chopped red chilies and cilantro leaves.

Curried Shrimp in Coconut Milk

A curry-like dish where the shrimp are cooked in a spicy coconut gravy.

INGREDIENTS

Serves 4–6

2½ cups unsweetened coconut milk
2 tablespoons yellow curry paste
  (see Cook's Tip)
1 tablespoon fish sauce
½ teaspoon salt
1 teaspoon sugar
1 pound jumbo shrimp, shelled, tails
  left intact and deveined
8 ounces cherry tomatoes
juice of ½ lime, to serve
2 red chilies, cut into strips, and
  cilantro leaves, to garnish

1 Put half the coconut milk into a pan or wok and bring to a boil.

2 Add the yellow curry paste to the coconut milk, stir until it disperses, then simmer for about 10 minutes.

3 Add the fish sauce, salt, sugar and remaining coconut milk. Simmer for another 5 minutes.

4 Add the shrimp and cherry tomatoes. Simmer very gently for about 5 minutes until the shrimp are pink and tender.

5 Serve sprinkled with lime juice and garnished with chilies and cilantro.

COOK'S TIP

To make yellow curry paste, process 6–8 yellow chilies, 1 chopped lemongrass stalk, 4 peeled shallots, 4 garlic cloves, 1 tablespoon peeled chopped fresh ginger, 1 teaspoon coriander seeds, 1 teaspoon mustard powder, 1 teaspoon salt, ½ teaspoon ground cinnamon, 1 tablespoon light brown sugar and 2 tablespoons oil in a blender or food processor. When a paste forms, transfer to a jar and keep in the fridge.

Water Spinach with Brown Bean Sauce

Water spinach, often known as Siamese watercress, is a green vegetable with arrowhead-shaped leaves. If you can't find it, use spinach, watercress, *bok choy* or even broccoli, and adjust the cooking time accordingly. There are excellent variations to this recipe using black bean sauce, instead of brown bean sauce.

INGREDIENTS

Serves 4–6
1 bunch water spinach, about
  2¼ pounds in weight
3 tablespoons vegetable oil
1 tablespoon chopped garlic
1 tablespoon brown bean sauce
2 tablespoons fish sauce
1 tablespoon sugar
freshly ground black pepper

1 Trim and discard the bottom coarse, woody end of the water spinach. Cut the remaining part into 2-inch lengths, keeping the leaves separate from the stems.

2 Heat the oil in a wok or large frying pan. When it starts to smoke, add the chopped garlic and toss for 10 seconds.

3 Add the stem part of the water spinach, let it sizzle and cook for 1 minute, then add the leafy parts.

4 Stir in the brown bean sauce, fish sauce, sugar and pepper. Toss and turn over the spinach until it begins to wilt, about 3–4 minutes. Transfer to a serving dish and serve immediately.

Mixed Vegetables in Coconut Milk

A most delicious way of cooking vegetables. If you don't like highly spiced food, use fewer red chili peppers.

INGREDIENTS

Serves 4–6
1 pound mixed vegetables, such as
  eggplant, baby canned corn, carrots,
  snake beans and patty pan squash
8 red chilies, seeded
2 lemongrass stalks, chopped
4 kaffir lime leaves, torn
2 tablespoons vegetable oil
1 cup unsweetened coconut milk
2 tablespoons fish sauce
a pinch of salt
15–20 Thai basil leaves, to garnish

1 Cut the vegetables into similar size shapes using a sharp knife.

2 Put the red chilies, lemongrass and kaffir lime leaves in a mortar and grind together with a pestle.

3 Heat the oil in a wok or large deep frying pan. Add the chili mixture and fry for 2–3 minutes.

4 Stir in the coconut milk and bring to a boil. Add the vegetables and cook for about 5 minutes, or until they are tender. Season with the fish sauce and salt, and garnish with basil leaves.

Cabbage Salad

A simple and delicious way of using cabbage. Other vegetables such as broccoli, cauliflower, beansprouts and Chinese cabbage can also be prepared this way.

INGREDIENTS

Serves 4–6

2 tablespoons fish sauce
grated rind of 1 lime
2 tablespoons lime juice
½ cup unsweetened coconut milk
2 tablespoons vegetable oil
2 large red chilies, seeded and finely cut into strips
6 garlic cloves, finely sliced
6 shallots, finely sliced
1 small cabbage, shredded
2 tablespoons coarsely chopped roasted peanuts, to serve

1 Make the dressing by combining the fish sauce, lime rind and juice and coconut milk. Set aside.

2 Heat the oil in a wok or frying pan. Stir-fry the chilies, garlic and shallots, until the shallots are brown and crisp. Remove and set aside.

3 Blanch the cabbage in boiling salted water for about 2–3 minutes, drain and put into a bowl.

4 Stir the dressing into the cabbage, toss and mix well. Transfer the salad to a serving dish. Sprinkle with the fried shallot mixture and the chopped roasted peanuts.

Bamboo Shoot Salad

This salad, which has a hot and sharp flavor, originated in north-east Thailand. Use fresh young bamboo shoots when you can find them, otherwise substitute canned bamboo shoots.

INGREDIENTS

Serves 4

14-ounce can whole bamboo shoots
1 ounce glutinous (sticky) rice
2 tablespoons chopped shallots
1 tablespoon chopped garlic
3 tablespoons chopped scallions
2 tablespoons fish sauce
2 tablespoons lime juice
1 teaspoon sugar
½ teaspoon dried flaked chilies
20–25 small mint leaves
1 tablespoon toasted sesame seeds

3 Turn the rice into a bowl, add the shallots, garlic, scallions, fish sauce, lime juice, sugar, chilies and half the mint leaves.

4 Mix thoroughly, then pour over the bamboo shoots and toss together. Serve sprinkled with sesame seeds and the remaining mint leaves.

1 Rinse and drain the bamboo shoots, finely slice and set aside.

2 Dry-roast the rice in a frying pan until it is golden brown. Remove and grind to fine crumbs with a mortar and pestle.

Jasmine Rice

A naturally aromatic, long-grain white rice, jasmine rice is the staple of most Thai meals. If you eat rice regularly, you might invest in an electric rice cooker.

INGREDIENTS

Serves 4–6

2 cups jasmine rice
3 cups cold water

COOK'S TIP

An electric rice cooker cooks the rice and keeps it warm. Different sizes and models of rice cookers are available. The top of the range is a nonstick version, which is expensive, but well worth the money.

1 Rinse the rice thoroughly, at least three times, in cold water until the water runs clear.

2 Put the rice in a heavy-bottomed saucepan and add the water. Bring the rice to a vigorous boil, uncovered, over high heat.

3 Stir and reduce the heat to low. Cover and simmer for up to 20 minutes, or until all the water has been absorbed. Remove from the heat and allow to stand for 10 minutes.

4 Remove the lid and stir the rice gently with a rice paddle or a pair of wooden chopsticks, to fluff up and separate the grains.

Fried Jasmine Rice with Shrimp and Thai Basil

Thai basil (*bai grapao*), also known as Holy basil, has a unique, pungent flavor that is both spicy and sharp. It can be found in most Asian food markets.

INGREDIENTS

Serves 4–6

3 tablespoons vegetable oil
1 egg, beaten
1 onion, chopped
1 tablespoon chopped garlic
1 tablespoon shrimp paste
4 cups cooked jasmine rice
12 ounces cooked shelled shrimp
½ cup thawed frozen peas
oyster sauce, to taste
2 scallions, chopped
15–20 Thai basil leaves, coarsely chopped, plus an extra sprig, to garnish

1 Heat 1 tablespoon of the oil in a wok or frying pan. Add the beaten egg and swirl it around the pan to set like a thin pancake.

2 Cook until golden, slide out on to a board, roll up and cut into thin strips. Set aside.

3 Heat the remaining oil in the wok, add the onion and garlic and fry for 2–3 minutes. Stir in the shrimp paste and mix thoroughly.

4 Add the rice, shrimp and peas and toss together until everything is heated through.

5 Season with oyster sauce to taste, taking great care as the shrimp paste is salty. Add the scallions and basil leaves. Transfer to a serving dish and serve topped with the strips of egg pancake. Garnish with a sprig of basil.

Coconut Rice

This rich dish is usually served with a tangy papaya salad.

INGREDIENTS

Serves 4–6
2 cups jasmine rice
1 cup water
2 cups unsweetened coconut milk
½ teaspoon salt
2 tablespoons sugar
fresh shredded coconut, to garnish
   (optional)

1 Wash the rice in several changes of cold water until it runs clear. Place the water, coconut milk, salt and sugar in a heavy-bottomed saucepan.

2 Add the rice, cover, and bring to a boil. Reduce the heat to low and simmer for about 15–20 minutes, or until the rice is tender to the bite and cooked through.

3 Turn off the heat and allow the rice to rest in the saucepan for about 5–10 minutes.

4 Fluff up the rice with chopsticks before serving.

Pineapple Fried Rice

This dish is ideal to prepare for a special occasion meal. Served in the pineapple skin shells, it is certain to be the talking point of the dinner.

INGREDIENTS

Serves 4–6
1 pineapple
2 tablespoons vegetable oil
1 small onion, finely chopped
2 green chilies, seeded and chopped
8 ounces lean pork, cut into
   small dice
4 ounces cooked shelled shrimp
3–4 cups cooked cold rice
½ cup roasted cashews
2 scallions, chopped
2 tablespoons fish sauce
1 tablespoon soy sauce
10–12 mint leaves, 2 red chilies, sliced,
   and 1 green chili, sliced, to garnish

1 Cut the pineapple in half lengthwise and remove the flesh from both halves by cutting around inside the skin. Reserve the skin shells. You need 4 ounces of fruit, chopped finely (keep the rest for a dessert).

---- COOK'S TIP ----

When buying a pineapple, look for a sweet-smelling fruit with an even brownish-yellow skin. To test for ripeness, tap the base – a dull sound indicates that the fruit is ripe. The flesh should also give slightly when pressed.

2 Heat the oil in a wok or large frying pan. Add the onion and chilies and fry for about 3–5 minutes, until softened. Add the pork and cook until it is brown on all sides.

3 Stir in the shrimp and rice and toss well together. Continue to stir-fry until the rice is thoroughly heated.

4 Add the chopped pineapple, cashews and scallions. Season with fish sauce and soy sauce.

5 Spoon into the pineapple skin shells. Garnish with shredded mint leaves and red and green chilies.

Crisp Fried Rice Vermicelli

Mee Krob is usually served at celebratory meals. It is a crisp tangle of fried rice vermicelli, which is tossed in a piquant, garlic, sweet-and-sour sauce.

INGREDIENTS

Serves 4–6

oil for frying
6 ounces rice vermicelli
1 tablespoon chopped garlic
4–6 dried chilies, seeded and chopped
2 tablespoons chopped shallot
1 tablespoon dried shrimp, rinsed
4 ounces ground pork
4 ounces cooked shelled shrimp, chopped
2 tablespoons brown bean sauce
2 tablespoons rice wine vinegar
3 tablespoons fish sauce
3 tablespoons palm sugar
2 tablespoons tamarind or lime juice
½ cup bean sprouts

For the garnish

2 scallions, shredded
2 tablespoons fresh cilantro leaves
2 heads pickled garlic (optional)
2-egg omelet, rolled and sliced
2 red chilies, chopped

1 Heat the oil in a wok. Break the rice vermicelli apart into small handfuls about 3 inches long. Deep-fry in the hot oil until they puff up. Remove and drain on paper towels.

2 Leave 2 tablespoons of the hot oil in the wok, add the garlic, chilies, shallots and shrimp. Fry until fragrant.

3 Add the ground pork and stir-fry for about 3–4 minutes, until it is no longer pink. Add the shrimp and fry for 2 minutes more. Remove the mixture and set aside.

4 To the same wok, add the brown bean sauce, vinegar, fish sauce and palm sugar. Bring to a gentle boil, stir to dissolve the sugar and cook until thick and syrupy.

5 Add the tamarind or lime juice and adjust the seasoning. It should be sweet, sour and salty.

6 Reduce the heat. Add the pork and shrimp mixture and the bean sprouts to the sauce. Stir to mix.

7 Add the rice noodles and toss gently to coat them with the sauce, without breaking the noodles too much. Transfer the noodles to a platter. Garnish with scallions, cilantro leaves, pickled garlic, omelet strips and chilies.

Thai Fried Noodles

Phat Thai has a fascinating flavor and texture. It's made with fine rice noodles and is considered one of the national dishes of Thailand.

INGREDIENTS

Serves 4–6

12 ounces rice noodles
3 tablespoons vegetable oil
1 tablespoon chopped garlic
16 uncooked jumbo shrimp, shelled, tails left intact, and deveined
2 eggs, lightly beaten
1 tablespoon dried shrimp, rinsed
2 tablespoons pickled white radish
2 ounces fried tofu, cut into small slivers
½ teaspoon dried chili flakes
4 ounces garlic chives, cut into 2-inch lengths
1 cup bean sprouts
½ cup roasted peanuts, coarsely ground
1 teaspoon sugar
1 tablespoon dark soy sauce
2 tablespoons fish sauce
2 tablespoons tamarind juice
2 tablespoons cilantro leaves and 1 kaffir lime, to garnish

1 Soak the noodles in warm water for 20–30 minutes, then drain.

2 Heat 1 tablespoon of the oil in a wok or large frying pan. Add the garlic and fry until golden. Stir in the shrimp and cook for about 1–2 minutes, until pink, tossing from time to time. Remove and set aside.

3 Heat another 1 tablespoon of oil in the wok. Add the eggs and tilt the wok to spread them into a thin sheet. Stir to scramble and break the eggs into small pieces. Remove from the wok and set aside with the shrimp.

4 Heat the remaining oil in the same wok. Add the dried shrimp, pickled radish, tofu and dried chilies. Stir briefly. Add the soaked noodles and stir-fry for 5 minutes.

5 Add the garlic chives, half the bean sprouts and half the peanuts. Season with the sugar, soy sauce, fish sauce and tamarind juice. Mix together well and cook until the noodles are completely heated through.

6 Return the shrimp and egg mixture to the wok and mix with the noodles. Serve garnished with the rest of the bean sprouts, peanuts, cilantro leaves and lime wedges.

INDIA

Spicy Pepper Soup

This is a highly soothing broth for winter evenings, also known as *Mulla-ga-tani*. Serve with the whole spices, or strain and reheat if you prefer. The lemon juice may be adjusted to taste, but this dish should be distinctly sour.

INGREDIENTS

Serves 4

2 tbsp vegetable oil
½ tsp freshly ground black pepper
1 tsp cumin seeds
½ tsp mustard seeds
¼ tsp asafoetida
2 whole dried red chilies
4-6 curry leaves
½ tsp ground turmeric
2 garlic cloves, crushed
½ pint/1¼ cups tomato juice
juice of 2 lemons
4fl oz/½ cup water
salt, to taste
cilantro leaves, chopped, to garnish

----------- COOK'S TIP -----------

Don't be put off by the unpleasant smell of asafoetida as it disappears when cooked. Used in small quantities, as here, asafoetida adds an oniony flavor to foods.

----------- VARIATION -----------

For a slightly more bitter flavor, use lime juice instead of lemon juice. Add 1 tsp tamarind paste for extra sourness.

1 In a heavy-based saucepan, heat the oil and fry the pepper, cumin and mustard seeds, asafoetida, chilies, curry leaves, turmeric and garlic until the chilies are nearly black and the garlic is golden brown.

2 Lower the heat and add the tomato juice, lemon juice, water and salt. Bring the soup to the boil, then lower the heat and simmer gently for about 10 minutes. Pour the soup into bowls, garnish with the chopped cilantro and serve immediately.

Vegetable Samosas

A selection of highly spiced vegetables in a pastry casing makes these samosas a delicious snack at any time of the day.

INGREDIENTS

Makes 28

14 sheets of filo pastry, thawed and
  wrapped in a damp dish towel
oil for brushing the pastries

For the filling

3 large potatoes, boiled and
  coarsely mashed
3oz/¾ cup frozen peas, thawed
2oz/⅓ cup canned
  sweetcorn, drained
1 tsp ground coriander
1 tsp ground cumin
1 tsp dry mango powder (*amchur*)
1 small onion, finely chopped
2 green chilies, finely chopped
2 tbsp coriander leaves, chopped
2 tbsp mint leaves, chopped
juice of 1 lemon
salt, to taste

1 Preheat the oven to 400°F. Cut each sheet of filo pastry in half lengthways and fold each piece in half lengthways to give 28 thin strips. Lightly brush with oil.

COOK'S TIP

Work with one or two sheets of filo pastry at a time and keep the rest covered with a damp dish towel to prevent it drying out.

2 Toss all the filling ingredients together in a large mixing bowl until they are well blended. Adjust the seasoning with salt and lemon juice if necessary.

3 Using one strip of the pastry at a time, place 1 tbsp of the filling mixture at one end of the strip and diagonally fold the pastry up to form a triangle shape. Brush the samosas with oil and bake in the oven for 10–15 minutes, until golden brown.

Ginger Chicken Wings

INGREDIENTS

Serves 4

10–12 chicken wings, skinned
6fl oz/³⁄4 cup plain yogurt
1½ tsp ginger pulp
1 tsp salt
1 tsp Tabasco sauce
1 tbsp tomato ketchup
1 tsp garlic pulp
1 tbsp lemon juice
1 tbsp fresh cilantro leaves
1 tbsp oil
2 medium onions, sliced
1 tbsp shredded root ginger

1 Place the chicken wings in a glass or china bowl. Pour the yogurt into a separate bowl along with the ginger pulp, salt, Tabasco sauce, tomato ketchup, garlic pulp, lemon juice and half the fresh cilantro leaves. Whisk everything together, then pour the mixture over the chicken wings and stir gently to coat the chicken.

2 Heat the oil in a wok or heavy-based frying pan and fry the onions until soft.

3 Pour in the chicken wings and cook over a medium heat, stirring occasionally, for 10–15 minutes.

4 Add the remaining cilantro and the shredded ginger and serve hot.

_____ COOK'S TIP _____

You can substitute drumsticks or other chicken portions for the wings in this recipe, but remember to increase the cooking time.

Glazed Garlic Shrimp

It is best to peel the shrimp for this dish as it helps them to absorb maximum flavor. Serve with salad as an appetizer or with rice and accompaniments for a more substantial meal.

INGREDIENTS

Serves 4
1 tbsp oil
3 garlic cloves, roughly chopped
3 tomatoes, chopped
½ tsp salt
1 tsp crushed red chilies
1 tsp lemon juice
1 tbsp mango chutney
1 fresh green chili, chopped
15–20 cooked jumbo shrimp, peeled
fresh cilantro sprigs, to garnish

1 In a medium heavy-based saucepan, heat the oil and add the garlic, cooking gently for a few minutes.

COOK'S TIP

Use a skewer or the point of a knife to remove the black intestinal vein running down the back of the shrimps.

2 Lower the heat and add the chopped tomatoes to the saucepan along with the salt, crushed red chilies, lemon juice, mango chutney and fresh green chili.

3 Finally, add the shrimp, turn up the heat and stir-fry these quickly, until heated through.

4 Transfer the shrimp to a serving dish. Serve garnished with fresh cilantro sprigs.

Balti Keema with Curry Leaves and Chilies

Ground lamb is cooked in its own juices with a few spices and herbs, but no other liquid.

INGREDIENTS

Serves 4
2 tsp oil
2 medium onions, chopped
10 curry leaves
6 green chilies
12oz lean ground lamb
1 tsp garlic pulp
1 tsp ginger pulp
1 tsp chili powder
¼ tsp ground turmeric
1 tsp salt
2 tomatoes, peeled and quartered
1 tbsp chopped fresh cilantro

1 Heat the oil in a wok or heavy-based frying pan and fry the onions together with the curry leaves and 3 of the whole green chilies.

_____ COOK'S TIP _____

This curry also makes a terrific brunch if served with fried eggs.

2 Put the lamb into a bowl and blend thoroughly with the garlic, ginger, chili powder, turmeric and salt.

3 Add the lamb to the onions and stir-fry for 7–10 minutes.

4 Add the tomatoes, cilantro and chilies and stir-fry for 2 minutes.

Creamy Lamb Korma

Cutting the lamb into strips for this lovely dish makes it easier and quicker to cook.

INGREDIENTS

Serves 4

2 green chilies
4fl oz/½ cup plain yogurt
2fl oz/¼ cup coconut milk
1 tbsp ground almonds
1 tsp salt
1 tsp garlic pulp
1 tsp ginger pulp
1 tsp garam masala
¼ tsp ground cardamom
large pinch of ground cinnamon
1 tbsp chopped fresh mint
1 tbsp oil
2 medium onions, diced
1 bay leaf
4 black peppercorns
8oz lean lamb, cut into strips
¼ pint/⅔ cup water
fresh mint leaves, to garnish

2 Heat the oil in a wok or heavy-based frying pan and fry the onions with the bay leaf and peppercorns for about 5 mintues.

4 Pour in the yogurt mixture and water, lower the heat, cover and cook for about 15 minutes or until the lamb is cooked through, stirring occasionally. Stir-fry for a further 2 minutes. Serve garnished with fresh mint leaves.

___ COOK'S TIP ___

Pea and Mushroom Pilau goes very well with this korma.

3 When the onions are soft and golden brown, add the lamb and stir-fry for about 2 minutes.

1 Finely chop the chilies. Whisk the yogurt with the chilies, coconut milk, ground almonds, salt, garlic, ginger, garam masala, cardamom, cinnamon and mint.

Beef Madras

Madras curries originate from southern India and are aromatic, robust and pungent in flavor. This recipe uses beef, but you can replace it with lean lamb if you prefer.

INGREDIENTS

Serves 4

2lb lean stewing beef
1 tbsp oil
1 large onion, finely chopped
4 cloves
4 green cardamom pods
2 green chilies, finely chopped
1in piece root ginger,
　finely chopped
2 garlic cloves, crushed
2 dried red chilies
1 tbsp curry paste
2 tsp ground coriander
1 tsp ground cumin
½ tsp salt
¼ pint/⅔ cup beef stock
fresh cilantro, to garnish
rice, to serve

1 Remove any visible fat from the beef and cut the meat into 1in cubes.

2 Heat the oil in a large heavy-based frying pan and stir-fry the onion, cloves and cardamom pods for about 5 minutes. Add the fresh green chilies, ginger, garlic and dried red chilies and fry for a further 2 minutes.

3 Add the curry paste and fry for about 2 minutes. Add the beef and fry for 5–8 minutes until all the meat pieces are lightly browned.

4 Add the coriander, cumin, salt and stock. Cover and simmer gently for 1–1½ hours or until the meat is tender. Serve with rice and garnish with fresh cilantro.

COOK'S TIP

When whole cardamom pods are used as a flavoring, they are not meant to be eaten. In India, they are left on the side of the plate, along with any bones.

Balti Beef

INGREDIENTS

Serves 4

1 red bell pepper
1 green bell pepper
1 tbsp oil
1 tsp cumin seeds
½ tsp fennel seeds
1 onion, cut into thick wedges
1 garlic clove, crushed
1in piece root ginger,
  finely chopped
1 red chili, finely chopped
1 tbsp curry paste
½ tsp salt
1½lb lean rump or fillet steak, cut
  into thick strips
naan bread, to serve

1 Cut the red and green bell peppers into 1in chunks.

2 Heat the oil in a non-stick wok or frying pan and fry the cumin and fennel seeds for about 2 minutes or until they begin to splutter. Add the onion, garlic, ginger and chili and fry for a further 5 minutes.

3 Add the curry paste and salt and fry for a further 3–4 minutes.

4 Add the bell peppers and stir-fry for about 5 minutes. Stir in the beef strips and continue to fry for 10–12 minutes or until the meat is tender. Serve with warm naan bread.

Chicken Tikka Masala

Tender chicken pieces are cooked in a creamy, spicy tomato sauce and served on naan bread.

INGREDIENTS

Serves 4

1½lb chicken breasts, skinned
6 tbsp tikka paste
4fl oz/½ cup plain yogurt
1 tbsp oil
1 onion, chopped
1 garlic clove, crushed
1 green chili, seeded and chopped
1in piece root ginger, grated
1 tbsp tomato purée
8fl oz/1 cup water
a little melted butter
1 tbsp lemon juice
fresh cilantro sprigs, plain yogurt and
   toasted cumin seeds, to garnish
naan bread, to serve

COOK'S TIP

Soak the wooden skewers in cold water before using to prevent them from burning while under the broiler.

1 Remove any visible fat from the chicken and cut the meat into 1in cubes. Put 3 tbsp of the tikka paste and 4 tbsp of the plain yogurt into a bowl. Add the chicken and leave to marinate for at least 20 minutes.

4 Brush the chicken pieces lightly with melted butter and broil under a medium heat for 15 minutes, turning the skewers occasionally.

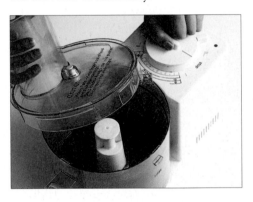

2 For the tikka sauce, heat the oil in a heavy-based pan and fry the onion, garlic, chili and ginger for 5 minutes. Add the remaining tikka paste and fry for 2 minutes. Add the tomato purée and water, bring to the boil and simmer for 15 minutes.

5 Put the tikka sauce into a food processor or blender and process until smooth. Return to the pan.

3 Meanwhile, thread the chicken pieces on to wooden kebab skewers. Preheat the broiler.

6 Add the remaining yogurt and lemon juice, remove the chicken pieces from the skewers and add to the saucepan, then simmer for 5 minutes. Garnish with fresh cilantro, plain yogurt and toasted cumin seeds and serve on naan bread.

Tandoori Chicken

A most popular Indian/Pakistani chicken dish which is cooked in a clay oven called a *tandoor*, this is extremely popular in the West and appears on the majority of restaurant menus. Although the authentic tandoori flavor is very difficult to achieve in conventional ovens, this version still makes a very tasty dish.

INGREDIENTS

Serves 4
4 chicken quarters, skinned
6fl oz/¾ cup plain yogurt
1 tsp garam masala
1 tsp ginger pulp
1 tsp garlic pulp
1½ tsp chili powder
¼ tsp ground turmeric
1 tsp ground coriander
1 tbsp lemon juice
1 tsp salt
few drops of red food coloring
1 tbsp oil
mixed salad leaves and lime wedges, to garnish

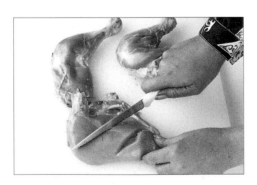

1 Rinse and pat dry the chicken quarters. Make two deep slits in the flesh of each piece, place in a dish and set aside.

2 Mix together the yogurt, garam masala, ginger, garlic, chili powder, turmeric, coriander, lemon juice, salt, red food coloring and oil, and beat well, so that all the ingredients are thoroughly combined.

3 Cover the chicken quarters with the spice mixture and leave to marinate for about 3 hours.

4 Preheat the oven to 475°F. Transfer the chicken pieces to an ovenproof dish.

5 Bake the chicken in the oven for 20–25 minutes or until the chicken is cooked right through and evenly browned on top.

6 Remove from the oven, transfer to a serving dish and garnish with the salad leaves and lime wedges.

_____ COOK'S TIP _____

The traditional bright red color is derived from food coloring. This is only optional and may be omitted if you wish.

Chicken Jalfrezi

A Jalfrezi curry is a stir-fried dish cooked with onions, ginger and garlic in a rich bell pepper sauce.

INGREDIENTS

Serves 4

1½lb chicken breasts, skinned
1 tbsp oil
1 tsp cumin seeds
1 onion, finely chopped
1 green bell pepper, seeded and
  finely chopped
1 red bell pepper, seeded and
  finely chopped
1 garlic clove, crushed
¾in piece root ginger,
  finely chopped
1 tbsp curry paste
¼ tsp chili powder
1 tsp ground coriander
1 tsp ground cumin
½ tsp salt
14oz can chopped tomatoes
2 tbsp chopped fresh cilantro
fresh cilantro sprig, to garnish
plain rice, to serve

1 Remove any visible fat from the chicken and cut the meat into 1in cubes.

2 Heat the oil in a wok or heavy-based frying pan and fry the cumin seeds for 2 minutes until they splutter. Add the onion, bell peppers, garlic and ginger and fry for 6–8 minutes.

3 Add the curry paste and fry for about 2 minutes. Stir in the chili powder, ground coriander, cumin and salt and add 1 tbsp water; fry for a further 2 minutes.

4 Add the chicken cubes and fry for about 5 minutes. Add the canned tomatoes and chopped fresh cilantro. Cover the wok or frying pan with a lid and cook for about 15 minutes or until the chicken cubes are tender. Garnish with a sprig of fresh cilantro and serve with plain rice.

Balti Chicken Curry

Tender pieces of chicken are lightly cooked with fresh vegetables and aromatic spices in the traditional Balti style.

INGREDIENTS

Serves 4

1½lb chicken breasts, skinned
1 tbsp oil
½ tsp cumin seeds
½ tsp fennel seeds
1 onion, thickly sliced
2 garlic cloves, crushed
1in piece root ginger, finely chopped
1 tbsp curry paste
8oz broccoli, broken into florets
4 tomatoes, cut into thick wedges
1 tsp garam masala
2 tbsp chopped fresh cilantro
naan bread, to serve

1 Remove any visible fat from the chicken and cut the meat into 1in cubes.

2 Heat the oil in a wok or heavy-based frying pan and fry the cumin and fennel seeds for 2 minutes until the seeds begin to splutter. Add the onion, garlic and ginger and cook for 5–7 minutes. Stir in the curry paste and cook for a further 2–3 minutes.

3 Add the broccoli florets and fry for about 5 minutes. Add the chicken cubes and fry for 5–8 minutes.

4 Add the tomato wedges to the wok with the garam masala and the chopped fresh cilantro. Cook the curry for a further 5–10 minutes or until the chicken cubes are tender. Serve with naan bread.

Balti Chicken in a Thick Creamy Coconut Sauce

If you like the flavor of coconut, you will really love this aromatic curry.

INGREDIENTS

Serves 4

1 tbsp ground almonds
1 tbsp desiccated coconut
3fl oz/⅓ cup coconut milk
6oz/⅔ cup fromage frais
1½ tsp ground coriander
1 tsp chili powder
1 tsp garlic pulp
1½ tsp ginger pulp
1 tsp salt
1 tbsp oil
8oz boneless chicken, skinned and cubed
3 green cardamom pods
1 bay leaf
1 dried red chili, crushed
2 tbsp chopped fresh cilantro

1 Using a heavy-based saucepan, dry-roast the ground almonds and desiccated coconut until they turn just a shade darker. Transfer the nut mixture to a mixing bowl.

2 Add the coconut milk, fromage frais, ground coriander, chili powder, garlic, ginger and salt to the mixing bowl.

3 Heat the oil in a wok or heavy-based frying pan and add the chicken cubes, cardamoms and bay leaf. Stir-fry for about 2 minutes to seal the chicken but not cook it.

4 Pour in the coconut milk mixture and blend everything together. Lower the heat, add the chili and fresh cilantro, cover and cook for 10–12 minutes, stirring occasionally. Uncover, then stir and cook for a further 2 minutes before serving, making sure the chicken is cooked.

Chicken Biryani

Biryanis originated in Persia and are traditionally made with a combination of meat and rice. They are often served at dinner parties and on festive occasions.

INGREDIENTS

Serves 4

10oz/1½ cups basmati rice
2 tbsp oil
1 onion, thinly sliced
2 garlic cloves, crushed
1 green chili, finely chopped
1in piece root ginger,
   finely chopped
1½lb chicken breast fillets, skinned
   and cut into 1in cubes
3 tbsp curry paste
¼ tsp salt
¼ tsp garam masala
3 tomatoes, cut into thin wedges
¼ tsp ground turmeric
2 bay leaves
4 green cardamom pods
4 cloves
¼ tsp saffron strands
Tomato and Onion Chutney, to serve

1 Wash the rice in several changes of cold water. Put into a large bowl, cover with plenty of water and leave to soak for 30 minutes.

2 Meanwhile, heat the oil in a large heavy-based frying pan and fry the onion for about 5–7 minutes until lightly browned. Add the garlic, chili and ginger and fry for about 2 minutes.

3 Add the chicken and fry for about 5 minutes, stirring occasionally.

4 Add the curry paste, salt and garam masala to the chicken mixture and cook for 5 minutes. Gently stir in the tomato wedges and continue cooking for another 3–4 minutes, then remove from the heat and set aside.

5 Preheat the oven to 375°F. Bring a large saucepan of water to the boil. Drain the rice and add it to the pan with the turmeric. Cook for about 10 minutes, or until the rice is almost tender. Drain the rice and toss together with the bay leaves, cardamoms, cloves and saffron.

6 Layer the rice and chicken in a shallow, ovenproof dish until all the mixture has been used, finishing off with a layer of rice. Cover and bake in the oven for 15–20 minutes or until the chicken is tender. Serve with Tomato and Onion Chutney.

Shrimp Curry

A rich flavorsome curry made with shrimp and a delicious blend of aromatic spices.

INGREDIENTS

Serves 4

1½lb uncooked jumbo shrimp
4 dried red chilies
1oz/½ cup desiccated coconut
1 tsp black mustard seeds
1 large onion, chopped
2 tbsp oil
4 bay leaves
1in piece root ginger, finely chopped
2 garlic cloves, crushed
1 tbsp ground coriander
1 tsp chili powder
1 tsp salt
4 tomatoes, finely chopped
plain rice, to serve

2 Put the dried red chilies, coconut, mustard seeds and onion in a large heavy-based frying pan and dry-fry for 8–10 minutes or until the spices begin to brown but not burn. Put into a food processor or blender and process to a coarse paste.

3 Heat the oil in the frying pan and fry the bay leaves for 1 minute. Add the chopped ginger and the garlic and fry for 2–3 minutes.

4 Add the coriander, chili powder, salt and the coconut paste and fry gently for 5 minutes.

5 Stir in the chopped tomatoes and about 6fl oz/¾ cup water and simmer gently for 5–6 minutes or until the sauce has thickened.

6 Add the shrimp and cook for about 4–5 minutes or until they turn pink and the edges are curling slightly. Serve with plain boiled rice.

1 Peel the shrimp and discard the shells. Run a sharp knife along the center back of each shrimp to make a shallow cut and carefully remove the thin black intestinal vein.

COOK'S TIP

Serve extra tiger shrimps unpeeled, on the edge of each plate, for an attractive garnish. Cook them with the peeled shrimps.

Green Fish Curry

This dish combines all the flavors of the East.

INGREDIENTS

Serves 4

¼ tsp ground turmeric
2 tbsp lime juice
pinch of salt
4 cod fillets, skinned and cut into
  2in chunks
1 onion, chopped
1 green chili, roughly chopped
1 garlic clove, crushed
1oz/¼ cup cashew nuts
½ tsp fennel seeds
2 tbsp desiccated coconut
2 tbsp oil
¼ tsp cumin seeds
¼ tsp ground coriander
¼ tsp ground cumin
¼ tsp salt
¼ pint/⅔ cup water
6fl oz/¾ cup plain yogurt
3 tbsp finely chopped fresh cilantro
fresh cilantro sprig, to garnish
Pea and Mushroom Pilau, to serve

1 Mix together the turmeric, lime juice and salt and rub over the fish. Cover and marinate for 15 minutes.

2 Meanwhile, process the onion, chili, garlic, cashew nuts, fennel seeds and coconut to a paste. Spoon the paste into a bowl and set aside.

3 Heat the oil in a large heavy-based frying pan and fry the cumin seeds for 2 minutes or until they begin to splutter. Add the paste and fry for 5 minutes, then stir in the ground coriander, cumin, salt and water and cook for about 2–3 minutes.

4 Add the yogurt and the chopped fresh cilantro. Simmer gently for 5 minutes. Add the fish fillets and gently stir in. Cover and cook gently for 10 minutes until the fish is tender. Serve with Pea and Mushroom Pilau, garnished with a cilantro sprig.

Stir-fried Vegetables with Monkfish

Monkfish is a rather expensive fish, but ideal to use in stir-fry recipes as it is quite tough and does not break easily.

INGREDIENTS

Serves 4
2 tbsp oil
2 medium onions, sliced
1 tsp garlic pulp
1 tsp ground cumin
1 tsp ground coriander
1 tsp chili powder
6oz monkfish, cut into cubes
2 tbsp fresh fenugreek leaves
2 tomatoes, seeded and sliced
1 zucchini, sliced
salt
1 tbsp lime juice

1 Heat the oil in a wok or heavy-based frying pan and fry the onions over a low heat until soft.

2 Meanwhile mix together the garlic, cumin, coriander and chili powder. Add this spice mixture to the onions and stir-fry for about 1 minute.

3 Add the fish and continue to stir-fry for 3–5 minutes until the fish is well cooked through.

4 Add the fenugreek, tomatoes and zucchini, followed by salt to taste, and stir-fry for a further 2 minutes. Sprinkle with lime juice before serving.

COOK'S TIP

Try to use monkfish for this recipe, but if it is not available, either cod or shrimp make suitable substitutes.

Vegetable Kashmiri

This is a wonderful vegetable curry, in which fresh mixed vegetables are cooked in a spicy aromatic yogurt sauce.

INGREDIENTS

Serves 4

2 tsp cumin seeds
8 black peppercorns
2 green cardamom pods, seeds only
2in cinnamon stick
½ tsp grated nutmeg
2 tbsp oil
1 green chili, chopped
1in piece root ginger, grated
1 tsp chili powder
½ tsp salt
2 large potatoes, cut into 1in chunks
8oz cauliflower, broken
  into florets
8oz okra, trimmed and
  thickly sliced
¼ pint/⅔ cup plain yogurt
¼ pint/⅔ cup vegetable stock
toasted flaked almonds (optional) and
  fresh cilantro sprigs, to garnish

1 Grind the cumin seeds, peppercorns, cardamom seeds, cinnamon stick and nutmeg to a fine powder using a coffee blender or a pestle and mortar.

2 Heat the oil in a large heavy-based saucepan and fry the chili powder and ginger for 2 minutes, stirring all the time.

3 Add the chili powder, salt and ground spice mixture and fry for about 2–3 minutes, stirring all the time to prevent the spices from sticking.

COOK'S TIP

Instead of the vegetable mixture used here, try cooking other ones of your choice in this lovely yogurt sauce.

4 Stir in the potatoes, cover and cook for 10 minutes over a low heat, stirring from time to time.

5 Add the cauliflower and okra and cook for 5 minutes.

6 Add the yogurt and stock. Bring to the boil, then reduce the heat. Cover and simmer for 20 minutes, or until all the vegetables are tender. Garnish with toasted almonds, if using, and cilantro sprigs.

Aloo Saag

Spinach, potatoes and traditional
Indian spices are the main
ingredients in this simple
but authentic curry.

INGREDIENTS

Serves 4

1lb spinach
1 tbsp oil
1 tsp black mustard seeds
1 onion, thinly sliced
2 garlic cloves, crushed
1in piece root ginger,
   finely chopped
1½lb potatoes, cut into 1in chunks
1 tsp chili powder
1 tsp salt
4fl oz/½ cup water

COOK'S TIP

To make certain that the spinach is
completely dry, put it in a clean dish towel,
roll up tightly and squeeze gently to
remove any excess liquid. Use a waxy
variety of potato for this dish so that the
pieces do not break up during cooking.

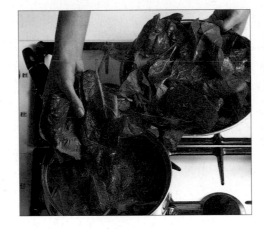

1 Wash and trim the spinach, then
blanch it in a saucepan of boiling
water for about 3–4 minutes.

2 Drain the spinach thoroughly and
set aside. When it is cool enough
to handle, use your hands to squeeze
out any remaining liquid (see Cook's
Tip) and set aside.

3 Heat the oil in a large heavy-based
saucepan and fry the mustard seeds
for 2 minutes or until they splutter.

4 Add the sliced onion, garlic cloves
and chopped ginger to the mustard
seeds and fry for 5 minutes, stirring.

5 Add the potato chunks, chili
powder, salt and water and
stir-fry for a further 8 minutes.

6 Add the drained spinach. Cover
the pan with a lid and simmer for
10–15 minutes or until the potatoes
are tender. Serve hot.

Balti Stir-fried Vegetables with Cashew Nuts

This quick and versatile stir-fry will accommodate most other combinations of vegetables – you do not have to use the selection suggested here.

INGREDIENTS

Serves 4

2 medium carrots
1 medium red bell pepper, seeded
1 medium green bell pepper, seeded
2 zucchini
4oz green beans
1 medium bunch scallions
1 tbsp oil
4–6 curry leaves
½ tsp cumin seeds
4 dried red chilies
10–12 cashew nuts
1 tsp salt
2 tbsp lemon juice
fresh mint leaves, to garnish

1 Prepare the vegetables: cut the carrots, peppers and zucchini into matchsticks, halve the beans and chop the scallions. Set aside.

2 Heat the oil in a wok or heavy-based frying pan and fry the curry leaves, cumin seeds and dried chilies for about 1 minute.

3 Add the vegetables and nuts and stir them around gently. Add the salt and lemon juice. Continue to stir and cook for about 3–5 minutes.

4 Transfer the vegetables to a serving dish, garnish with fresh mint leaves and serve immediately.

COOK'S TIP

If you are short of time, substitute frozen mixed vegetables for the carrots, bell peppers, zucchini and green beans; they work equally well in this dish.

Tarka Dhal

Tarka Dhal is probably the most popular of Indian lentil dishes and is found today in most Indian/Pakistani restaurants.

INGREDIENTS

Serves 4

4oz/¼ cup *masoor dhal*
2oz/¼ cup *moong dhal*
1 pint/2½ cups water
1 tsp ginger pulp
1 tsp garlic pulp
¼ tsp ground turmeric
2 fresh green chilies, chopped
1½ tsp salt

For the *tarka*

2 tbsp oil
1 onion, sliced
¼ tsp mixed mustard and
  onion seeds
4 dried red chilies
1 tomato, sliced

For the garnish

1 tbsp chopped fresh cilantro
1–2 fresh green chilies, seeded
  and sliced
1 tbsp chopped fresh mint

1 Boil the two lentils in the water with the ginger and garlic pulp, turmeric and chopped green chillies for 15–20 minutes until soft.

2 Mash the lentil mixture with a fork or pound with a rolling pin until the consistency of a creamy chicken soup.

3 If the lentil mixture looks too dry, add a little more water. Season with the salt. To prepare the *tarka*, heat the oil in a heavy-based frying pan and fry the onion with the mustard and onion seeds, dried red chilies and tomato for 2 minutes.

4 Pour the *tarka* over the mashed lentils and garnish with fresh coriander, green chilies and mint.

———— COOK'S TIP ————

Dried red chilies are available in many different sizes. If the ones you have are large, or if you want a less spicy flavor, reduce the quantity specified to 1–2.

Mung Beans with Potatoes

Mung beans are one of the quicker-cooking pulses which do not require soaking and are very easy and convenient to use. In this recipe they are cooked with potatoes and Indian spices to give a tasty nutritious dish.

INGREDIENTS

Serves 4

6oz/1 cup mung beans
1¼ pints/3 cups water
8oz potatoes, cut into ¾in chunks
2 tbsp oil
½ tsp cumin seeds
1 green chili, finely chopped
1 garlic clove, crushed
1in piece root ginger,
    finely chopped
¼ tsp ground turmeric
½ tsp chili powder
1 tsp salt
1 tsp sugar
4 curry leaves
5 tomatoes, skinned and
    finely chopped
1 tbsp tomato purée
curry leaves, to garnish
plain rice, to serve

1 Wash the beans. Bring to the boil in the water, cover and simmer until soft, about 30 minutes. Drain. Par-boil the potatoes for 10 minutes in another saucepan, then drain well.

2 Heat the oil in a heavy-based pan and fry the cumin seeds until they splutter. Add the chili, garlic and ginger and fry for 3–4 minutes.

3 Add the turmeric, chili powder, salt and sugar and cook for about 2 minutes, stirring to prevent the mixture from sticking to the pan.

4 Add the 4 curry leaves, chopped tomatoes and tomato purée and simmer for about 5 minutes until the sauce thickens. Add the tomato sauce and the potatoes to the mung beans and mix well together. Garnish with the extra curry leaves and serve with plain boiled rice.

Madras Sambal

There are many variations of this popular dish but it is regularly cooked in one form or another in almost every south–Indian home. You can use any combination of vegetables that are in season.

INGREDIENTS

Serves 4

8oz/1 cup *toovar dhal* or red
 split lentils
1 pint/2½ cups water
½ tsp ground turmeric
2 large potatoes, cut into 1in chunks
2 tbsp oil
½ tsp black mustard seeds
¼ tsp fenugreek seeds
4 curry leaves
1 onion, thinly sliced
4oz French beans, cut into 1in lengths
1 tsp salt
½ tsp chili powder
1 tbsp lemon juice
toasted coconut, to garnish
Tomato and Onion Chutney, to serve

1 Wash the *toovar dhal* or lentils in several changes of water. Place in a heavy-based saucepan with the water and the turmeric. Bring to the boil, cover and simmer for 30–35 minutes until the lentils are soft.

2 Par-boil the potatoes in a large pan of boiling water for 10 minutes. Drain well and set aside.

3 Heat the oil in a large frying pan and fry the mustard and fenugreek seeds and curry leaves for 2–3 minutes until the seeds begin to splutter. Add the sliced onion and the French beans and stir-fry for 7–8 minutes. Add the par-boiled potatoes and cook for a further 2 minutes.

4 Stir in the lentils with the salt, chilli powder and lemon juice and simmer for 2 minutes. Garnish with toasted coconut and serve with freshly made Tomato and Onion Chutney.

Pea and Mushroom Pilau

It is best to use button mushrooms and petits pois for this delectable rice dish as they make the pilau look truly attractive and appetizing.

Ingredients

Serves 6

1lb/2¼ cups basmati rice
1 tbsp oil
½ tsp cumin seeds
2 black cardamom pods
2 cinnamon sticks
3 garlic cloves, sliced
1 tsp salt
1 medium tomato, sliced
⅔ cup button mushrooms
3oz/generous ⅓ cup petits pois
1¼ pints/3 cups water

1 Wash the rice well and leave it to soak in water for 30 minutes.

2 In a medium heavy-based saucepan, heat the oil and add the spices, garlic and salt.

3 Add the tomato and mushrooms and stir-fry for 2–3 minutes.

4 Drain the rice and add it to the pan with the peas. Stir gently, making sure that you do not break up the grains of rice.

5 Add the water and bring to the boil. Lower the heat, cover and continue to cook for 15–20 minutes.

--- COOK'S TIP ---

Petits pois are small green peas, picked when very young. The tender, sweet peas inside are ideal for this delicately flavored rice dish. However, if you can't find petit pois, garden peas can be used instead.

Basmati Rice with Potato

Rice is eaten at all meals in Indian and Pakistani homes. There are several ways of cooking rice and mostly whole spices are used. Always choose a good-quality basmati rice.

INGREDIENTS

Serves 4

11oz/1½ cups basmati rice
1 tbsp oil
1 small cinnamon stick
1 bay leaf
¼ tsp black cumin seeds
3 green cardamom pods
1 medium onion, sliced
1 tsp ginger pulp
1 tsp garlic pulp
¼ tsp ground turmeric
1½ tsp salt
1 large potato, roughly diced
16fl oz/2 cups water
1 tbsp chopped fresh cilantro

1 Wash the rice well and leave it to soak in water for 30 minutes. Heat the oil in a heavy-based saucepan, add the cinnamon, bay leaf, black cumin seeds, cardamoms and onion and cook for about 2 minutes.

_____ COOK'S TIP _____

Serve the rice and potato mixture using a slotted spoon and handle it gently to avoid breaking the delicate grains of rice.

2 Add the ginger, garlic, turmeric, salt and potato and cook for 1 minute.

3 Drain the rice and add to the potato and spices in the pan.

4 Stir to mix, then pour in the water followed by the cilantro. Cover the pan with a lid and cook for 15–20 minutes. Remove from the heat and leave to stand, still covered, for 5–10 minutes before serving.

Tomato and Onion Chutney

Chutneys are served with most meat dishes in Indian cuisine.

INGREDIENTS

Serves 4

8 tomatoes
1 medium onion, chopped
3 tbsp brown sugar
1 tsp garam masala
1 tsp ginger powder
6fl oz/¾ cup malt vinegar
1 tsp salt
1 tbsp clear honey
plain yogurt, sliced green chili and
    fresh mint leaves, to garnish

COOK'S TIP

This chutney will keep for about 2 weeks in a covered jar in the refrigerator.

1 Wash the tomatoes and cut them into quarters.

2 Place them with the onion in a heavy-based saucepan.

3 Add the sugar, garam masala, ginger, vinegar, salt and honey, half-cover the pan with a lid and cook over a low heat for about 20 minutes.

4 Mash the tomatoes with a fork to break them up, then continue to cook on a slightly higher heat until the chutney thickens. Serve chilled, garnished with plain yogurt, sliced chili and mint leaves.

Sweet-and-sour Raita

Raitas are traditionally served with most Indian meals as accompaniments which are cooling to the palate. They go particularly well with biryanis.

INGREDIENTS

Serves 4

16fl oz/2 cups plain yogurt
1 tsp salt
1 tsp sugar
2 tbsp honey
1½ tsp mint sauce
2 tbsp roughly chopped
    fresh cilantro
1 green chili, seeded and
    finely chopped
1 medium onion, diced
2fl oz/¼ cup water

1 Pour the yogurt into a bowl and whisk it well. Add the salt, sugar, honey and mint sauce.

2 Taste to check the sweetness and add more honey, if desired.

3 Reserve a little chopped cilantro for the garnish and add the rest to the yogurt mixture, with the chili, onion and water.

4 Whisk once again and pour into a serving bowl. Garnish with the reserved cilantro and place in the refrigerator until ready to serve.

COOK'S TIP

A 2–4in piece of peeled, seeded and grated cucumber can also be added to raita. Alternatively, cut it into small dice.

Ground Rice Pudding

This delicious and light ground rice pudding is the perfect end to a spicy meal. It can be served either hot or cold.

INGREDIENTS

Serves 4–6

2oz/½ cup coarsely ground rice
4 green cardamom pods, crushed
1½ pints/3¾ cups semi-skimmed milk
6 tbsp sugar
1 tbsp rose water
1 tbsp crushed pistachio nuts,
   to garnish

1 Place the ground rice in a saucepan with the cardamoms. Add 1 pint/2½ cups milk and bring to the boil over a medium heat, stirring occasionally.

2 Add the remaining milk and cook over a medium heat for about 10 minutes or until the rice mixture thickens to a creamy consistency.

3 Stir in the sugar and rose water and continue to cook for a further 2 minutes. Serve garnished with the pistachio nuts.

—— COOK'S TIP ——

Rose water is a distillation of scented rose petals which has the intense fragrance and flavor of roses. It is a popular flavoring in Indian cooking. Use it cautiously, adding just enough to suit your taste.

Vermicelli

Indian vermicelli, made from wheat, is much finer than Italian vermicelli and is readily available from Asian stores.

INGREDIENTS

Serves 4
4oz/1 cup vermicelli
2 pints/5 cups water
½ tsp saffron strands
1 tbsp sugar
4 tbsp fromage frais, to serve (optional)

For the garnish
1 tbsp shredded fresh or desiccated
    coconut
1 tbsp flaked almonds
1 tbsp chopped pistachio nuts
1 tbsp sugar

1 Crush the vermicelli in your hands and place in a saucepan. Pour in the water, add the saffron and bring to the boil. Boil for about 5 minutes.

2 Stir in the sugar and continue cooking until the water has evaporated. Strain through a sieve, if necessary, to remove any excess liquid.

3 Place the vermicelli in a serving dish and garnish with the coconut, almonds, pistachio nuts and sugar. Serve with fromage frais, if wished.

COOK'S TIP

You can use a variety of fruits instead of nuts to garnish this dessert. Try a few soft fruits such as blackberries, raspberries or strawberries, or add some chopped dried apricots or sultanas.

MIDDLE EAST

Beef and Herb Soup with Yogurt

This classic Iranian soup, *Aashe Maste*, is almost a meal in itself. It is full of invigorating herbs, and is a popular cold weather dish.

INGREDIENTS

Serves 6

2 large onions
2 tablespoons oil
1 tablespoon ground turmeric
½ cup yellow split peas
5 cups water
8 ounces ground beef
1 cup rice
3 tablespoons each fresh chopped
parsley, cilantro and chives
1 tablespoon butter
1 large garlic clove, finely chopped
4 tablespoons chopped mint
2–3 saffron strands dissolved in
1 tablespoon boiling water (optional)
salt and freshly ground black pepper
yogurt and nan bread, to serve

1 Chop one of the onions, then heat the oil in a large saucepan and fry the onion until golden brown. Add the turmeric, split peas and water, bring to a boil, then reduce the heat and simmer for 20 minutes.

2 Grate the other onion into a bowl, add the ground beef and seasoning and mix well. Using your hands, form the mixture into small balls, about the size of walnuts. Carefully add to the pan and simmer for 10 minutes.

— COOK'S TIP —

Fresh spinach is also delicious in this soup. Add 2 ounces finely chopped spinach leaves to the soup with the parsley, cilantro and chives.

3 Add the rice, then stir in the parsley, cilantro, and chives and simmer for about 30 minutes, until the rice is tender, stirring frequently.

4 Melt the butter in a small pan and gently fry the garlic. Add the mint, stir briefly and sprinkle over the soup with the saffron, if using.

5 Spoon the soup into warmed serving dishes and serve with yogurt and nan bread.

Spinach and Lemon Soup with Meatballs

Aarshe Saak is almost standard fare in many parts of the Middle East. In Greece it is made with rice and chicken stock only and called Avgolemono.

INGREDIENTS

Serves 6
2 large onions
3 tablespoons oil
1 tablespoon ground turmeric
½ cup yellow split peas
5 cups water
8 ounces ground lamb
1 pound spinach, chopped
½ cup rice flour or cornstarch
juice of 2 lemons
1–2 garlic cloves, very
   finely chopped
2 tablespoons chopped fresh mint
4 eggs, beaten
salt and freshly ground black pepper

1 Chop one of the onions, heat 2 tablespoons of the oil in a large frying pan and fry the onion until golden. Add the turmeric, split peas and water and bring to a boil. Reduce the heat to medium and simmer for about 20 minutes.

2 Grate the other onion. Put it into a bowl, add the ground lamb and seasoning and mix well. Using your hands, form the mixture into small balls, about the size of walnuts. Carefully add to the pan and simmer for 10 minutes, then add the chopped spinach, cover and simmer for 20 minutes.

3 Mix the rice flour or cornstarch with about 1 cup cold water to make a smooth paste, then slowly add to the pan, stirring all the time to prevent lumps. Stir in the lemon juice, season with salt and pepper and cook over a gentle heat for 20 minutes.

4 Meanwhile, heat the remaining oil in a small pan and fry the garlic briefly until golden. Stir in the mint and remove the pan from the heat.

5 Remove the soup from the heat and stir in the beaten eggs. Sprinkle the garlic and mint garnish over the soup and serve.

--- COOK'S TIP ---

If preferred, use less lemon juice to begin with and then add more to taste once the soup is cooked.

Böreks

In Turkey, little stuffed pastries are very popular. They are easy to make and are ideal for parties or as finger canapés.

INGREDIENTS

Makes 35–40
8 ounces feta cheese, grated
8 ounces mozzarella, grated
2 eggs, beaten
3 tablespoons chopped fresh parsley
3 tablespoons chopped fresh chives
3 tablespoons chopped fresh mint
pinch of nutmeg
8 ounces filo pastry
3–4 tablespoon melted butter
freshly ground black pepper

1 Preheat the oven to 350°F. In a bowl, blend the feta and mozzarella cheeses with the beaten eggs. Add the chopped parsley, chives and mint, and season with black pepper and nutmeg. Stir well to mix.

2 Cut the sheets of pastry into four rectangular strips about 3 inches wide. Cover all but one or two strips of the pastry with a damp cloth to prevent them from drying out.

3 Brush one strip of pastry at a time with a little melted butter.

4 Place 1 teaspoon of filling at the bottom edge. Fold one corner over the filling to make a triangle shape. Continue folding the pastry over itself until you get to the end of the strip. Keep making triangles until all the mixture is used up.

5 Place the *böreks* on a greased baking tray and bake in the oven for about 30 minutes until golden brown and crisp. Serve warm or cold.

— COOK'S TIP —

A mixture of almost any cheeses can be used but avoid cream cheeses.

Baked Eggs with Herbs and Vegetables

Eggs, baked or fried as omelets with vegetables and herbs and sometimes meat, too, are popular throughout the Middle East. This particular dish, *Kuku Sabzi*, comes from Persia and is a traditional New Year favorite.

INGREDIENTS

Serves 4–6
2–3 saffron strands
8 eggs
2 leeks
4 ounces fresh spinach
½ iceberg lettuce
4 scallions
3 tablespoons chopped fresh parsley
3 tablespoons chopped fresh chives
3 tablespoons chopped fresh cilantro
1 garlic clove, crushed
2 tablespoons chopped walnuts
  (optional)
2 tablespoons butter
salt and freshly ground black pepper
yogurt and pita bread, to serve

1 Preheat the oven to 350°F. Soak the saffron strands in 1 tablespoon boiling water.

COOK'S TIP

To bring out their flavor, lightly toast the walnuts in a moderate oven, or under a hot broiler before chopping.

2 Beat the eggs in a large bowl. Chop the leeks, spinach, lettuce and scallions finely and add to the eggs together with the chopped herbs, garlic, and walnuts, if using. Season with salt and pepper, add the saffron water and stir thoroughly to mix.

3 Melt the butter in a large shallow casserole and pour in the vegetable and egg mixture.

4 Bake in the oven for 35–40 minutes until the egg mixture is set and the top is golden. Serve hot or cold, cut into wedges, with yogurt and pita bread.

Falafel

These tasty patties are one of the national dishes of Egypt. They can also be made with dried fava beans or chick-peas, and make an excellent appetizer.

INGREDIENTS

Serves 6
2½ cups dried white beans
2 red onions, chopped
2 large garlic cloves, crushed
3 tablespoons finely chopped
   fresh parsley
1 teaspoon ground coriander
1 teaspoon ground cumin
1½ teaspoons baking powder
oil, for deep frying
salt and freshly ground black pepper
tomato salad, to serve

1 Soak the white beans overnight in water. Remove the skins and process in a blender or food processor. Add the chopped onions, garlic, parsley, coriander, cumin, baking powder and seasoning and blend again to make a very smooth paste. Allow the mixture to stand at room temperature for at least 30 minutes.

2 Take walnut-sized pieces of mixture and flatten into small patties. Set aside again for about 15 minutes.

3 Heat the oil until it's very hot and then fry the patties in batches until golden brown. Drain on kitchen paper and then serve with a tomato salad.

Hummus

This popular Middle Eastern dip is widely available in supermarkets, but nothing compares with the delicious home-made variety.

INGREDIENTS

Serves 4–6
1 cup cooked chick-peas
½ cup tahini
3 garlic cloves
juice of 2 lemons
3–4 tablespoons water
salt and freshly ground black pepper
fresh radishes, to serve

For the garnish
1 tablespoon olive oil
1 tablespoon finely chopped
   fresh parsley
½ teaspoon paprika
4 black olives

1 Place the chick-peas, tahini, garlic, lemon juice, seasoning and a little of the water in a blender or food processor. Process until smooth, adding a little more water, if necessary.

2 Alternatively, if you don't have a blender or food processor, mix the ingredients together in a small bowl until smooth.

3 Spoon the mixture into a shallow dish. Make a dent in the middle and pour the olive oil into it. Garnish with parsley, paprika and olives and serve with the radishes.

--- COOK'S TIP ---

Canned chick-peas can be used for hummus. Drain and rinse under cold water before processing.

Persian Kebabs

Kebabs are eaten throughout the Middle East and almost always cooked over a wood or charcoal fire. There are many variations; this particular recipe, *Kabab Bahrg*, comes from Iran and many restaurants serve only this dish.

INGREDIENTS

Serves 4
1 pound lean lamb or beef fillet
2–3 saffron strands
1 large onion, grated
4–6 tomatoes, halved
1 tablespoon butter, melted
salt and freshly ground black pepper
3 tablespoons *sumac*, to garnish
   (optional)
rice, to serve

1 Place the meat on a chopping board. Using a sharp knife remove any excess fat from the meat and cut the meat into strips, about ½ inch thick and 1½ inches long.

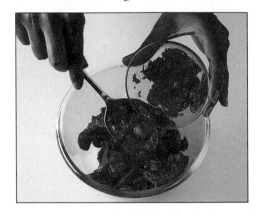

2 Soak the saffron in 1 tablespoon boiling water, pour into a small bowl and mix with the grated onion. Add to the meat and stir a few times so that the meat is coated thoroughly. Cover loosely with plastic wrap and let marinate overnight in the fridge.

3 Season the meat with salt and pepper and then thread onto flat skewers, aligning the strips in neat rows. Thread the tomatoes onto two separate skewers.

4 Grill the kebabs and tomatoes over hot charcoal for 10–12 minutes, basting with butter and turning occasionally. Serve with rice, sprinkled with *sumac*, if you like.

Shish Kebab

INGREDIENTS

Serves 4
1 pound boned leg of lamb, cubed
1 large green bell pepper, seeded and
   cut into squares
1 large yellow bell pepper, seeded and
   cut into squares
8 baby onions, halved
8 ounces button mushrooms
4 tomatoes, halved
1 tablespoon melted butter
bulgur wheat, to serve

For the marinade
3 tablespoons olive oil
juice of 1 lemon
2 garlic cloves, crushed
1 large onion, grated
1 tablespoon fresh oregano
salt and freshly ground black pepper

1 First make the marinade: blend together the oil, lemon juice, garlic, onion, oregano and seasoning. Place the meat in a shallow dish and pour over the marinade.

2 Cover with plastic wrap and let marinate overnight in the fridge.

3 Thread the cubes of lamb on to skewers, alternating with pieces of green and yellow pepper, onions and mushrooms. Thread the tomatoes on to separate skewers. Grill the kebabs and tomatoes over hot charcoal for 10–12 minutes, basting with butter. Serve with bulgur wheat.

Tangy Beef and Herb Khoresh

Lamb, beef or poultry stews combined with vegetables, fruit, herbs and spices, are called *khoresh* in Farsi and are among the most loved of Persian dishes. Like this beef stew, *Khoreshe Gormeh Sabzi*, they are mildly spiced and are ideal for a simple but delicious dinner party.

INGREDIENTS

Serves 4

3 tablespoons oil
1 large onion, chopped
1 pound lean stewing beef, cubed
1 tablespoon chopped fenugreek leaf
2 teaspoons ground turmeric
½ teaspoon ground cinnamon
2½ cups water
1 ounce fresh parsley, chopped
1 ounce fresh chives, chopped
15-ounce can red kidney beans
juice of 1 lemon
salt and freshly ground black pepper
rice, to serve

1 Heat 2 tablespoons of the oil in a large saucepan or flameproof casserole and fry the onion for about 3–4 minutes until light golden. Add the beef and fry for another 5–10 minutes until browned, stirring so that the meat browns on all sides.

2 Add the fenugreek, turmeric and cinnamon and cook for about 1 minute, stirring, then add the water and bring to a boil. Cover and simmer over a low heat for 45 minutes, stirring occasionally.

3 Heat the remaining oil in a small frying pan and fry the parsley and chives over a moderate heat for 2–3 minutes, stirring frequently.

4 Drain the kidney beans and stir them into the beef with the herbs and lemon juice. Season with salt and pepper. Simmer the stew for another 30–35 minutes, until the meat is tender. Serve on a bed of rice.

Sautéed Lamb with Yogurt

In the Middle East meat is normally stewed or barbecued. Here's a delicious exception from Turkey where the lamb is pan-fried instead.

INGREDIENTS

Serves 4

1 pound lean lamb, preferably boned leg, cubed
3 tablespoons butter
4 tomatoes, skinned and chopped
4 thick slices of bread, crusts removed
1 cup strained plain yogurt
2 garlic cloves, crushed
salt and freshly ground black pepper
paprika and mint leaves, to garnish

For the marinade
½ cup strained plain yogurt
1 large onion, grated

1 First make the marinade: blend together the yogurt, onion and a little seasoning in a large bowl. Add the cubed lamb, cover loosely with plastic wrap and set aside to marinate in a cool place for at least 1 hour.

2 Melt half the butter in a frying pan and fry the meat for 5–10 minutes, until tender but still moist. Transfer to a plate with a slotted spoon and keep warm while cooking the tomatoes.

3 Melt the remaining butter in the same pan and fry the tomatoes for 4–5 minutes until soft. Meanwhile, toast the bread and arrange in the bottom of a shallow serving dish.

4 Season the tomatoes and then spread over the toasted bread in an even layer.

5 Blend the yogurt and garlic and season with salt and pepper. Spoon over the tomatoes.

6 Arrange the meat in a layer on top. Sprinkle with paprika and mint leaves and serve at once.

Stuffed Spring Chickens

This dish is widely found in the Lebanon and Syria. The stuffing is a delicious blend of meat, nuts and rice and makes a great dinner party dish.

INGREDIENTS

Serves 6–8
2 x 2¼-pound chickens
1 tablespoon butter
yogurt and salad, to serve

For the stuffing
3 tablespoons oil
1 onion, chopped
1 pound ground lamb
¾ cup almonds, chopped
¾ cup pine nuts
2 cups cooked rice
salt and freshly ground black pepper

1 Preheat the oven to 350°F. If necessary, remove the giblets from the chickens and rinse the body cavities in cold water.

2 Heat the oil in a large frying pan and sauté the onion until slightly softened. Add the ground lamb and cook over a moderate heat for 4–8 minutes until well browned, stirring frequently. Set aside.

3 Heat a small pan over a moderate heat and dry-fry the almonds and pine nuts for 2–3 minutes until golden, shaking the pan frequently.

4 Mix together the meat mixture, almonds, pine nuts and cooked rice. Season with salt and pepper, and then spoon the mixture into the body cavities of the chickens. Rub the chickens all over with the butter.

5 Place the chickens in a large roasting dish, cover with foil and bake in the oven for 45–60 minutes. After about 30 minutes, remove the foil and baste the chickens with the pan juices. Continue cooking without the foil until the chickens are cooked through and the meat juices run clear. Serve the chickens, cut into portions, with yogurt and a salad.

Chicken and Eggplant Khoresh

In Persian or Farsi this dish is known as *Khoreshe Bademjun*, *khoresh* meaning stew and *bademjun* meaning eggplant. It is often served on festive occasions and is believed to have been a favorite of kings.

INGREDIENTS

Serves 4

2 tablespoons oil
1 whole chicken or 4 large
　chicken pieces
1 large onion, chopped
2 garlic cloves, crushed
14-ounce can chopped tomatoes
1 cup water
3 eggplants, sliced
3 bell peppers, preferably red, green
　and yellow, seeded and sliced
2 tablespoons lemon juice
1 tablespoon ground cinnamon
salt and freshly ground black pepper
Persian rice, to serve

1 Heat 1 tablespoon of the oil in a large saucepan or flameproof casserole and fry the chicken or chicken pieces on both sides for about 10 minutes. Add the onion and fry for another 4–5 minutes, until the onion is golden brown.

2 Add the garlic, the chopped tomatoes and their liquid, water and seasoning. Bring to a boil, then reduce the heat and simmer slowly, covered, for 10 minutes.

3 Meanwhile, heat the remaining oil and fry the eggplant in batches until light golden. Transfer to a plate with a slotted spoon. Add the peppers to the pan and fry for a few minutes until slightly softened.

4 Place the eggplant over the chicken or chicken pieces and then add the peppers. Sprinkle over the lemon juice and cinnamon, then cover and continue cooking over a low heat for about 45 minutes, or until the chicken is cooked.

5 Transfer the chicken to a serving plate and spoon the eggplant and peppers around the edge. Reheat the sauce if necessary, adjust the seasoning and pour over the chicken. Serve the *khoresh* with Persian rice.

Chicken Kebabs

Chicken kebabs are prepared in very much the same way all over the Middle East and are a great favorite everywhere. They are ideal for barbecues on hot summer evenings.

INGREDIENTS

Serves 6–8
2 young chickens
1 large onion, grated
2 garlic cloves, crushed
½ cup olive oil
juice of 1 lemon
1 teaspoon paprika
2–3 saffron strands, soaked in
   1 tablespoon boiling water
salt and freshly ground black pepper
nan or pita bread, to serve

1 Cut the chicken into small pieces, removing the bone if preferred, and place in a shallow bowl. Mix the onion, garlic, olive oil, lemon juice, paprika and saffron, and season with salt and pepper.

2 Pour the marinade over the chicken, turning the chicken so that all the pieces are covered evenly. Cover the bowl loosely with plastic wrap and set aside in a cool place to marinate for at least 2 hours.

3 Thread the chicken onto long, preferably metal, skewers. If barbecuing, once the coals are ready, cook for 10–15 minutes, turning occasionally. Or, if you prefer, cook under a moderately hot broiler for 10–15 minutes, turning occasionally.

4 Serve with nan or pita bread. Or you could remove boneless chicken from the skewers and serve it in pita bread as a sandwich accompanied by a garlicky yogurt sauce.

Baked Rock Cornish Hens

This dish is ideal for dinner parties. It is easy to make and tasty too. Allow ample time to make this recipe, however. The Rock Cornish hens should be allowed to marinate overnight to make them extra delicious.

INGREDIENTS

Serves 4
2 cups plain yogurt
4 tablespoons olive oil
1 large onion, grated
2 garlic cloves, crushed
½ teaspoon paprika
2–3 saffron strands, soaked in
   1 tablespoon boiling water
juice of 1 lemon
4 Rock Cornish hens, halved
salt and freshly ground black pepper
Romaine lettuce salad, to serve

1 Blend together the yogurt, olive oil, onion, garlic, paprika, saffron and lemon juice, and season with salt and pepper.

2 Place the Rock Cornish hen halves in a shallow dish, pour over the marinade and then cover and allow to marinate overnight in a cool place or for at least 4 hours in the fridge.

3 Preheat the oven to 350°F. Arrange the Rock Cornish hens in a greased baking pan and bake in the oven for 30–45 minutes, basting frequently until cooked. Serve with Romaine lettuce salad.

---- COOK'S TIP ----

The hens can also be barbecued, for an authentic and even more delicious taste.

Shrimp in Tomato Sauce

Shrimp are popular everywhere in the Middle East. This delicious recipe is an easy way of making the most of them.

INGREDIENTS

Serves 4
2 tablespoons oil
2 onions, finely chopped
2–3 garlic cloves, crushed
5–6 tomatoes, peeled and chopped
2 tablespoons tomato paste
½ cup fish stock
    or water
½ teaspoon ground cumin
½ teaspoon ground cinnamon
1 pound raw, peeled medium to
    large shrimp
juice of 1 lemon
salt and freshly ground black pepper
fresh parsley, to garnish
rice, to serve

1 Heat the oil in a large frying pan or saucepan and fry the onions for 3–4 minutes until golden. Add the garlic, fry for about 1 minute, and then stir in the tomatoes.

2 Blend the tomato paste with the stock or water and stir into the pan with the cumin, cinnamon and seasoning. Simmer, covered, over a low heat for 15 minutes, stirring occasionally. Do not allow to boil.

3 Add the shrimp and lemon juice and simmer the sauce for another 10–15 minutes over a low to moderate heat until the shrimp are cooked and the stock is reduced by about half.

4 Serve with plain rice or in a decorative ring of Persian rice, garnished with parsley.

Swordfish Kebabs

Fish is most delicious when cooked over hot charcoal.

INGREDIENTS

Serves 4–6
2 pounds swordfish steaks
3 tablespoons olive oil
juice of ½ lemon
1 garlic clove, crushed
1 teaspoon paprika
3 tomatoes, quartered
2 onions, cut into wedges
salt and freshly ground black pepper
salad and pita bread, to serve

COOK'S TIP

Almost any type of firm white fish can be used for this recipe.

1 Cut the fish into large cubes and place in a dish.

2 Blend together the oil, lemon juice, garlic, paprika and seasoning in a small mixing bowl and pour over the fish. Cover loosely with plastic wrap and set aside to marinate in a cool place for up to 2 hours.

3 Thread the fish cubes onto skewers, alternating with pieces of tomato and onion.

4 Grill the kebabs over hot charcoal for 5–10 minutes, basting frequently with the remaining marinade and turning occasionally. Serve with salad and pita bread.

Tahini Baked Fish

This simple dish is a great favorite in many Arab countries, particularly Egypt, the Lebanon and Syria.

INGREDIENTS

Serves 6

6 cod or haddock fillets
juice of 2 lemons
4 tablespoons olive oil
2 large onions, chopped
1 cup tahini
1 garlic clove, crushed
3–4 tablespoons water
salt and freshly ground black pepper
rice and salad, to serve

1 Preheat the oven to 350°F. Arrange the cod or haddock fillets in a shallow casserole or baking dish, pour over 1 tablespoon each of the lemon juice and olive oil and bake in the oven for 20 minutes.

2 Meanwhile heat the remaining oil in a large frying pan and fry the onions for 6–8 minutes until well browned and almost crisp.

3 Put the tahini, garlic and seasoning in a small bowl and slowly beat in the remaining lemon juice and water, a little at a time, until the sauce is light and creamy.

4 Sprinkle the onions over the fish, pour over the tahini sauce and bake for another 15 minutes, until the fish is cooked through and the sauce is bubbling. Serve the fish at once with rice and a salad.

Baked Fish with Nuts

This specialty comes from Egypt and is as delicious as it is unusual.

INGREDIENTS

Serves 4

3 tablespoons oil
4 small porgy, about 2 pounds in all
1 large onion, finely chopped
¾ cup hazelnuts, chopped
¾ cup pine nuts
3–4 tomatoes, sliced
3–4 tablespoons finely chopped
  fresh parsley
1 cup fish stock
salt and freshly ground black pepper
parsley sprigs, to garnish
new potatoes or rice, and vegetables or
  salad, to serve

1 Preheat the oven to 375°F. Heat 2 tablespoons of the oil in a frying pan and fry the fish, two at a time, until crisp on both sides.

2 Heat the remaining oil in a large saucepan or flameproof casserole and fry the onion for 3–4 minutes until golden. Add the chopped hazelnuts and pine nuts and stir-fry for a few minutes.

3 Stir in the tomatoes, cook for a few minutes and then add the parsley, seasoning and stock and simmer for 10–15 minutes, stirring occasionally.

4 Place the fish in a shallow casserole and spoon the sauce over. Bake in the oven for 20 minutes or until the fish is cooked through and flakes easily if pierced with a fork.

5 Serve the fish at once accompanied by new potatoes or rice, and vegetables or salad.

COOK'S TIP

Other small whole fish, such as snapper, sea perch or butterfish, can be used for this recipe if porgy is unavailable.

Eggplant Bake

Eggplants are extremely popular all over the Middle East. This particular dish, *Kuku Bademjan*, comes from Iran.

INGREDIENTS

Serves 4
4 tablespoons oil
1 onion, finely chopped
3–4 garlic cloves, crushed
4 eggplants, cut into quarters
6 eggs
2–3 saffron strands, soaked in
   1 tablespoon boiling water
1 teaspoon paprika
salt and freshly ground black pepper
chopped fresh parsley, to garnish
bread and salad, to serve

1 Preheat the oven to 350°F. Heat about 2 tablespoons of the oil in a frying pan and fry the onion until golden. Add the garlic, fry for about 2 minutes and then add the eggplants and cook for 10–12 minutes until soft and golden brown. Cool and then chop the eggplants.

2 Beat the eggs in a large bowl and stir in the eggplant mixture, saffron water, paprika and seasoning. Place the remaining oil in a deep casserole. Heat in the oven for a few minutes, then add the egg and eggplant mixture. Bake for 30–40 minutes until set. Garnish with parsley and serve with bread and salad.

Turkish-style Vegetable Casserole

INGREDIENTS

Serves 4
4 tablespoons olive oil
1 large onion, chopped
2 eggplants, cut into small cubes
4 zucchini, cut into small chunks
4–5 okra, soaked in vinegar for
   30 minutes, cut into short lengths
1 green bell pepper, seeded and
   chopped
1 red bell pepper, seeded and chopped
1 cup fresh or frozen peas
4 ounces green beans
1 pound new potatoes, cubed
½ teaspoon ground cinnamon
/2 teaspoon ground cumin
1 teaspoon paprika
4–5 tomatoes, skinned
14-ounce can chopped tomatoes
2 tablespoons chopped fresh parsley
3–4 garlic cloves, crushed
1½ cups vegetable stock
salt and freshly ground black pepper
black olives, to garnish

1 Preheat the oven to 375°F. Heat 3 tablespoons of the oil in a heavy-bottomed pan and fry the onion until golden. Add the eggplants and sauté for about 3 minutes, then add the zucchini, okra, green and red bell pepper, peas, green beans and potatoes, together with the spices and seasoning. Cook for another 3 minutes, stirring all the time, then transfer the vegetable mixture to a shallow casserole.

2 Chop and seed the fresh tomatoes and mix with the canned tomatoes, parsley, garlic and the remaining olive oil in a bowl.

3 Pour the stock over the vegetables and then spoon over the tomato mixture. Cover and cook in the oven for 45–60 minutes. Serve, garnished with black olives.

Baked Stuffed Eggplant

The name of this famous Turkish *mezze* dish, *Imam Bayaldi*, literally means, "the Imam fainted" – perhaps with pleasure at the deliciousness of the dish.

INGREDIENTS

Serves 6
3 eggplants
4 tablespoons olive oil
1 large onion, chopped
2 small bell peppers (1 red and
   1 green), seeded and diced
3 garlic cloves, crushed
5–6 tomatoes, peeled and chopped
2 tablespoons chopped fresh parsley
about 1 cup boiling water
1 tablespoon lemon juice
salt and freshly ground black pepper
chopped fresh parsley, to garnish
bread, salad and yogurt dip,
   to serve

COOK'S TIP

This flavorful dish can be made in advance and is ideal for a buffet table.

1 Preheat the oven to 375°F. Cut the eggplants in half lengthwise and scoop out the flesh, reserving the shells.

2 Heat 2 tablespoons of the olive oil and fry the onion and peppers for 5–6 minutes until both are slightly softened but not too tender.

3 Add the garlic and continue to cook for another 2 minutes then stir in the tomatoes, parsley and eggplant flesh. Season and then stir well and fry over a moderate heat for 2–3 minutes.

4 Heat the remaining oil in a separate pan and fry the eggplant shells, two at a time, on both sides.

5 Stuff the shells with the sautéed vegetables. Arrange the eggplants closely together in a shallow casserole and pour enough boiling water around the eggplants to come about halfway up their sides.

6 Cover with foil and bake in the oven for 45–60 minutes until the eggplants are tender and most of the liquid has been absorbed.

7 Place a half eggplant on each serving plate and sprinkle with a little lemon juice. Serve the eggplants hot or cold, garnished with parsley and accompanied by bread, salad and a yogurt dip.

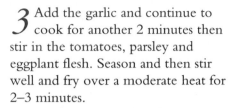

Spinach Pie

This Turkish dish, *Fatayer*, makes a healthy vegetarian dish.

INGREDIENTS

Serves 6

2 pounds fresh spinach, chopped
2 tablespoons butter or margarine
2 onions, chopped
2 garlic cloves, crushed
10 ounces feta cheese, crumbled
¾ cup pine nuts
5 eggs, beaten
2 saffron strands, soaked in
  2 tablespoons boiling water
1 teaspoon paprika
¼ teaspoon ground cumin
¼ teaspoon ground cinnamon
14 sheets filo pastry
about 4 tablespoons olive oil
salt and freshly ground black pepper
lettuce, to serve

1 Place the spinach in a large colander, sprinkle with a little salt, rub into the leaves and leave for 30 minutes to drain the excess liquid.

2 Preheat the oven to 350°F. Melt the butter or margarine in a large pan and fry the onions until golden. Add the garlic, cheese and nuts. Remove from the heat and stir in the eggs, spinach, saffron and spices. Season with salt and pepper and mix well.

COOK'S TIP

Cheddar, Parmesan or any hard cheese can be added to this dish as well as the feta.

3 Grease a large rectangular baking pan. Take seven of the sheets of filo and brush one side of each with a little olive oil. Place on the bottom of the pan, overlapping the sides.

4 Spoon all of the spinach mixture over the pastry and carefully drizzle 2 tablespoons of the remaining olive oil over the top.

5 Fold the overlapping pastry over the filling. Cut the remaining pastry sheets to the pan size and brush each one with more olive oil. Arrange on top of the filling.

6 Brush with water to prevent curling and then bake in the oven for about 30 minutes, until the pastry is golden brown. Serve with the lettuce.

Turkish Salad

This classic salad is a wonderful combination of textures and flavors. The saltiness of the cheese is perfectly balanced by the refreshing salad vegetables.

INGREDIENTS

Serves 4
1 Romaine lettuce heart
1 green bell pepper
1 red bell pepper
½ cucumber
4 tomatoes
1 red onion
8 ounces feta cheese, crumbled
black olives, to garnish

For the dressing
3 tablespoons olive oil
3 tablespoons lemon juice
1 garlic clove, crushed
1 tablespoon chopped fresh parsley
1 tablespoon chopped fresh mint
salt and freshly ground black pepper

1 Chop the lettuce into bite-size pieces. Seed the peppers, remove the cores and cut the flesh into thin strips. Chop the cucumber and slice or chop the tomatoes. Cut the onion in half, then slice finely.

2 Place the chopped lettuce, peppers, cucumber, tomatoes and onion in a large bowl. Sprinkle the feta over the top and toss together lightly.

3 To make the dressing: blend together the olive oil, lemon juice and garlic in a small bowl. Stir in the parsley and mint and season with salt and pepper to taste.

4 Pour the dressing over the salad, toss lightly and serve garnished with a handful of black olives.

Persian Salad

This very simple, refreshing salad can be served with almost any Persian dish – don't add the dressing until just before you are ready to serve.

INGREDIENTS

Serves 4
4 tomatoes
½ cucumber
1 onion
1 Romaine lettuce heart

For the dressing
2 tablespoons olive oil
juice of 1 lemon
1 garlic clove, crushed
salt and freshly ground black pepper

1 Cut the tomatoes and cucumber into small cubes. Finely chop the onion and tear the lettuce into pieces.

2 Place the tomatoes, cucumber, onion and lettuce in a large salad bowl and mix lightly together.

3 To make the dressing, pour the olive oil into a small bowl. Add the lemon juice, garlic and seasoning and blend together well. Pour over the salad and toss lightly to mix. Sprinkle with black pepper and serve with meat or rice dishes.

Tabbouleh

This classic Lebanese salad has become very popular in other countries. It makes an ideal substitute for a rice dish on a buffet table and is excellent served with cold sliced lamb.

INGREDIENTS

Serves 4

1 cup fine bulgur wheat
juice of 1 lemon
3 tablespoons olive oil
½ cup finely chopped fresh parsley
3 tablespoons fresh mint, chopped
4–5 scallions, chopped
1 green bell pepper, seeded and sliced
salt and freshly ground black pepper
2 large tomatoes, diced, and black
   olives, to garnish

1 Put the bulgur wheat in a bowl. Add enough cold water to cover it and let it stand for at least 30 minutes and up to 2 hours.

2 Drain and squeeze with your hands to remove excess water. The bulgur wheat will swell to double the size. Spread on paper towels to dry the bulgur wheat completely.

3 Place the bulgur wheat in a large bowl, add the lemon juice, the oil and a little salt and pepper. Allow to stand for 1–2 hours if possible, in order for the flavors to develop.

4 Add the chopped parsley, mint, scallions and bell pepper and mix well. Garnish with diced tomatoes and olives and serve.

Yogurt with Cucumber

INGREDIENTS

Serves 4–6

½ cucumber
1 small onion
2 garlic cloves
1 tablespoon fresh parsley
2 cups plain yogurt
¼ teaspoon paprika
salt and white pepper
mint leaves, to garnish

1 Finely chop the cucumber and onion, crush the garlic and finely chop the parsley.

--- COOK'S TIP ---

It's not traditional, but other herbs, such as mint or chives, would be equally good in this dish.

2 Lightly beat the yogurt and then add the cucumber, onion, garlic and parsley and season with salt and pepper to taste.

3 Sprinkle with a little paprika and chill for at least 1 hour. Garnish with mint leaves and serve with warm pita bread or as an accompaniment to meat, poultry and rice dishes.

Sweet Rice

In Iran, sweet rice, *Shirin Polo,* is always served at wedding banquets and on other traditional special occasions.

INGREDIENTS

Serves 8–10

3 oranges
6 tablespoons sugar
3 tablespoons melted butter
5–6 carrots, cut into julienne strips
1/2 cup mixed chopped pistachios, almonds and pine nuts
3 1/2 cups basmati rice, soaked in salted water for 2 hours
2–3 saffron strands, soaked in 1 tablespoon boiling water
salt

> ——— COOK'S TIP ———
>
> Take care to cook this rice over a very low heat as it can burn easily owing to the sugar in the carrots.

1 Cut the peel from the oranges in wide strips using a potato peeler, and cut the peel into thin shreds.

2 Place the strips of peel in a saucepan with enough water to cover and bring to a boil. Simmer for a few minutes, drain and repeat this process until you have removed the bitter flavor of the peel.

3 Place the peel back in the pan with 3 tablespoons of the sugar and 4 tablespoons water. Bring to a boil and then simmer until the water is reduced by half. Set aside.

4 Heat 1 tablespoon of the butter in a pan and fry the carrots for 2–3 minutes. Add the remaining sugar and 4 tablespoons water and simmer for 10 minutes until almost evaporated.

5 Stir the carrots and half of the nuts into the orange peel and set aside. Drain the rice, boil in salted water for 5 minutes, then reduce the heat and simmer very gently for 10 minutes until half cooked. Drain and rinse.

6 Heat 1 tablespoon of the remaining butter in the pan and add about 3 tablespoons water. Fork a little of the rice into the pan and spoon on some of the orange mixture. Make layers until all the mixture has been used.

7 Cook gently for 10 minutes. Pour over the remaining butter and cover with a clean dish towel. Secure with a lid and steam for 30–45 minutes. Serve garnished with the remaining nuts and the saffron water.

Rice with Fresh Herbs

INGREDIENTS

Serves 4

scant 2 cups basmati rice, soaked in salted water for 2 hours
2 tablespoons finely chopped fresh parsley
2 tablespoons finely chopped fresh cilantro
2 tablespoons finely chopped fresh chives
1 tablespoon finely chopped fresh dill
3–4 scallions, finely chopped
4 tablespoons butter
1 teaspoon ground cinnamon
2–3 saffron strands, soaked in 1 tablespoon boiling water
salt

1 Drain the rice, and then boil in salted water for 5 minutes, reduce the heat and simmer for 10 minutes.

2 Stir in the herbs and scallions and mix well with a fork. Simmer for a few minutes more, then drain but do not rinse. Wash and dry the pan.

3 Heat half of the butter in the pan, add 1 tablespoon water, then stir in the rice. Cook over a very low heat for 10 minutes, then test to see if it is half cooked. Add the remaining butter, the cinnamon and saffron water and cover the pan with a clean dish towel. Secure with a tightly fitting lid, and steam over a very low heat for 30–40 minutes.

Persian Melon

Called *Paludeh Garmac*, this is a typical Persian dessert, using delicious, sweet fresh fruits flavored with rose water and a hint of aromatic mint.

INGREDIENTS

Serves 4

2 small melons
1 cup strawberries, sliced
3 peaches, peeled and cut into small cubes
1 bunch of seedless grapes (green or red)
2 tablespoons sugar
1 tablespoon rose water
1 tablespoon lemon juice
crushed ice (optional)
4 sprigs of mint, to decorate

1 Carefully cut the melons in half and remove the seeds. Scoop out the flesh with a melon baller, making sure not to damage the skin. Reserve the melon shells. Alternatively, if you don't have a melon baller, scoop out the flesh using a large spoon and cut into bite-size pieces.

2 Reserve four strawberries and slice the others. Place in a bowl with the melon balls, the peaches, grapes, sugar, rose water and lemon juice.

3 Pile the fruit into the melon shells and chill in the fridge for 2 hours.

4 To serve, sprinkle with crushed ice, decorating each melon with a whole strawberry and a sprig of mint.

COOK'S TIP

To peel peaches, cover with boiling water and leave to stand for a couple of minutes. Cool under cold water before peeling.

Oranges in Syrup

This is a favorite classic dessert. It
is light and simple-to-make,
refreshing and delicious.

INGREDIENTS

Serves 4

4 oranges
2½ cups water
1½ cups sugar
2 tablespoons lemon juice
2 tablespoons orange blossom water or
  rose water
½ cup pistachio nuts, shelled and
  chopped

--- COOK'S TIP ---

A perfect dessert to serve after a heavy
main course dish. Almonds could be substituted for the pistachio nuts, if you like.

1 Peel the oranges with a vegetable
peeler down to the pith.

2 Cut the orange peel into fine strips
and boil in water several times to
remove the bitterness. Drain and set
aside until needed.

3 Place the water, sugar and lemon
juice in a saucepan. Bring to a
boil and then add the orange peel and
simmer until the syrup thickens. Add
the orange blossom or rose water, stir
and set aside to cool.

4 Completely peel the pith from the
oranges and cut them into thick
slices. Arrange in a shallow serving dish
and pour over the syrup. Chill for
about 1–2 hours and then decorate
with pistachio nuts and serve.

Baklava

This is queen of all pastries with its exotic flavors and is usually served for the Persian New Year on March 21, celebrating the first day of spring.

INGREDIENTS

Serves 6–8

3¾ cups ground
   pistachio nuts
1¼ cups confectioner's sugar
1 tablespoon ground cardamom
about ⅔ cup unsalted butter,
   melted
1 pound filo pastry

For the syrup
2 cups granulated or
   superfine sugar
1¼ cups water
2 tablespoons rose water

1 First make the syrup: place the sugar and water in a saucepan, bring to a boil and then simmer for about 10 minutes until syrupy. Stir in the rose water and set aside to cool.

2 Mix together the pistachio nuts, confectioner's sugar and ground cardamom. Preheat the oven to 325°F and brush a large rectangular baking pan with a little melted butter.

3 Taking one sheet of filo pastry at a time, and keeping the remainder covered with a damp cloth, brush with melted butter and lay on the bottom of the pan. Continue until you have six buttered layers in the pan. Spread half of the nut mixture over, pressing down with a spoon.

4 Take another six sheets of filo pastry, brush each with butter and lay over the nut mixture. Sprinkle over the remaining nuts and top with a final layer of six filo sheets each brushed again with butter. Cut the pastry diagonally into small lozenge shapes using a sharp knife. Pour the remaining melted butter over the top.

5 Bake for 20 minutes, then increase the heat to 400°F and bake for about 15 minutes until light golden in color and puffed.

6 Remove from the oven and drizzle about three quarters of the syrup over the pastry, reserving the remainder for serving. Arrange the baklava lozenges on a large glass dish and serve with extra syrup.

Omm Ali

Here's an Egyptian version of bread and butter pudding.

INGREDIENTS

Serves 4

10–12 sheets filo pastry
2½ cups milk
1 cup heavy or whipping cream
1 egg, beaten
2 tablespoons rose water
½ cup each chopped pistachio nuts,
  almonds and hazelnuts
⅔ cup raisins
1 tablespoon ground cinnamon
light cream, to serve

1 Preheat the oven to 325°F. Bake the filo pastry, on a baking sheet, for 15–20 minutes until crisp. Remove the baking sheet from the oven and raise the temperature to 400°F.

2 Scald the milk and heavy or whipping cream by pouring into a pan and heating very gently until hot but not boiling. Slowly add the beaten egg and the rose water. Cook over a very low heat, until the mixture begins to thicken, stirring all the time.

3 Crumble the pastry using your hands and then spread in layers with the nuts and raisins into the bottom of a shallow baking dish.

4 Pour the custard mixture over the nut and pastry base and bake in the oven for 20 minutes until golden. Sprinkle with cinnamon and serve with light cream.

MOROCCO

Harira

INGREDIENTS

Serves 6

¹⁄₂ cup chickpeas, soaked overnight
1 tablespoon butter
8 ounces boneless leg of lamb, cubed
1 onion, chopped
1 pound tomatoes, peeled
  and chopped
a few celery leaves, chopped
2 tablespoons chopped fresh parsley
1 tablespoon chopped fresh cilantro
¹⁄₂ teaspoon ground ginger
¹⁄₂ teaspoon ground turmeric
1 teaspoon ground cinnamon
scant ¹⁄₂ cup green lentils
4 ounces vermicelli
2 egg yolks
juice of ¹⁄₂–1 lemon
salt and freshly ground black pepper
fresh cilantro, to garnish
lemon wedges, to serve

1 Drain the chickpeas, rinse under cold water and set aside. Melt the butter in a large flameproof casserole or saucepan and fry the lamb and onion for 2–3 minutes, stirring, until the lamb is just browned.

2 Add the tomatoes, celery leaves, herbs and spices and season well with black pepper. Cook for about 1 minute and then stir in 7¹⁄₂ cups water and add the lentils and chickpeas.

3 Slowly bring to a boil and skim the surface to remove the surplus froth. Boil rapidly for 10 minutes, then reduce the heat and simmer very gently for about 2 hours or until the chickpeas are very tender. Season with salt and a little more pepper if necessary.

4 Add the vermicelli and cook for 5–6 minutes, until it is just cooked through. If the soup is very thick at this stage, add a little more water.

5 Beat the egg yolks with the lemon juice and stir into the simmering soup. Immediately remove the soup from the heat and stir until thickened. Pour into warmed serving bowls and garnish with fresh cilantro. Serve with lemon wedges.

— COOK'S TIP —

If you have forgotten to soak the chickpeas, place them in a pan with about four times their volume of cold water. Bring very slowly to a boil, then cover and remove from the heat. Let stand for 45 minutes. They can then be drained and used as described in the recipe.

Chickpea and Parsley Soup

INGREDIENTS

Serves 6

1⅓ cups chickpeas, soaked overnight
1 small onion
1 bunch fresh parsley
2 tablespoons olive and sunflower
    oil, mixed
5 cups chicken stock
juice of ½ lemon
salt and freshly ground black pepper
lemon wedges and finely pared strips of
    rind, to garnish
fresh crusty bread, to serve

1 Drain the chickpeas and rinse under cold water. Cook them in boiling water for 1–1½ hours, until tender. Drain and peel (see Cook's Tip).

2 Place the onion and parsley in a food processor or blender and process until finely chopped.

3 Heat the olive and sunflower oils in a saucepan or flameproof casserole and fry the onion mixture for about 4 minutes over low heat, until the onion is slightly softened.

4 Add the chickpeas, cook gently for 1–2 minutes and add the stock. Season well with salt and pepper. Bring the soup to a boil, then cover and simmer for 20 minutes, until the chickpeas are very tender.

5 Let the soup cool a little and then purée part of it in a food processor or blender, or by mashing the chickpeas fairly roughly with a fork, so that the soup is thick but still quite chunky.

— COOK'S TIP —

Chickpeas, particularly canned ones, blend better in soups and other dishes if the outer skin is rubbed off with your fingers. Although this will take you some time, the final result is much better, so it is well worth doing.

6 Return the soup to a clean pan, add the lemon juice and adjust the seasoning if necessary. Heat gently and then serve garnished with lemon wedges and finely pared rind, and accompanied by fresh crusty bread.

Olives with Moroccan Marinades

INGREDIENTS

Serves 6–8
1⅓ cups green olives (unpitted) for
   each marinade

For the Moroccan marinade
3 tablespoons chopped fresh cilantro
3 tablespoons chopped fresh flat-
   leaf parsley
1 garlic clove, finely chopped
generous pinch of cayenne pepper
generous pinch of ground cumin
2–3 tablespoons olive oil
2–3 tablespoons lemon juice

For the spicy herb marinade
¼ cup chopped fresh cilantro
¼ cup chopped fresh flat-leaf parsley
1 garlic clove, finely chopped
1 teaspoon grated fresh ginger
1 red chili, seeded and finely sliced
¼ preserved lemon, cut into thin strips

1 Crack the olives, hard enough
to break the flesh, but not hard
enough to crack the pit. Place them
in a bowl of cold water and let sit
overnight to remove the excess brine.
Drain thoroughly and place in a jar.

2 Blend the ingredients for the
Moroccan marinade and pour it
over half the olives, adding more olive
oil and lemon juice to cover, if necessary.

3 To make the spicy herb marinade,
combine the cilantro, parsley,
garlic, ginger, chili and preserved
lemon. Add the remaining olives. Store
the olives in the fridge for at least
1 week, shaking the jars occasionally.

Byesar

The Arab dish Byesar is similar
to Middle Eastern hummus,
but uses fava beans instead of
chickpeas. In Morocco, it is eaten
by dipping bread into ground
spices and then scooping up
the purée.

INGREDIENTS

Serves 4–6
4 ounces dried fava beans, soaked
2 garlic cloves, peeled
1 teaspoon cumin seeds
¼ cup olive oil
salt
mint sprigs, to garnish
extra cumin seeds, cayenne pepper and
   bread, to serve

1 Put the dried fava beans in a pan
with the whole garlic cloves and
cumin seeds and add enough water just
to cover. Bring to a boil, then reduce
the heat and simmer, until the beans
are tender. Drain, cool and then slip off
the outer skin of each bean.

2 Purée the beans in a blender or
food processor, adding enough
olive oil and water to make a smooth
soft dip. Season to taste with plenty of
salt. Garnish with sprigs of mint and
serve with extra cumin seeds, cayenne
pepper and bread.

Moroccan Rabbit

The subtle spices make the perfect accompaniments to rabbit.

INGREDIENTS

Serves 4
1½ pounds prepared rabbit pieces
pinch of saffron
1 garlic clove, crushed
pinch of ground turmeric
1 teaspoon paprika
good pinch of ground cumin
1 onion, grated
2 tablespoons butter
1 tablespoon finely chopped fresh
   cilantro
½ cup raisins
1 teaspoon garam masala or pumpkin
   pie spice
salt and freshly ground black pepper
2 tablespoons sliced almonds, toasted,
   to garnish

1 Preheat the oven to 350°F and place the rabbit pieces in a casserole.

2 Combine the saffron and 2 tablespoons boiling water and stir to dissolve. Add the garlic, turmeric, paprika, cumin and salt and pepper and rub this mixture into the rabbit pieces.

3 Add the onion, half the butter, the cilantro and 2½ cups boiling water. Cover and cook in the oven for 50 minutes, then transfer the rabbit pieces to a shallow heatproof dish and rub with the remaining butter.

4 Increase the oven temperature to 375°F. Cook the rabbit pieces for 8–10 minutes, until browned, and place on a serving plate.

5 Meanwhile, pour the sauce into a small saucepan, add the raisins and garam masala and simmer until reduced by about half. Pour the sauce over the rabbit and garnish with the sliced almonds.

Moroccan-style Roast Lamb

Lamb is by far the most popular meat in Morocco, where whole or half lambs are still cooked over open fires. In this oven-roasted variation of *M'choui* the meat is cooked in a very hot oven to start and then finished in a cooler oven until it is so tender that it falls from the bone.

INGREDIENTS

Serves 6
1 leg of lamb, 3–3½ pounds
3 tablespoons butter
2 garlic cloves, crushed
½ teaspoon cumin seeds
¼ teaspoon paprika
pinch of cayenne pepper
salt
fresh cilantro, to garnish
bread or roast potatoes, to serve

1 Trim the lamb of excess fat and make several shallow diagonal cuts in the meat.

2 Combine the butter, garlic, cumin, paprika, cayenne pepper and salt and spread over the surface of the lamb, pressing the mixture into the slits. Set aside for at least 2 hours or overnight.

3 Preheat the oven to 425°F. Place the meat in a large roasting pan and cook for 15 minutes. (Be warned: The butter will burn, but the resulting flavor is delicious.) Reduce the oven temperature to 350°F and continue cooking for 1½–2 hours, until the meat is well cooked and very tender, basting several times with the meat juices.

4 Place the cooked meat on a serving plate and serve immediately. In Morocco, it is customary to pull the meat away from the bone using a fork; however, it may be carved if you prefer. Garnish with fresh cilantro and serve Moroccan-style with bread, or with roast potatoes.

Beef Tagine with Sweet Potatoes

This warming dish is eaten during the winter in Morocco, where, especially in the mountains, the weather can be surprisingly cold. Tagines, by definition, are cooked on the stove (or, more often in Morocco, over coals). However, this works well cooked in the oven.

INGREDIENTS

Serves 4

1¹⁄₂–2 pounds stewing beef
2 tablespoons sunflower oil
good pinch of ground turmeric
1 large onion, chopped
1 fresh red or green chili, seeded and chopped
1¹⁄₂ teaspoons paprika
generous pinch of cayenne pepper
¹⁄₂ teaspoon ground cumin
1 pound sweet potatoes
1 tablespoon chopped fresh parsley
1 tablespoon chopped fresh cilantro
1 tablespoon butter
salt and freshly ground black pepper

1 Trim the meat and cut into ³⁄₄-inch cubes. Heat the oil in a flameproof casserole and fry the meat, together with the turmeric and seasoning, over medium heat for 3–4 minutes, until evenly brown, stirring frequently.

2 Cover the pan tightly and cook for 15 minutes over fairly low heat, without lifting the lid. Preheat the oven to 350°F.

3 Add the onion, chili, paprika, cayenne pepper and cumin to the pan together with just enough water to cover the meat. Cover tightly and cook for 1–1¹⁄₂ hours until the meat is very tender, checking occasionally and adding a little extra water to keep the stew fairly moist.

4 Meanwhile, peel the sweet potatoes and slice them straight into a bowl of salted water (sweet potatoes discolor very quickly). Transfer to a pan, bring to a boil and then simmer for 2–3 minutes, until just tender. Drain.

5 Stir the herbs into the meat, adding a little extra water if the stew appears dry. Arrange the potato slices over the meat and dot with the butter. Cover and cook for another 10 minutes or until the potatoes feel very tender. Increase the oven temperature to 400°F or heat the broiler.

6 Remove the lid of the casserole and cook in the oven or under the broiler for another 5–10 minutes, until the potatoes are golden.

Grilled Poussins

These little chickens can be cooked under the broiler, but taste best if cooked, Moroccan-style, over charcoal.

INGREDIENTS

Serves 4
2 large or 4 small poussins
green salad, to serve

For the marinade
²/₃ cup olive oil
1 onion, grated
1 garlic clove, crushed
1 tablespoon chopped fresh mint
1 tablespoon chopped fresh flat-
   leaf parsley
1 tablespoon chopped fresh cilantro
1–2 teaspoons ground cumin
1 teaspoon paprika
pinch of cayenne pepper

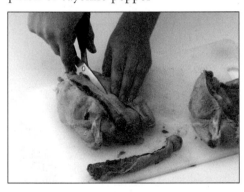

1 Tuck the wings of each poussin under the body and remove the wishbone. Turn the birds over and cut along each side of the backbone with poultry shears and remove.

2 Push down on each bird to break the breast bone. Keeping the bird flat, push a skewer through the wings and breast. Push another skewer through the thighs.

3 Combine all the marinade ingredients and spread over both sides of the poussins. Place in a large shallow dish, cover with plastic wrap and marinate for at least 4 hours or overnight.

4 Prepare a grill or preheat the broiler. Barbecue the poussins for about 25–35 minutes, turning occasionally and brushing with the marinade. If broiling, cook under a medium broiler about 3 inches from the heat for 25–35 minutes or until cooked through, turning and basting occasionally.

5 When ready to serve, cut the birds in half. Serve with a green salad.

Chicken Kdra with Chickpeas and Almonds

A *kdra* is a type of tagine, traditionally cooked with *smen*, a strong Moroccan butter, and a lot of onions. The almonds in this recipe are precooked until soft, adding an interesting texture and flavor to the chicken.

INGREDIENTS

Serves 4

½ cup blanched almonds
½ cup chickpeas, soaked overnight
4 chicken breast halves, skinned
4 tablespoons (½ stick) butter
½ teaspoon saffron threads
2 Spanish onions, finely sliced
4 cups chicken stock
1 small cinnamon stick
¼ cup chopped fresh flat-leaf parsley,
    plus extra to garnish
lemon juice, to taste
salt and freshly ground black pepper

1 Place the almonds in a pan of water and simmer for 1½–2 hours, until fairly soft, then drain. Cook the chickpeas for 1–1½ hours, until soft. Drain the chickpeas, then place in a bowl of cold water and rub with your fingers to remove the skins. Discard the skins and drain.

2 Place the chicken breasts in a pan, together with the butter, half of the saffron, salt and plenty of black pepper. Heat gently, stirring, until the butter has melted.

3 Add the onions and stock, bring to a boil and then add the chickpeas and cinnamon stick. Cover and cook very gently for 45–60 minutes, until the chicken is completely tender.

4 Transfer the chicken to a serving plate and keep warm. Bring the sauce to a boil and simmer until well reduced, stirring frequently. Add the almonds, parsley and remaining saffron and cook for another 2–3 minutes. Sharpen the sauce with a little lemon juice, then pour it over the chicken and serve, garnished with extra parsley.

Chicken with Tomatoes and Honey

INGREDIENTS

Serves 4

2 tablespoons sunflower oil
2 tablespoons butter
4 chicken quarters or 1 whole chicken,
    quartered
1 onion, grated or very finely chopped
1 garlic clove, crushed
1 teaspoon ground cinnamon
good pinch of ground ginger
3–3½ pounds tomatoes, peeled, cored
    and roughly chopped
2 tablespoons honey
⅓ cup blanched almonds
1 tablespoon sesame seeds
salt and freshly ground black pepper
corn bread, to serve

1 Heat the oil and butter in a large casserole. Add the chicken pieces and cook over medium heat for about 3 minutes, until the chicken is lightly browned.

2 Add the onion, garlic, cinnamon, ginger, tomatoes and seasoning, and heat gently until the tomatoes begin to bubble.

3 Lower the heat, cover and simmer very gently for 1 hour, stirring and turning the chicken occasionally, until it is completely cooked through.

4 Transfer the chicken pieces to a plate and then increase the heat and cook the tomatoes until the sauce is reduced to a thick purée, stirring frequently. Stir in the honey, cook for a minute and then return the chicken to the pan and cook for 2–3 minutes to heat through. Dry-fry the almonds and sesame seeds or toast under the broiler until golden.

5 Transfer the chicken and sauce to a warmed serving dish and sprinkle with the almonds and sesame seeds. Serve with corn bread.

Sea Bream with Artichokes and Zucchini

INGREDIENTS

Serves 4

1 or 2 whole sea bream or sea bass
   (about 3 pounds), cleaned and scaled,
   with the head and tail left on
2 onions
2–3 zucchini
4 tomatoes
3 tablespoons olive oil
1 teaspoon fresh thyme
1 can (14 ounces) artichoke hearts
lemon wedges and finely pared rind,
   black olives and fresh cilantro leaves,
   to garnish

For the *charmoula*

1 onion, chopped
2 garlic cloves, halved
½ bunch fresh parsley
3–4 fresh cilantro sprigs
pinch of paprika
3 tablespoons olive oil
2 tablespoons white wine vinegar
1 tablespoon lemon juice
salt and freshly ground black pepper

1 First make the *charmoula*. Place the ingredients in a food processor with 3 tablespoons water and process until the onion is finely chopped and the ingredients are well combined. Alternatively, chop the onion, garlic and herbs finely and blend with the other ingredients and the water.

2 Make three or four slashes on both sides of the fish. Place in a bowl and spread with the *charmoula* marinade, pressing into both sides of the fish. Set aside for 2–3 hours, turning the fish occasionally.

3 Slice the onions. Trim the zucchini and cut into julienne strips. Peel the tomatoes, discard the seeds and chop roughly.

4 Preheat the oven to 425°F. Place the onions, zucchini and tomatoes in a shallow ovenproof dish. Sprinkle with the olive oil, salt and thyme and roast for 15–20 minutes, until softened and slightly charred, stirring occasionally.

5 Reduce the oven temperature to 350°F. Add the artichokes to the dish and place the fish, together with the marinade, on top of the vegetables. Pour on ⅔ cup water and cover with foil.

6 Bake for 30–35 minutes or until the fish is tender. (It will depend on whether you are cooking 1 large or 2 smaller fish.) For the last 5 minutes of cooking, remove the foil to let the skin brown lightly. Alternatively, place under a hot broiler for 2–3 minutes.

7 Arrange the fish on a large, warmed serving platter and spoon the vegetables around the sides. Garnish with lemon wedges and finely pared strips of rind, black olives and fresh cilantro leaves before serving.

Fish Boulettes in Hot Tomato Sauce

This is an unusual and tasty dish that needs hardly any preparation and produces very little mess, as it is all cooked in one pan. It serves four people as a main course, but also makes a great appetizer for eight.

INGREDIENTS

Serves 4
4 cod, haddock or sea bass fillets, about
   6 ounces each
pinch of saffron
½ bunch flat-leaf parsley
1 egg
½ cup white bread crumbs
1½ tablespoons olive oil
1 tablespoon lemon juice
salt and freshly ground black pepper
fresh flat-leaf parsley and lemon
   wedges, to garnish

For the sauce
1 onion, very finely chopped
2 garlic cloves, crushed
6 tomatoes, peeled, seeded and
   chopped
1 green or red chili, seeded and
   finely sliced
6 tablespoons olive oil
⅔ cup water
1 tablespoon lemon juice

1 Skin the fish and, if necessary, remove any bones. Cut the fish into large chunks and place in a blender or a food processor.

2 Dissolve the saffron in 2 tablespoons boiling water and pour into the blender or food processor with the parsley, egg, bread crumbs, olive oil and lemon juice. Season well with salt and pepper and process for 10–20 seconds, until the fish is finely chopped and all the ingredients are combined.

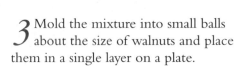

3 Mold the mixture into small balls about the size of walnuts and place them in a single layer on a plate.

4 To make the sauce, place the onion, garlic, tomatoes, chili, olive oil and water in a saucepan. Bring to a boil and then simmer, partially covered, for 10–15 minutes, until the sauce is slightly reduced.

5 Add the lemon juice and then place the fish balls in the simmering sauce. Cover and simmer very gently for 12–15 minutes, until the fish balls are cooked through, turning them over occasionally.

6 Serve the fish balls and sauce immediately, garnished with flat-leaf parsley and lemon wedges.

Monkfish Couscous

Since fish needs very little cooking, it is quickest and easiest to cook the couscous using this simple method. However, if you prefer to steam couscous, steam it over the onions and peppers.

INGREDIENTS

Serves 4
1½ pounds monkfish
2 tablespoons olive oil
1 onion, very thinly sliced into rings
3 tablespoons raisins
¼ cup cashews
1 small red bell pepper, cored, seeded and sliced
1 small yellow bell pepper, cored, seeded and sliced
4 tomatoes, peeled, seeded and sliced
1½ cups fish stock
1 tablespoon chopped fresh parsley
salt and freshly ground black pepper

For the couscous
1⅔ cups couscous
2¼ cups boiling vegetable stock or water

1 Bone and skin the monkfish, if necessary, and cut into bite-size chunks using a sharp knife.

2 Heat half the oil in a saucepan or flameproof casserole and fry about a quarter of the onion rings for 5–6 minutes, until they are a dark golden brown. Transfer to a plate lined with paper towels.

3 Add the raisins and stir-fry for 30–60 seconds, until they begin to plump up. Add to the plate with the onion rings. Add the cashews to the pan and stir-fry for 30–60 seconds, until golden. Place on the plate with the onion and raisins and set aside.

4 Heat the remaining oil in the pan and add the remaining onion rings. Cook for 4–5 minutes, until golden, and then add the pepper slices. Cook over fairly high heat for 6–8 minutes, until the peppers are soft, stirring occasionally. Add the tomatoes and fish stock, reduce the heat and simmer for 10 minutes.

5 Meanwhile, prepare the couscous. Place in a bowl, pour the boiling stock over it and stir once or twice. Set aside for 10 minutes so that the couscous can absorb the liquid, then fluff up with a fork. Cover and keep warm. Alternatively, prepare according to the instructions on the package.

6 Add the fish to the peppers and onion, partially cover and simmer for 6–8 minutes, until the fish is tender, stirring occasionally. Season.

7 Pile the couscous on a large serving plate and make a hollow in the middle. Pour in the monkfish and peppers together with all the sauce. Sprinkle with the parsley and the reserved onion rings, raisins and cashews, and serve.

Sea Bass and Fennel Tagine

This is a delicious tagine featuring fish that is flavored with *charmoula*, a popular blend of herbs and spices used especially in fish dishes.

INGREDIENTS

Serves 4

4 sea bass, monkfish or cod fillets, about 6 ounces each
8 ounces (about 30) medium shrimp
2 tablespoons olive oil
1 onion, chopped
1 fennel bulb, sliced
8 ounces small new potatoes, halved
2 cups fish stock
lemon wedges, to serve (optional)

For the *charmoula*

2 garlic cloves, crushed
4 teaspoons ground cumin
4 teaspoons paprika
pinch of chili powder or cayenne pepper
2 tablespoons chopped fresh parsley
2 tablespoons chopped fresh cilantro
3 tablespoons white vinegar
1 tablespoon lemon juice

1 First make the *charmoula* by blending the crushed garlic, spices, herbs, vinegar and lemon juice in a bowl.

2 Skin the fish, if necessary, and remove any bones, then cut into large bite-size chunks. Peel the shrimp and pull off the tails. Using a sharp knife, cut along the back of each shrimp and pull out and discard the dark thread.

3 Place the fish and shrimp in two separate shallow dishes, add half the *charmoula* marinade to each dish and stir well to coat evenly. Cover with plastic wrap and set aside in a cool place for 30 minutes–2 hours.

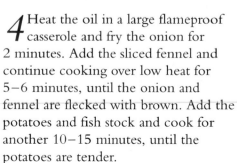

4 Heat the oil in a large flameproof casserole and fry the onion for 2 minutes. Add the sliced fennel and continue cooking over low heat for 5–6 minutes, until the onion and fennel are flecked with brown. Add the potatoes and fish stock and cook for another 10–15 minutes, until the potatoes are tender.

5 Add the marinated fish, stir gently and cook for 4 minutes, then add the shrimp and all the remaining marinade and cook for another 5–6 minutes, until the fish is tender and the shrimp are pink.

6 Serve in bowls, with lemon wedges for squeezing, if desired.

ITALY

Marinated Vegetable Antipasto

INGREDIENTS

Serves 4
3 red bell peppers
3 yellow bell peppers
4 garlic cloves, sliced
handful fresh basil leaves, plus extra to
    garnish
extra virgin olive oil

For the mushrooms
1 pound open cap mushrooms
4 tablespoons extra virgin olive oil
1 large garlic clove, crushed
1 tablespoon chopped fresh rosemary
1 cup dry white wine
fresh rosemary sprigs, to garnish
salt and freshly ground black pepper

For the olives
1 dried red chili, crushed
grated rind of 1 lemon
½ cup extra virgin olive oil
1⅓ cups Italian black olives
2 tablespoons chopped fresh Italian
    parsley
1 lemon wedge, to serve

1 Place the peppers under a hot broiler. Turn occasionally until blackened and blistered all over. Remove from the heat and place in a plastic bag. When cool, remove the skin, halve the peppers and remove the seeds. Cut the flesh into strips lengthwise and place in a bowl with the garlic and basil leaves. Add salt, cover with oil and marinate for 3 hours, tossing occasionally. Garnish with more basil leaves before serving.

2 Thickly slice the mushrooms and place in a large bowl. Heat the oil in a small pan and add the garlic and rosemary. Pour in the wine. Bring the mixture to a boil, then lower the heat and simmer for about 3 minutes. Season to taste.

3 Pour the mixture over the mushrooms. Mix well and let cool, stirring occasionally. Cover and marinate overnight. Serve at room temperature, garnished with rosemary.

4 Prepare the olives. Place the chili and lemon rind in a small pan with the oil. Heat gently for about 3 minutes. Add the olives and heat for 1 more minute. Pour into a bowl and let cool. Marinate overnight. Sprinkle on the parsley just before serving with the lemon wedge.

Pan-fried Chicken Liver Salad

INGREDIENTS

Serves 4

3 ounces fresh baby spinach leaves
3 ounces red leaf lettuce
5 tablespoons olive oil
1 tablespoon butter
8 ounces chicken livers, thinly sliced
3 tablespoons vin santo
2–3 ounces Parmesan cheese, shaved
salt and freshly ground black pepper

1 Wash and dry the spinach and red leaf lettuce. Tear the leaves into a large bowl, season with salt and pepper to taste, and toss gently to mix.

2 Heat 2 tablespoons of the oil with the butter in a large heavy frying pan. When foaming, add the chicken livers and toss over medium to high heat for 5 minutes or until the livers are browned on the outside but still pink in the center. Remove the pan from the heat.

3 Remove the livers from the pan with a slotted spoon, drain them on paper towels, then place on top of the spinach.

4 Return the pan to medium heat, add the remaining oil and the vin santo and stir until sizzling.

5 Pour the hot dressing over the spinach and livers and toss to coat. Put the salad in a serving bowl and sprinkle shavings of Parmesan on top. Serve immediately.

Three-cheese Lasagne

The cheese makes this lasagne quite expensive, so reserve it for a special occasion.

INGREDIENTS

Serves 6–8
2 tablespoons olive oil
1 onion, finely chopped
1 carrot, finely chopped
1 celery stalk, finely chopped
1 garlic clove, crushed
1½ pounds ground beef
14 ounce can chopped tomatoes
1¼ cups beef stock
1¼ cups red wine
2 tablespoons sun-dried tomato paste
2 teaspoons dried oregano
9 sheets no-cook lasagne
3 x 5 ounce packages mozzarella
    cheese, thinly sliced
2 cups ricotta cheese
4 ounces Parmesan cheese, grated
salt and freshly ground black pepper

1 Heat the olive oil and gently cook the onion, carrot, celery and garlic for about 10 minutes, until softened.

2 Add the beef and cook until it changes color, stirring constantly and breaking up the meat.

3 Add the tomatoes, stock, wine, tomato paste, oregano, salt and pepper and bring to a boil, stirring. Cover, lower the heat and simmer gently for 1 hour, stirring.

4 Preheat the oven to 375°F. Check for seasoning, then ladle one-third of the meat sauce into a 9 x 13-inch baking dish and cover with 3 sheets of lasagne. Arrange one-third of the mozzarella slices over the top, dot with one-third of the ricotta, then sprinkle with one-third of the grated Parmesan.

5 Repeat these layers twice, then bake for 40 minutes. Let cool for 10 minutes before serving.

Tortiglioni with Spicy Sausage Sauce

INGREDIENTS

Serves 4
2 tablespoons olive oil
1 onion, finely chopped
1 celery stalk, finely chopped
2 large garlic cloves, crushed
1 fresh red chili, seeded and chopped
1 pound ripe Italian plum tomatoes,
    peeled and finely chopped
2 tablespoons tomato paste
⅔ cup red wine
1 teaspoon sugar
12 ounces dried tortiglioni
6 ounces spicy salami, rind removed
salt and freshly ground black pepper
2 tablespoons chopped fresh parsley,
    to garnish
grated Parmesan cheese, to serve

1 Heat the oil, then add the onion, celery, garlic and chili and cook gently, stirring frequently, for about 10 minutes, until softened.

2 Add the tomatoes, tomato paste, wine, sugar and salt and pepper to taste and bring to a boil, stirring. Lower the heat, cover and simmer gently, stirring, for 20 minutes. Add a little water occasionally if the sauce becomes too thick.

3 Drop the pasta into a saucepan of rapidly boiling salted water and simmer, uncovered, for 10 minutes.

4 Chop the salami into bite-size chunks and add to the sauce. Heat through, then season to taste.

5 Drain the pasta, tip it into a large bowl, then pour the sauce over and toss to mix. Sprinkle the parsley and grated Parmesan on top.

Tagliatelle with Bolognese Sauce

INGREDIENTS

Serves 4

2 tablespoons olive oil
1 onion, finely chopped
1 carrot, finely chopped
1 celery stick, finely chopped
1 garlic clove, crushed
12 ounces ground beef
⅔ cup red wine
1 cup milk
14 ounce can chopped tomatoes
1 tablespoon sun-dried tomato paste
12 ounces dried tagliatelle
salt and freshly ground black pepper
shredded fresh basil, to garnish
grated Parmesan cheese, to serve

1 Heat the oil in a large pan. Add the onion, carrot, celery and garlic and cook gently, stirring, for about 10 minutes, until softened. Do not let the vegetables color.

2 Add the ground beef to the pan with the vegetables and cook over medium heat until the meat changes color, stirring constantly and breaking up any lumps with a wooden spoon.

3 Pour in the wine. Stir frequently until it has evaporated, then add the milk and continue cooking and stirring until this has evaporated, too.

COOK'S TIP

Don't skimp on the cooking time—it is essential for a full-flavored Bolognese sauce. Some Italian cooks insist on cooking it for 3–4 hours, so the longer you can leave it the better.

4 Stir in the tomatoes and tomato paste, with salt and pepper to taste. Simmer the sauce uncovered, over the lowest possible heat for at least 45 minutes.

5 Cook the tagliatelle in a pan of rapidly boiling salted water for 8–10 minutes or until *al dente*. Drain and pour into a warmed bowl. Pour on the sauce and toss to combine. Garnish with basil and serve at once, with Parmesan cheese on the side.

Penne alla Carbonara

INGREDIENTS

Serves 3–4

12 ounces dried penne
2 tablespoons olive oil
1 small onion, finely chopped
6 ounces pancetta rashers, any rinds
   removed, cut into bite-size strips
1–2 garlic cloves, crushed
5 egg yolks
¾ cup heavy cream
1⅓ cups grated Parmesan cheese, plus
   extra to serve
salt and freshly ground black pepper

1 Cook the penne in a large pan of rapidly boiling salted water for about 10 minutes or until *al dente*.

2 Meanwhile, heat the oil in a large flameproof casserole. Add the onion and cook for about 5 minutes, stirring, until softened. Add the pancetta and garlic. Cook over medium heat until the pancetta is cooked but not crisp. Remove the pan from the heat and set aside.

3 Put the egg yolks in a jug and add the cream and Parmesan cheese. Grind in plenty of black pepper. Beat well to mix.

4 Drain the penne and tip into the casserole. Toss over medium heat, stirring, so the pancetta mixture blends evenly with the pasta.

5 Remove from the heat, pour in the egg yolk mixture and toss well to combine. Spoon into a large shallow serving dish, grind a little black pepper over and sprinkle with some of the extra Parmesan. Serve the rest of the Parmesan separately.

—————— COOK'S TIP ——————

Don't return the pan to the heat after adding the egg yolks as they will scramble and give the pasta a curdled appearance.

Spinach and Ricotta Gnocchi

The mixture for these tasty little herb dumplings should be handled very carefully to achieve light and fluffy results. Serve with sage butter and grated Parmesan.

INGREDIENTS

Serves 4

6 garlic cloves, unpeeled
1 ounce mixed fresh herbs, such as parsley, basil, thyme, coriander and chives, finely chopped
8 ounces fresh spinach leaves
generous 1 cup ricotta cheese
1 egg yolk
⅔ cup grated Parmesan cheese
⅔ cup flour
¼ cup butter
2 tablespoons fresh sage, chopped
salt

2 Mix the ricotta with the egg yolk, spinach, herbs and garlic. Add half the Parmesan and the flour.

3 Using floured hands, break off pieces of the spinach mixture slightly smaller than a walnut and roll them into small dumplings.

4 Cook the gnocchi in boiling salted water. They will rise to the top of the pan when cooked.

5 The gnocchi should be light and fluffy all the way through. If not, simmer for another minute. Drain well. Meanwhile, melt the butter in a frying pan and add the sage. Simmer gently for 1 minute. Add the gnocchi to the frying pan and toss in the butter over gentle heat for about 1 minute, then serve sprinkled with the remaining Parmesan.

1 Cook the garlic cloves in boiling water for 4 minutes. Drain and pop out of the skins. Place in a food processor with the herbs and blend to a purée, or mash the garlic with a fork, add the herbs and mix well. Place the spinach in a large pan with just the water that clings to the leaves and cook gently until wilted. Let the spinach leaves cool, then squeeze out as much liquid as possible. Chop the leaves finely.

Pasta all' arrabbiata

This is a speciality of Lazio – the word *arrabbiata* means rabid or angry, and describes the heat that comes from the chili. This quick version of the dish is made with bottled sugocasa, or crushed Italian tomatoes.

INGREDIENTS

Serves 4
1 pound sugocasa
2 garlic cloves, crushed
⅔ cup dry white wine
1 tablespoon sun-dried tomato purée
1 fresh red chili
12 ounces penne or tortiglioni
¼ cup chopped Italian parsley
salt and freshly ground black pepper
freshly grated Pecorino cheese, to serve

1 Put the sugocasa, garlic, wine, tomato purée and whole chili in a saucepan and bring to the boil. Cover and simmer gently.

2 Drop the penne or tortiglioni into a large saucepan of rapidly boiling salted water and simmer for 10–12 minutes or until the pasta is *al dente*.

3 Remove the chili from the sauce and add half the chopped fresh parsley. Taste for seasoning. If you prefer a hotter taste, chop some or all of the chili and return it to the sauce.

4 Drain the pasta and tip into a warmed large bowl. Pour the sauce over the pasta and toss to mix. Serve at once, sprinkled with grated Pecorino and the remaining parsley.

Saffron Risotto

This classic risotto makes a delicious first course, or a light supper dish in its own right.

INGREDIENTS

Serves 4
about 5 cups beef or chicken stock
good pinch of saffron threads or
  1 envelope of saffron powder
6 tablespoons butter
1 onion, finely chopped
1½ cups risotto rice
1 cup grated Parmesan cheese
salt and freshly ground black pepper

1 Bring the stock to a boil, then reduce to a low simmer. Ladle a little stock into a small bowl. Add the saffron threads or powder and set aside to infuse.

2 Melt 4 tablespoons of butter in a saucepan until foaming. Add the onion and cook gently for about 3 minutes, stirring, until softened.

3 Add the rice. Stir until the grains start to swell and burst, then add a few ladlefuls of the stock, with the saffron liquid, and season to taste. Stir over low heat until the stock is absorbed. Add the remaining stock, allowing the rice to absorb the liquid before adding more, and stirring constantly. After 20–25 minutes, the rice should be *al dente* and the risotto golden yellow, moist and creamy.

4 Gently stir in about two-thirds of the grated Parmesan and the remaining butter. Heat through until the butter has melted, then taste for seasoning. Transfer the risotto to a warmed serving bowl or platter and serve hot, with the remaining grated Parmesan sprinkled on top.

Polenta Elisa

INGREDIENTS

Serves 4
1 cup milk
1 teaspoon salt
2 cups pre-cooked polenta
1 cup grated Gruyère cheese
1 cup torta di Dolcelatte cheese,
  crumbled·
4 tablespoons butter
2 garlic cloves, roughly chopped
a few fresh sage leaves, chopped
freshly ground black pepper
prosciutto, to serve

1 Preheat the oven to 400°F. Lightly butter an 8–10-inch glass baking dish.

2 Bring the milk and 3 cups water to a boil in a pan, add 1 teaspoon salt, then pour in the polenta. Cook for 8 minutes or according to the instructions on the package.

3 Spoon half the polenta into the baking dish and level the surface with the back of a spoon. Cover with half the grated Gruyère and crumbled Dolcelatte. Spoon the remaining polenta evenly over the top and sprinkle with the remaining cheese.

4 Melt the butter in a pan until foaming, add the garlic and sage and fry until the butter browns.

5 Drizzle the butter mixture over the polenta and cheese and grind black pepper liberally over the top. Bake in the oven for 5 minutes. Serve hot, with slices of prosciutto.

Pizza Margherita

The Margherita is named after the nineteenth century Queen of Italy and is one of the most popular of all pizzas.

INGREDIENTS

Serves 4

1 pound peeled plum tomatoes, fresh or canned
1 quantity pizza dough, rolled out
12 ounces mozzarella cheese, diced
10–12 leaves fresh basil, torn into pieces
4 tablespoons freshly grated Parmesan cheese (optional)
3 tablespoons olive oil
salt and freshly ground black pepper

1 Preheat the oven to 475°F for at least 20 minutes before baking. Strain the tomatoes through the medium holes of a food mill placed over a bowl, scraping in all of the tomato pulp.

2 Spread the puréed tomatoes over the prepared pizza dough, leaving the rim uncovered.

3 Sprinkle mozzarella cheese over the pizza base. Dot with the torn pieces of basil and sprinkle with the Parmesan, if using. Season with salt and freshly ground black pepper and drizzle with olive oil. Immediately place the pizzas in the oven. Bake for about 15–20 minutes, or until the crust is golden brown and the cheeses are melted and bubbling.

Pizza Napoletana

If you ask for a pizza in the Neapolitan manner anywhere in Italy other than Naples, you will be given this pizza with anchovies.

INGREDIENTS

Serves 4

1 pound peeled tomatoes, fresh or canned
1 quantity pizza dough, rolled out
1½ ounces anchovy fillets in oil, drained and cut into strips
12 ounces mozzarella cheese, diced
1 teaspoon oregano leaves, fresh or dried
3 tablespoons olive oil
salt and freshly ground black pepper

1 Preheat the oven to 475°F for at least 20 minutes before baking. Strain the tomatoes through the medium holes of a food mill placed over a bowl, scraping in all the tomato pulp.

2 Spread the puréed tomatoes over the prepared pizza dough, leaving the rim uncovered. Dot evenly with the anchovy strips and the diced mozzarella cheese.

3 Sprinkle the pizza with oregano, salt and freshly ground black pepper and drizzle with olive oil. Immediately place the pizza in the preheated oven. Bake for about 15–20 minutes, or until the crust is golden brown and the cheese is melted and bubbling.

Italian Olive Bread

INGREDIENTS

Makes 1 loaf
12 ounces all-purpose flour
½ teaspoon salt
1 teaspoon easy-blend dry yeast
1 teaspoon dried thyme
3 tablespoons olive oil
4 black olives, stoned and chopped
3 sun-dried tomatoes in oil, chopped
crushed rock salt

1 Place the flour and salt in a bowl and sprinkle over the yeast and thyme. Make a well in the center and pour in 7 fluid ounces of warm water and 2 tablespoons olive oil.

2 Mix to a dough and knead on a floured surface for 10 minutes, until elastic (or use a food processor or a mixer with a dough attachment).

3 Place the dough in a large oiled plastic bag. Seal and leave in a warm place for about 2 hours, or until the dough has doubled in size.

4 Turn out the dough on a floured surface and knead lightly. Flatten with your hands. Sprinkle over the olives and tomatoes and knead in until well distributed. Shape the dough into a long oval and place on a greased baking sheet. Cover and leave to rise in a warm place for 45 minutes. Preheat the oven to 375°F.

5 When risen, press your finger several times into the dough, drizzle over the remaining oil and sprinkle with the rock salt. Bake in the oven for 35–40 minutes, until the loaf is golden and sounds hollow when tapped on the bottom.

Focaccia with Onions

INGREDIENTS

Serves 6–8

1 pound all-purpose flour
1 sachet easy-blend yeast
1 teaspoon salt
pinch of sugar
5 tablespoons olive oil
1 medium onion, sliced thinly and
   cut into short lengths
½ teaspoon fresh thyme leaves
coarse sea salt

1 Place the flour, yeast, salt and sugar in a bowl. Make a well in the center and pour in 8 fluid ounces lukewarm water and 1 tablespoon oil. Mix to a dough and knead until smooth and elastic.

2 Place the dough in a large oiled bowl, cover with plastic wrap and leave in a warm place until doubled in size. Turn out the dough onto a floured surface and knead for 4 minutes.

3 After punching the dough down, knead it on a lightly floured surface for 3–4 minutes. Brush a shallow baking pan with 1 tablespoon of the oil. Place the dough in the pan, and use your fingers to press it into an even layer 1-inch thick. Cover the dough with a cloth, and leave to rise in a warm place for 30 minutes. Preheat the oven to 400°F.

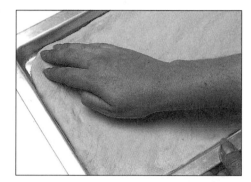

4 While the focaccia is rising, heat 3 tablespoons of the oil in a medium frying pan. Add the onion and cook over low heat until soft. Stir in the thyme leaves.

5 Just before baking, use your fingers to press rows of light indentations into the surface of the focaccia. Brush with the remaining oil.

6 Spread the onions evenly over the top, and sprinkle lightly with coarse sea salt. Bake for 25 minutes or until just golden. Cut into large squares or wedges and serve as an accompaniment to a meal or alone, warm or at room temperature.

Chocolate Bread

In Italy it is the custom to serve this dessert bread with mascarpone or Gorgonzola cheese and a glass of red wine.

INGREDIENTS

Makes 2 loaves
4 cups flour
½ teaspoon salt
2 tablespoons butter
2 tablespoons superfine sugar
2 teaspoons active dry yeast
2 tablespoons cocoa powder
½ cup chocolate chips
melted butter, for brushing

5 Preheat the oven to 425°F. Bake the loaves for 10 minutes. Reduce the oven temperature to 375°F and bake for 15–20 more minutes.

4 Cut the dough in half and knead half the chocolate chips into each piece of dough until they are evenly distributed. Shape into rounds, place on lightly oiled baking sheets and cover with oiled plastic wrap. Let rise in a warm place for 1–2 hours, until the dough has doubled in bulk.

6 Place the loaves on a wire rack and brush liberally with butter. Cover with a dish towel and let cool.

1 Sift the flour and salt into a mixing bowl, cut in the butter with a knife, then stir in the sugar, yeast and cocoa powder.

2 Gradually add 1¼ cups of tepid water to the flour mixture in the bowl, and gather the dough together with your hands.

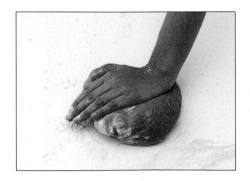

3 Turn the dough out onto a lightly floured surface and knead for about 10 minutes, until it is smooth and elastic.

Spicy Fruit Cake from Siena

This flat cake has a wonderful spicy flavor. *Panforte* is very rich, so should be cut into small wedges. Offer a glass of sparkling wine to go with it.

INGREDIENTS

Serves 12–14
butter, for greasing
1 cup hazelnuts, roughly chopped
½ cup whole almonds,
   roughly chopped
1⅓ cups mixed candied fruits, diced
¼ teaspoon ground coriander
¾ teaspoon ground cinnamon
¼ teaspoon ground cloves
¼ teaspoon grated nutmeg
½ cup flour
½ cup honey
generous 1 cup sugar
confectioners' sugar, for dusting

2 In a heavy saucepan, mix the honey with the sugar and bring to a boil. Cook until it reaches 280°F on a sugar thermometer or when a small bit forms a hard ball when pressed between fingertips in ice water. (Take care as the mixture will be very hot.)

— COOK'S TIP —

The cake can be stored in an airtight container for up to 2 weeks.

3 Immediately pour the sugar syrup into the dry ingredients and stir in well until coated. Pour into the prepared cake pan. Use the back of the spoon to press the mixture into the pan. Bake for 1 hour.

4 When ready the cake will still feel quite soft, but it will harden as it cools. Cool completely in the pan and then turn out onto a serving plate. Dust the cake lightly with confectioners' sugar before serving.

1 Preheat the oven to 350°F. Grease an 8-inch round cake pan with the butter. Line the base of the pan with parchment paper. Spread the nuts on a baking tray and place in the oven for about 10 minutes, until lightly toasted. Remove and set aside. Lower the oven temperature to 300°F. In a large mixing bowl, combine the candied fruits, all the spices and the flour and stir together with a wooden spoon. Add the nuts to the bowl and stir well, so they are evenly distributed.

Zabaglione

This sumptuous warm dessert is quick and easy to make, but it needs to be served right away. For a dinner party, assemble the ingredients ahead of time so that all you need to do is quickly combine everything once the main course is over.

INGREDIENTS

Serves 6
4 egg yolks
½ cup superfine sugar
½ cup dry Marsala
savoiardi (Italian ladyfingers),
   to serve

1 Half fill a saucepan with water and bring it to the simmering point. Put the egg yolks and sugar in a large heatproof bowl and beat with a hand-held electric mixer until the mixture is pale and creamy.

2 Put the bowl over the pan and gradually pour in the Marsala, whisking the mixture until it is very thick and has increased in volume.

3 Remove the bowl from the water and pour the zabaglione into six heatproof, long-stemmed glasses. Serve at once, with ladyfingers.

Lovers' Knots

The literal translation of these *cenci* is "rags and tatters", but they are often referred to by the more endearing term of lovers' knots. They are eaten at carnival time in February.

INGREDIENTS

1¼ cups flour
½ teaspoon baking powder
pinch of salt
2 tablespoons superfine sugar, plus
   extra for dusting
1 egg, beaten
about 1½ tablespoons rum
vegetable oil, for deep frying

COOK'S TIP

If you do not have a deep-fat fryer with a built-in thermostat, or a deep-fat thermometer, test the temperature of the oil by dropping in a scrap of the dough trimmings – it should turn crisp and golden in about 30 seconds.

1 Sift the flour, baking powder and salt into a large mixing bowl, then stir in the sugar. Add the egg. Stir with a fork until it is evenly mixed with the flour, then add the rum gradually and continue mixing until the dough draws together. Knead the dough on a lightly floured surface until it is smooth and elastic. Divide the dough into quarters.

2 Roll each piece of dough out to a 6 x 3-inch rectangle and trim the rectangles to make them straight. Cut the rectangles lengthwise into six strips, ½-inch wide, and tie into a simple knot.

3 Heat the oil in a deep-fat fryer to a temperature of 375°F. Deep fry the knots in batches for 1–2 minutes until they are crisp and golden. Transfer to paper towels with a slotted spoon. Serve warm, dusted with sugar.

Tiramisu

The name of this popular dessert translates as "pick me up" and is said to derive from the fact that it tastes so good that it makes you swoon when you eat it.

INGREDIENTS

Serves 6–8

3 eggs, separated
2 cups mascarpone cheese, at
    room temperature
1 tablespoon vanilla sugar
¾ cup cold, strong, black coffee
½ cup Kahlúa or other
    coffee-flavored liqueur
18 savoiardi (Italian ladyfingers)
sifted cocoa powder and grated
    bittersweet chocolate, to finish

1 Whisk the egg whites in a grease-free bowl until stiff and in peaks.

2 Mix the mascarpone, vanilla sugar and egg yolks in a separate large bowl and whisk with the electric mixer until evenly combined. Fold in the egg whites, then put a few spoonfuls of the mixture in the bottom of a large serving bowl and spread it out evenly.

3 Mix the coffee and liqueur in a shallow dish. Dip a ladyfinger in the mixture, turn it quickly so that it becomes saturated, and place it on top of the mascarpone in the bowl. Add five more dipped ladyfingers, placing them side by side.

4 Spoon in about one-third of the remaining mixture and spread it out. Make more layers in the same way, ending with mascarpone. Sift with cocoa powder. Cover and chill overnight. Before serving, sprinkle with cocoa and grated chocolate.

Stuffed Peaches with Amaretto

INGREDIENTS

Serves 4

4 ripe but firm peaches
2 ounces amaretti cookies
2 tablespoons butter, softened
2 tablespoons confectioners' sugar
1 egg yolk
¼ cup amaretto liqueur
1 cup dry white wine
8 tiny basil sprigs, to decorate
vanilla ice cream, to serve

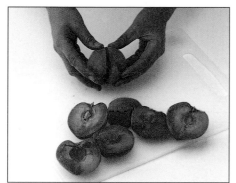

3 Cream the butter and sugar in a separate bowl until smooth. Stir in the reserved chopped peach flesh, the egg yolk and half the amaretto liqueur with the amaretti crumbs. Lightly butter a baking dish that is just large enough to hold the peach halves in a single layer.

4 Spoon the stuffing into the peaches, then stand them in the dish. Mix the remaining liqueur with the wine, pour over the peaches and bake for 25 minutes or until the peaches feel tender when tested with a skewer. Decorate with fresh basil and serve with vanilla ice cream.

1 Preheat the oven to 350°F. Following the indentation line on each peach, cut in half down to the pit, then twist the halves in opposite directions to separate them. Remove the pits, then cut out a little of the central flesh to make a larger hole for the stuffing. Chop this flesh finely and set aside.

2 Put the amaretti cookies in a bowl and crush them finely with the end of a rolling pin.

SPAIN

Marinated Olives

For the best flavor, marinate the olives for at least 10 days and serve at room temperature.

INGREDIENTS

Serves 4

1⅓ cups unpitted, green olives
3 garlic cloves
1 teaspoon coriander seeds
2 small red chilies
2–3 thick slices of lemon, cut into pieces
1 thyme or rosemary sprig
5 tablespoons white wine vinegar

COOK'S TIP

For a change, use a mix of caraway and cumin seeds in place of the coriander.

1 Spread out the olives and garlic on a chopping board. Using a rolling pin, crack and flatten them slightly.

2 Crack the coriander seeds in a mortar with a pestle.

3 Mix the olives, garlic, coriander seeds, chilies, lemon pieces, herb sprig and wine vinegar in a large bowl. Toss well, then transfer the mixture to a clean glass jar. Pour in water to cover. Store in the fridge for at least 5 days before serving.

Salted Almonds

These crunchy salted nuts are at their best when fresh, so, if you can, cook them on the day you plan to eat them.

INGREDIENTS

Serves 2–4

1 cup whole almonds in their skins
1 tablespoon egg white, lightly beaten
½ teaspoon coarse sea salt

COOK'S TIP

This traditional method of salt-roasting nuts gives a matte, dry-looking finish; if you want them to shine, turn the roasted nuts into a bowl, add 1 tablespoon of olive oil and shake well to mix.

1 Preheat the oven to 350°F. Spread out the almonds on a baking sheet and roast for about 20 minutes, until cracked and golden.

2 Mix the egg white and salt in a bowl, add the almonds and shake well to coat.

3 Turn out onto the baking sheet, give a shake to separate the nuts, then return them to the oven for 5 minutes, until they have dried. Let rest until cold, then store in an airtight container until ready to serve.

Butterflied Shrimp in Chocolate Sauce

Although the combination of flavors may seem odd, this is a truly delicious tapas. The use of bitter chocolate as a flavoring in savory dishes is popular.

INGREDIENTS

Serves 4

8 large raw shrimp, in the shell
1 tablespoon seasoned flour
1 tablespoon dry sherry
juice of 4 clementines or 1 large orange
½ ounce unsweetened, dark chocolate, chopped
2 tablespoons olive oil
2 garlic cloves, finely chopped
1-inch piece fresh ginger, finely chopped
1 small red chili, seeded and chopped
salt and freshly ground black pepper

1 Peel the shrimp, leaving just the tail sections intact. Make a shallow cut down the back of each shrimp and carefully pull out and discard the dark intestinal tract. Turn over the shrimp so that the undersides are uppermost, then carefully split them open from tail to top, using a small, sharp knife, cutting almost, but not quite, to the back.

2 Press the shrimp down firmly to flatten them out. Coat with the seasoned flour and set aside.

3 Gently heat the sherry and clementine or orange juice in a small saucepan. When warm, remove from the heat and stir in the chopped chocolate until melted.

4 Heat the olive oil in a frying pan. Fry the garlic, ginger and chili over medium heat for 2 minutes until golden. Remove with a slotted spoon and reserve. Add the shrimp, cut side down, to the pan and cook for 2–3 minutes until golden brown with pink edges. Turn and cook for 2 minutes more.

5 Return the garlic mixture to the pan and pour over the chocolate sauce. Cook for 1 minute, turning the shrimp to coat them in the glossy sauce. Season to taste and serve hot.

Charred Artichokes with Lemon Oil Dip

INGREDIENTS

Serves 4

1 tablespoon lemon juice or
   wine vinegar
2 artichokes, trimmed
12 garlic cloves, unpeeled
3 tablespoons olive oil
1 lemon
3 tablespoons olive oil
sea salt
sprigs of Italian parsley,
   to garnish

1 Preheat the oven to 400°F. Add the lemon juice or vinegar to a bowl of cold water. Cut each artichoke lengthwise into wedges. Pull the hairy choke out from the center of each wedge, then drop them into the acidulated water.

2 Drain the artichoke wedges and place in a roasting pan with the garlic. Add the oil and toss well to coat. Sprinkle with salt and roast for 40 minutes, stirring once or twice, until they are tender and a little charred.

3 Meanwhile, make the dip. Using a small, sharp knife thinly pare away two strips of rind from the lemon. Lay the strips of rind on a board and carefully scrape away any remaining pith. Place the rind in a small pan with water to cover. Bring to a boil, then simmer for 5 minutes. Drain the rind, refresh it in cold water, then chop it coarsely. Set it aside.

4 Arrange the cooked artichokes on a serving plate and set aside to cool for 5 minutes. Using the back of a fork, gently flatten the garlic cloves so that the flesh squeezes out of the skins. Transfer the garlic flesh to a bowl, mash to a paste, then add the lemon rind. Squeeze the juice from the lemon, then, using the fork, whisk the remaining olive oil and the lemon juice into the garlic mixture. Serve the artichokes warm with the lemon dip.

      COOK'S TIP

Artichokes are usually boiled, but dry-heat cooking also works very well. If you can get young artichokes, try roasting them over a barbecue.

Marinated Anchovies

Make these at least 1 hour and up to 24 hours in advance. Fresh anchovies are tiny, so be prepared to spend time filleting them – the results will be worth the effort.

INGREDIENTS

Serves 4
8 ounces fresh anchovies
juice of 3 lemons
2 tablespoons extra virgin olive oil
2 garlic cloves, finely chopped
1 tablespoon chopped fresh parsley
flaked sea salt

1 Cut off the ends from the anchovies, then split them open down one side.

2 Open each anchovy out flat and carefully lift out the bone.

3 Arrange the anchovies skin-side down in a single layer on a plate. Pour over two-thirds of the lemon juice and sprinkle with the salt. Cover and let stand for 1–24 hours, basting occasionally with the juices, until the flesh is white and no longer translucent.

4 Transfer the fish to a serving plate and drizzle over the olive oil and the remaining lemon juice. Sprinkle the garlic and parsley over the top, cover and chill until ready to serve.

Russian Salad

This colorful salad always makes a popular accompaniment.

INGREDIENTS

Serves 4

8 new potatoes, scrubbed
   and quartered
1 large carrot, diced
4 ounces fine green beans, cut into
   ³/₄-inch lengths
³/₄ cup peas
½ Spanish onion, chopped
4 cornichons or small gherkins, sliced
1 small red bell pepper, seeded and
   diced
⅓ cup pitted, black olives
1 tablespoon capers
4–6 tablespoons aïoli or mayonnaise
1 tablespoon freshly squeezed
   lemon juice
2 tablespoons chopped fresh dill
freshly ground black pepper
fresh dill, to garnish

COOK'S TIP

For a sweeter flavor, roast and skin the bell
pepper before adding it to the salad.

1 Cook the potatoes and diced carrot in a saucepan of boiling, lightly salted water for 5–8 minutes until almost tender. Add the beans and peas to the pan and cook for 2 minutes more, or until all the vegetables are tender. Drain well.

2 Turn the cooked vegetables into a large bowl. Add the onion, cornichons, red bell pepper, olives and capers. Stir the aïoli or mayonnaise and lemon juice together.

3 Add most of the dressing and the dill to the vegetables with plenty of freshly ground black pepper. Toss well to coat the vegetables lightly. Chill until ready to serve, then drizzle with the remaining dressing and garnish with the dill.

Spicy Meatballs

These meatballs are delicious served piping hot with chili sauce on the side, so guests can add as much heat as they like.

INGREDIENTS

Serves 6
4 ounces fresh, spicy sausages
4 ounces ground beef
2 shallots, finely chopped
2 garlic cloves, finely chopped
1½ cups fresh, white bread crumbs
1 egg, beaten
2 tablespoons chopped fresh parsley,
  plus extra to garnish
1 tablespoon olive oil
salt and freshly ground black pepper
Tabasco sauce or other hot chili sauce,
  to serve

1 Remove the skins from the sausages and place the sausage meat in a small mixing bowl.

--- COOK'S TIP ---

If you like, you can make the meatballs up to a day in advance, then cover and chill them until ready to cook.

2 Add the ground beef, shallots, garlic, bread crumbs, beaten egg and parsley, with plenty of salt and pepper. Mix well, then shape into 18 small balls.

3 Heat the olive oil in a frying pan and cook the meatballs, in batches if necessary, for 15–20 minutes, stirring regularly until evenly browned and cooked through.

4 Transfer the meatballs to a warm plate and sprinkle with chopped parsley. Serve with chili sauce. Offer toothpicks for spearing.

Sweet Crust Lamb

These little noisettes are just big enough for two mouthfuls, so are ideal for tapas. If you would prefer something a little more substantial, small lamb cutlets or chops can be prepared in the same way.

INGREDIENTS

Serves 8

6 ounces tender lamb fillet, sliced into ½-inch rounds
1 teaspoon English mustard
2 tablespoons light brown sugar
salt and freshly ground black pepper
toothpicks, to serve

1 Preheat the broiler to high. Sprinkle the lamb generously with salt and pepper and broil on one side for 2 minutes until well browned.

2 Remove the broiler tray from the broiler. Turn the lamb rounds over and spread with the mustard.

3 Sprinkle the sugar evenly over the lamb rounds, then return the broiler tray to the broiler.

COOK'S TIP

Watch the lamb carefully while it is broiling, as the sugar may burn if cooked for more than a few minutes.

4 Cook the lamb for 2–3 minutes more, until the sugar has melted, but the lamb is still pink in the center. Serve with toothpicks for spearing.

Skewered Lamb with Red Onion Salsa

This summery dish is ideal for chargrilling, although, if the weather fails, the skewers can be cooked under a conventional broiler. The simple salsa makes a refreshing accompaniment – make sure that you use a mild-flavored red onion that is fresh and crisp, and a tomato which is ripe and full of flavor.

INGREDIENTS

Serves 4
8 ounces lean lamb, cubed
½ teaspoon ground cumin
1 teaspoon paprika
1 tablespoon olive oil
salt and freshly ground black pepper

For the salsa
1 red onion, very thinly sliced
1 large tomato, seeded and chopped
1 tablespoon red wine vinegar
3–4 fresh basil or mint leaves,
  coarsely torn
small mint leaves, to garnish

1 Place the lamb in a bowl with the cumin, paprika, olive oil and plenty of salt and pepper. Toss well until the lamb is coated with spices.

2 Cover the bowl with plastic wrap and let rest in a cool place for a few hours, or in the fridge overnight, so that the lamb absorbs the flavors.

3 Spear the lamb cubes on four small skewers – if using wooden skewers, soak first in cold water for 30 minutes to prevent them from burning.

4 To make the salsa, put the sliced onion, tomato, vinegar and basil or mint leaves in a small bowl and stir together until thoroughly blended. Season to taste with salt, garnish with mint, then set aside while you cook the skewered lamb.

5 Cook the skewered lamb over hot coals or under a preheated broiler for about 5–10 minutes, turning the skewers frequently, until the lamb is well browned but still slightly pink in the center. Serve hot, with the salsa.

COOK'S TIP

For an alternative to the red onion salsa, stir chopped fresh mint or basil and a little lemon juice into a small pot of plain, strained yogurt. Drizzle the mixture over the cooked kebabs before serving.

Sausage Stew

This robust meat dish is good
served with a glass of cold beer.

INGREDIENTS

Serves 4
1 tablespoon olive oil
1 onion, chopped
2 garlic cloves, finely chopped
1 carrot, chopped
4 fresh, spicy sausages
²/₃ cup tomato juice
1 tablespoon brandy
¼ teaspoon Tabasco sauce
1 teaspoon sugar
salt and freshly ground black pepper
2 tablespoons chopped fresh cilantro,
   to garnish

1 Heat the oil in a large saucepan.
Cook the onion, garlic, carrot
and sausages for 10 minutes, stirring
occasionally until evenly browned.

2 Stir in the tomato juice, brandy,
Tabasco and sugar, with salt and
pepper to taste. Cover and simmer for
25 minutes until the sausages are
cooked through and the sauce has
thickened. Serve immediately,
garnished with chopped cilantro.

Stewed Beans and Pork

Fabada is a classic Spanish stew
that takes its name from a type of
white bean. It always contains
black pudding (*morcilla*) and
chorizo sausage and usually takes
a good 2 hours to prepare. Here
is a simple, speedy version that
serves well as a supper dish.

INGREDIENTS

Serves 4
1 tablespoon olive oil
6 ounces belly pork, rind removed
   and diced
4 ounces cured chorizo sausage, diced
1 onion, chopped
2 garlic cloves, finely chopped
1 large tomato, coarsely chopped
¼ teaspoon dried chili flakes
14-ounce can cannellini beans, drained
²/₃ cup chicken stock
salt and freshly ground black pepper
Italian parsley, to garnish

1 Heat the oil in a large frying pan
and fry the pork, chorizo, onion
and garlic for 5–10 minutes until the
onion has softened and browned. Add
the tomato and chili flakes and cook
for 1 minute more.

2 Stir in the beans and stock. Bring
to a boil, lower the heat, cover and
simmer for 15–20 minutes until the
pork is cooked through. Add salt and
pepper to taste and serve, garnished
with parsley.

COOK'S TIP

If preferred, smoked ham can be used in
place of belly pork in this recipe. Although
it isn't quite as authentic, the meat is a lot
less fatty and it adds a good, smoky flavor
to the stew.

Cheese and Ham Potato Patties

These soft patties can be served hot or cold – for a real treat, top each with a fried quail egg.

INGREDIENTS

Serves 4

1¼ pounds potatoes, peeled
  and cubed
2 tablespoons butter
¼ cup grated cheese, such as Manchego
  or aged Cheddar
4 slices of serrano ham, chopped
½ cup all-purpose flour
oil for greasing
salt and freshly ground black pepper

1 Cook the potatoes in a saucepan of boiling, lightly salted water for 10–15 minutes until tender. Drain well and mash with the butter and cheese until smooth.

2 Stir in the ham and flour with plenty of salt and pepper. Shape the mixture into eight rounds, each about ½ inch thick.

3 Lightly oil a griddle or heavy-bottomed frying pan and cook the patties for 4–5 minutes on each side until golden brown. Drain on paper towels and serve immediately.

---COOK'S TIP---

The patties have a very fluffy, soft center, so take care when turning them over. If preferred, brush them with oil and cook them under a moderately hot broiler, turning them halfway through cooking.

Chicken Croquettes

This recipe uses chicken but you could substitute other meat fillings if you like.

INGREDIENTS

Serves 4

2 tablespoons butter
¼ cup all-purpose flour
⅔ cup milk
1 tablespoon olive oil
1 boneless chicken breast with skin, about 3 ounces, diced
1 garlic clove, finely chopped
1 small egg, beaten
1 cup fresh, white bread crumbs
vegetable oil, for deep-frying
salt and freshly ground black pepper
Italian parsley, to garnish
lemon wedges, to serve

1 Melt the butter in a small saucepan. Add the flour and cook gently, stirring, for 1 minute. Gradually beat in the milk to make a smooth, very thick sauce. Cover with a lid and remove from the heat.

2 Heat the oil in a frying pan and cook the chicken with the garlic for 5 minutes, until the chicken is lightly browned and cooked through.

3 Turn the contents of the frying pan into a food processor or blender and process until finely chopped. Stir into the sauce. Add plenty of salt and pepper to taste. Let cool completely.

4 Shape into eight small sausages, then dip each in egg and then bread crumbs. Deep-fry in hot oil for 4 minutes until crisp and golden. Drain on paper towels and serve with lemon wedges, garnished with parsley.

Spicy Chicken Wings

These deliciously sticky bites will appeal to adults and children alike, although younger eaters might prefer a little less chili.

INGREDIENTS

Serves 4
8 plump chicken wings
2 large garlic cloves, cut into slivers
1 tablespoon olive oil
1 tablespoon paprika
1 teaspoon chili powder
1 teaspoon dried oregano
1 teaspoon salt
1 teaspoon ground black pepper
lime wedges, to serve

— COOK'S TIP —

Chunks of chicken breast and small thighs may also be cooked in this way.

1 Using a small, sharp knife, make one or two cuts in the skin of each chicken wing and carefully slide a sliver of garlic under the skin. Brush the wings with the olive oil.

2 In a large bowl, stir together the paprika, chili powder, oregano, salt and pepper. Add the chicken wings and toss together until very lightly coated in the mixture.

3 Broil or barbecue the chicken wings for 15 minutes until they are cooked through with a blackened, crispy skin. Serve with lime wedges to squeeze over.

Chicken with Lemon and Garlic

Extremely easy to cook and delicious to eat, serve this succulent dish with fried potatoes and aïoli.

INGREDIENTS

Serves 4
8 ounces skinless chicken breast fillets
2 tablespoons olive oil
1 shallot, finely chopped
4 garlic cloves, finely chopped
1 teaspoon paprika
juice of 1 lemon
2 tablespoons chopped fresh parsley
salt and freshly ground black pepper
Italian parsley, to garnish
lemon wedges, to serve

1 Sandwich the chicken breast fillets between two sheets of plastic wrap or wax paper. Beat out evenly with a rolling pin until the fillets are about ¼ inch thick.

— COOK'S TIP —

For a variation on this dish, try using strips of turkey breast or pork.

---

2 Cut the chicken into strips about ½ inch wide. Heat the oil in a large frying pan. Stir-fry the chicken strips with the shallot, garlic and paprika over high heat for about 3 minutes until lightly browned and cooked through. Add the lemon juice and parsley with salt and pepper to taste. Serve hot with lemon wedges, garnished with parsley.

Broiled Asparagus with Salt-cured Ham

Serve this wonderful vegetable dish when asparagus is plentiful and not too expensive.

INGREDIENTS

Serves 4
6 slices of serrano ham
12 asparagus spears
1 tablespoon olive oil
sea salt and coarsely ground black
pepper

COOK'S TIP

If you can't find serrano ham, use Italian prosciutto or Portuguese *presunto*.

1 Preheat the broiler to high. Halve each slice of ham lengthwise and wrap one half around each of the asparagus spears.

2 Brush the ham and asparagus lightly with oil and sprinkle with salt and pepper. Place on the broiler tray. Broil for 5–6 minutes, turning frequently, until the asparagus is tender but still firm. Serve immediately.

Braised Buttery Cabbage with Chorizo

This dish is equally delicious without the chorizo sausage, so just omit it when serving this to vegetarian guests.

INGREDIENTS

Serves 4
¼ cup butter
1 teaspoon caraway seeds
8 ounces green cabbage, shredded
2 garlic cloves, finely chopped
2 ounces cured chorizo sausage,
coarsely chopped
4 tablespoons dry sherry or white wine
salt and freshly ground black pepper

COOK'S TIP

Smoked bacon makes a good substitute for chorizo sausage in this recipe. Add it to the pan after the caraway seeds and cook for a few minutes before adding the cabbage.

1 Melt the butter in a frying pan, add the caraway seeds and cook for 1 minute. Add the cabbage to the pan with the garlic and chorizo. Stir-fry for 5 minutes until the cabbage is tender.

2 Add the sherry or wine and plenty of salt and pepper. Cover the pan and cook for 15–20 minutes until the cabbage is tender. Check the seasoning and serve.

FRANCE

French Onion Soup

In France this standard bistro fare is served so frequently that it is referred to simply as *gratinée*.

INGREDIENTS

Serves 6–8
1 tablespoon butter
2 tablespoons olive oil
4 large onions (about 1½ pounds), thinly sliced
2–4 garlic cloves, finely chopped
1 teaspoon sugar
½ teaspoon dried thyme
2 tablespoons flour
½ cup dry white wine
8 cups chicken or beef broth
2 tablespoons brandy (optional)
6–8 thick slices French bread, toasted
1 garlic clove
12 ounces Swiss cheese, grated

1 In a large heavy saucepan or flameproof casserole, heat the butter and oil over medium-high heat. Add the onions and cook for 10–12 minutes until they are softened and beginning to brown. Add the garlic, sugar and thyme and continue cooking over medium heat for 30–35 minutes, until the onions are well browned, stirring frequently.

2 Sprinkle over the flour and stir until well blended. Stir in the white wine and broth and bring to a boil. Skim off any foam that rises to the surface, then reduce the heat and simmer gently for 45 minutes. Stir in the brandy, if using.

3 Preheat the broiler. Rub each slice of toasted French bread with the garlic clove. Place six or eight ovenproof soup bowls on a baking sheet and fill about three-quarters full with the onion soup.

4 Float a piece of toast in each bowl. Top with grated cheese, dividing it evenly, and broil about 6 inches from the heat for about 3–4 minutes until the cheese begins to melt and bubble.

Shrimp Bisque

This di
on bist
Hemin
It make
or can
elegant

INGREI

Serves 2-
1 cup dr
½ cup w
2 shallot
1 bay le
1 pound
3 tablesp
3 tablesp
6 tablesp
freshly g
6 ounce
3–4 tabl
salt and

INGREDIENTS

Serves 6–8
1½ pounds small or medium cooked
   shrimp in the shell
1½ tablespoons vegetable oil
2 onions, halved and sliced
1 large carrot, sliced
2 celery sticks, sliced
8 cups water
a few drops of lemon juice
2 tablespoons tomato paste
bouquet garni
4 tablespoons butter
⅓ cup flour
3–4 tablespoons brandy
⅔ cup whipping cream

1 Remove the heads from the
shrimp and peel away the shells,
reserving the heads and shells for the
stock. Chill the peeled shrimp.

2 Heat the oil in a large saucepan,
add the shrimp heads and shells
and cook over high heat, stirring
frequently, until they start to brown.
Reduce the heat to medium, add the
onions, carrot and celery and fry
gently, stirring occasionally, for about
5 minutes until the onions turn
golden and start to soften.

3 Add the water, lemon juice,
tomato paste and bouquet garni.
Bring the broth to a boil, then reduce
the heat, cover and simmer gently
for 25 minutes. Strain broth stock
through a sieve. Melt the butter in a
heavy saucepan over medium heat.
Stir in the flour and cook until just
golden, stirring occasionally.

4 Add the brandy and half of the
shrimp broth, whisking until
smooth, then whisk in the remaining
liquid. Season as necessary.

5 Reduce the heat, cover and
simmer for 5 minutes, stirring
frequently. Strain the soup into a
clean saucepan. Add the cream and a
little extra lemon juice to taste, then
stir in most of the reserved shrimp
and cook over medium heat, stirring
frequently, until hot. Serve at once,
garnished with the reserved shrimp.

Goat Cheese Soufflé

Make sure everyone is seated before the soufflé comes out of the oven because it will begin to deflate almost immediately. This recipe works equally well with strong blue cheeses such as Roquefort.

INGREDIENTS

Serves 4-6
2 tablespoons butter
3 tablespoons flour
¾ cup milk
1 bay leaf
ground nutmeg
grated Parmesan cheese, for
  sprinkling
1½ ounces herb and garlic soft cheese
5 ounces firm goat cheese, diced
6 egg whites, at room temperature
¼ teaspoon cream of tartar
salt and freshly ground black pepper

1 Melt the butter in a saucepan over medium heat. Add the flour and cook until golden, stirring occasionally. Pour in half the milk, stirring vigorously until smooth, then stir in the remaining milk and add the bay leaf. Season with a pinch of salt and plenty of pepper and nutmeg. Reduce the heat to medium-low, cover and simmer gently for about 5 minutes, stirring occasionally. Preheat the oven to 375°F. Butter a 5-cup soufflé dish and sprinkle with the grated Parmesan cheese.

2 Remove the sauce from the heat and discard the bay leaf. Add both cheeses and stir until smooth.

3 In a clean greasefree bowl, using an electric mixer or balloon whisk, beat the egg whites slowly until they become frothy. Add the cream of tartar, increase the speed and continue beating until they form soft peaks. Continue to beat the mixture until the peaks begin to flop over a little at the top.

4 Stir a spoonful of the mixture into the cheese sauce to lighten it, then pour the cheese sauce over the remaining whites. Using a rubber spatula or large metal spoon, gently fold the sauce into the whites until well combined: try to work in one flowing movement, cutting down through the center to the bottom, then along the side of the bowl and up to the top.

5 Gently pour the soufflé mixture into the prepared dish and bake in the preheated oven for 25–30 minutes until puffed and golden brown. Serve the soufflé at once.

Provençal Swiss Chard Omelet

This traditional flat omelet can also be made with fresh spinach, but Swiss chard leaves are typical in Provence. It is delicious served with small black Niçoise olives.

INGREDIENTS

Serves 6
1½ pounds Swiss chard leaves, trimmed
4 tablespoons olive oil
1 large onion, sliced
5 eggs
salt and freshly ground black pepper

1 Wash the chard well and pat dry. Stack four or five leaves at a time and slice across into thin ribbons. Steam the chard until wilted, then drain in a strainer and press out any liquid with the back of a spoon.

2 Heat 2 tablespoons of the olive oil in a large frying pan. Add the onion and cook over medium-low heat for about 10 minutes until soft, stirring occasionally. Add the chard and cook for 2–4 minutes more until the leaves are tender.

3 In a large bowl, beat the eggs and season with salt and pepper, then stir in the cooked vegetables.

4 Heat the remaining 2 tablespoons of oil in a large non-stick frying pan over medium-high heat. Pour in the egg mixture and reduce the heat to medium-low. Cook the omelet, covered, for 5–7 minutes until the egg mixture is set around the edges and almost set on top

5 To turn the omelet over, loosen the edges and slide it onto a large plate. Place the frying pan over the omelette and, holding them tightly, carefully invert the pan and plate together. Lift off the plate and continue cooking for 2–3 minutes more. Slide the omelet onto a serving plate and serve hot or at room temperature, in wedges.

Pepper Steak

There are many versions of this French bistro classic. Some omit the cream, but it helps to balance the heat of the pepper. Use fairly thick steaks, such as fillet or lean sirloin.

INGREDIENTS

Serves 2
2 tablespoons black peppercorns
2 fillet or sirloin steaks, about
    8 ounces each
1 tablespoon butter
2 teaspoons vegetable oil
3 tablespoons brandy
⅔ cup heavy cream
1 garlic clove, finely chopped
salt, if needed

1 Place the peppercorns in a sturdy plastic bag. Crush with a rolling pin until medium-coarse or, using the flat base of a small heavy saucepan, press down on the peppercorns, rocking the pan to crush them.

2 Put the steaks on a board and trim away any extra fat. Press the pepper onto both sides of the meat, coating it completely.

3 Melt the butter with the oil in a heavy frying pan over medium-high heat. Add the meat and cook for 6–7 minutes, turning once, until done as preferred. (Medium-rare meat will still be slightly soft when pressed, medium will be springy and well-done firm.) Transfer the steaks to a warmed platter or plates and cover to keep warm.

4 Pour in the brandy to deglaze the pan. Allow to boil until reduced by half, scraping the base of the pan, then add the cream and garlic. Boil gently over medium heat for about 4 minutes until the cream has reduced by one-third. Stir any accumulated juices from the meat into the sauce, taste and add salt, if necessary. Pour the sauce over the steaks to serve.

Châteaubriand with Béarnaise

Châteaubriand is a lean and tender cut that is pounded to give it its characteristic shape. It is usually served for two, but could easily stretch to three.

INGREDIENTS

Serves 2
⅔ cup butter, cut into pieces
1½ tablespoons tarragon vinegar
1½ tablespoons dry white wine
1 shallot, finely chopped
2 egg yolks
1 pound beef fillet, about 6-inches long, cut from the thickest part of the fillet
1 tablespoon vegetable oil
salt and freshly ground black pepper
sautéed potatoes, to serve

1 Clarify the butter by melting it gently in a saucepan over low heat; do not boil. Skim off any foam and set aside.

2 Put the vinegar, wine and shallot in a small heavy saucepan over high heat and boil to reduce until the liquid has almost all evaporated. Remove from the heat and cool slightly. Add the egg yolks and whisk for 1 minute. Place the saucepan over very low heat and whisk constantly until the yolk mixture begins to thicken and the whisk begins to leave tracks on the base of the pan, then remove the pan from the heat.

3 Whisk in the melted butter, drop by drop until the sauce begins to thicken.

4 Season with salt and pepper and keep warm, stirring occasionally. Meanwhile, place the meat between two sheets of wax paper or plastic wrap and pound with the flat side of a meat pounder or roll with a rolling pin to flatten to about 1½-inches thick. Season with salt and pepper.

5 Heat the oil in a heavy frying pan over medium-high heat. Add the meat and cook for about 10–12 minutes, turning once, until done as preferred. (Medium-rare meat will be slightly soft when pressed, medium will be springy and well-done firm.)

6 Transfer the steak to a board and carve in thin diagonal slices. Strain the sauce, if you prefer, and serve with the steak, accompanied by sautéed potatoes.

— COOK'S TIP —

Beef fillet is often cheaper when bought whole than when it has been divided into steaks. If you buy a whole fillet, you can cut a *Châteaubriand* from the thickest part, *filet mignon* steaks from less thick parts, *tournedos* from the thinner part and use the thinnest tail part for stir-frying or Stroganoff. If you wish, wrap tightly and freeze until needed.

Toulouse Cassoulet

This is a regional specialty from the southwest of France.

INGREDIENTS

Serves 6–8

1 pound dried white beans (haricot or cannellini), soaked overnight in cold water, then rinsed and drained
1½ pounds French garlic sausages
1¼ pounds each boneless lamb and pork shoulder, cut into 2-in pieces
1 large onion, finely chopped
3 or 4 garlic cloves, finely chopped
4 tomatoes, peeled, seeded and chopped
1¼ cups chicken broth
bouquet garni
4 tablespoons fresh bread crumbs
salt and freshly ground black pepper

1 Put the beans in a saucepan with water to cover. Boil for about 10 minutes and drain, then return to a clean saucepan, cover with water and bring to a boil. Reduce the heat and simmer for 45 minutes, then add salt and let soak in the cooking water.

2 Preheat the oven to 350°F. Prick the sausages, place them in a large heavy frying pan over medium heat and cook for 20–25 minutes until browned, turning occasionally. Drain on paper towels and pour off all but 1 tbsp of the fat from the pan.

3 Increase the heat to medium-high. Season the lamb and pork and add enough of the meat to the pan to fit easily in one layer. Cook until browned, then transfer to a large dish. Continue browning in batches. Add the onion and garlic to the pan and cook for 3–4 minutes until just soft, stirring. Stir in the tomatoes and cook for 2–3 minutes more.

4 Transfer the vegetables to the meat dish. Add the chicken broth and bring to a boil, then skim off the fat. Spoon a quarter of the beans into a large casserole and top with a third of the sausages, meat and vegetables. Continue layering, ending with a layer of beans. Tuck in the bouquet garni, pour over the broth and top up with enough of the bean cooking liquid to just cover.

5 Cover the casserole and bake for 2 hours. (Check and add more bean cooking liquid if it seems dry.) Uncover the casserole, sprinkle over the bread crumbs and press with the back of a spoon to moisten them. Continue cooking the cassoulet, uncovered, for about 20 minutes more until browned.

Veal Kidneys with Mustard

INGREDIENTS

Serves 4

2 veal kidneys or 8–10 lamb kidneys,
 trimmed and membranes removed
2 tablespoons butter
1 tablespoon vegetable oil
4 ounces button mushrooms,
 quartered
4 tablespoons chicken broth
2 tablespoons brandy (optional)
¾ cup crème fraîche or heavy cream
2 tablespoons Dijon mustard
salt and freshly ground black pepper
snipped fresh chives, to garnish

1 Cut the veal kidneys into pieces, discarding any fat. If using lambs' kidneys, remove the central core by cutting a V-shape from the middle of each kidney. Cut each kidney into three or four pieces.

2 In a large frying pan, melt the butter with the oil over a high heat and swirl to blend. Add the kidneys and sauté for about 3–4 minutes, stirring frequently until well browned, then transfer them to a plate using a slotted spoon.

3 Add the mushrooms to the pan and sauté for 2–3 minutes until golden, stirring frequently. Pour in the chicken broth and brandy, if using, then bring to a boil and boil for 2 minutes.

4 Stir in the crème fraîche or heavy cream and cook for 2–3 minutes until the sauce has thickened slightly. Stir in the Dijon mustard and season to taste with salt and pepper, then add the kidneys and cook for 1 minute to reheat. Scatter over the chives before serving.

Roast Leg of Lamb with Beans

INGREDIENTS

Serves 8–10

6–7 pound leg of lamb
3 or 4 garlic cloves
olive oil
fresh or dried rosemary leaves
1 pound dried navy or fava beans,
  soaked overnight in cold water
1 bay leaf
2 tablespoons red wine
⅔ cup lamb or beef broth
2 tablespoons butter
salt and freshly ground black pepper
watercress, to garnish

1 Preheat the oven to 425°F. Wipe the leg of lamb with damp paper towels and dry the fat covering well. Cut 2 or 3 of the garlic cloves into 10–12 slivers, then with the tip of a knife, cut 10–12 slits into the lamb and insert the garlic slivers into the slits. Rub with oil, season with salt and pepper and sprinkle with the rosemary leaves.

2 Set the lamb on a rack in a shallow roasting pan and put in the oven. After 15 minutes, reduce the heat to 350°F and continue to roast for 1½–1¾ hours (about 18 minutes per 1 pound) or until a meat thermometer inserted into the thickest part of the meat registers 135–140°F for medium-rare to medium meat or 150°F if you want it well-done.

3 Meanwhile, rinse the beans and put in a saucepan with enough fresh water to cover generously. Add the remaining garlic and the bay leaf, then bring to a boil. Reduce the heat and simmer for 45 minutes–1 hour, or until tender.

4 Transfer the roast to a board and stand, loosely covered, for 10–15 minutes. Skim off the fat from the cooking juices, then add the wine and broth to the roasting pan. Boil over a medium heat, stirring and scraping the base of the pan, until slightly reduced. Strain into a warmed gravy boat.

5 Drain the beans, discard the bay leaf, then toss the beans with the butter until it melts and season with salt and pepper. Garnish the lamb with watercress and serve with the beans and the sauce.

Pork with Camembert

INGREDIENTS

Serves 3–4

¾–1 pound pork tenderloin
1 tablespoon butter
3 tablespoons sparkling dry cider or
    dry white wine
½–¾ cup crème fraîche or heavy
    cream
1 tablespoon chopped fresh mixed
    herbs, such as marjoram, thyme and
    sage
½ Camembert cheese (4 ounces), rind
    removed (2½ ounces without rind),
    sliced
1½ teaspoons Dijon mustard
freshly ground black pepper
fresh parsley, to garnish

1 Slice the pork tenderloin crosswise into small steaks about ¾-inch thick. Place between two sheets of greaseproof paper or clear film and pound with the flat side of a meat mallet or roll with a rolling pin to flatten to a thickness of ½-inch. Sprinkle with the black pepper.

2 Melt the butter in a heavy frying pan over medium-high heat until it begins to brown, then add the meat. Cook for 5 minutes, turning once, or until just cooked through and the meat is springy when pressed. Transfer to a warmed dish and cover to keep warm.

3 Add the cider or wine and bring to a boil, scraping the base of the pan. Stir in the cream and herbs and bring back to a boil.

4 Add the cheese and mustard and any accumulated juices from the meat. Add a little more cream if needed and adjust the seasoning. Serve the pork with the sauce and garnish with parsley.

Mussels Steamed in White Wine

INGREDIENTS

Serves 4

4½ pounds mussels
1¼ cups dry white wine
4–6 large shallots, finely chopped
bouquet garni
freshly ground black pepper

1 To prepare the mussels, discard any broken mussels and those with open shells that refuse to close when tapped. Under cold running water, scrape the mussel shells with a knife to remove any barnacles and pull out the stringy "beards". Soak the mussels in several changes of cold water for at least 1 hour.

2 In a large heavy flameproof casserole combine the wine, shallots, bouquet garni and plenty of pepper. Bring to a boil over medium-high heat and cook for 2 minutes.

3 Add the mussels and cook, tightly covered, for 5 minutes, or until the mussels open, shaking and tossing the pan occasionally. Discard any mussels that do not open.

4 Using a slotted spoon, divide the mussels among warmed soup plates. Tilt the casserole a little and hold for a few seconds to allow any sand to settle to the bottom.

5 Spoon or pour the cooking liquid over the mussels, dividing it evenly, then serve at once.

VARIATION

For Mussels with Cream Sauce (*Moules à la Crème*), cook as above, but transfer the mussels to a warmed bowl and cover. Strain the cooking liquid through a cheesecloth-lined colander into a large saucepan and boil for about 7–10 minutes to reduce by half. Stir in 6 tablespoons heavy cream and 2 tablespoons chopped parsley, then add the mussels. Cook for 1 minute more to reheat the mussels.

Lobster Thermidor

INGREDIENTS

Serves 2–4

2 live lobsters (1½ pounds each)
1½ tablespoons butter
2 tablespoons flour
2 tablespoons brandy
½ cup milk
6 tablespoons heavy cream
1 tablespoon Dijon mustard
lemon juice
salt and white pepper
grated Parmesan cheese, for
    sprinkling
fresh parsley and dill, to garnish

3 Melt the butter in a saucepan over medium-high heat. Stir in the flour and cook gently, stirring, until slightly golden. Pour in the brandy and milk, whisking vigorously until smooth, then whisk in the cream and Dijon mustard.

4 Push the lobster coral and liver through a sieve into the sauce and whisk to blend. Reduce the heat and simmer gently for 10 minutes, stirring, until thickened. Season to taste and add the lemon juice.

5 Preheat the broiler. Arrange the lobster shells in a gratin dish or shallow flameproof baking dish.

6 Stir the lobster meat into the sauce and divide the mixture evenly among the shells. Sprinkle lightly with Parmesan and grill until golden. Serve garnished with herbs.

1 Bring a large saucepan of salted water to a boil. Put the lobsters into the pan head first and cook for 8–10 minutes.

2 Cut the lobsters in half lengthwise and discard the dark sac behind the eyes, then pull out the string-like intestine from the tail. Remove the meat from the shells, reserving the coral and liver, then rinse the shells and wipe dry. Cut the meat into bite-size pieces.

Asparagus with Orange Sauce

INGREDIENTS

Serves 6

¾ cup unsalted butter, diced

3 egg yolks

1 tablespoon cold water

1 tablespoon fresh lemon juice

grated rind and juice of 1 unwaxed orange

30–36 thick asparagus spears

salt and cayenne pepper, to taste

shreds of orange zest, to garnish

1 Melt the butter in a small saucepan over low heat; do not boil. Skim off any foam and set aside.

2 In a heatproof bowl set over a saucepan of barely simmering water or in the top of a double boiler, whisk together the egg yolks, water, lemon juice, 1 tablespoon of the orange juice and season with salt. Place the saucepan or double boiler over very low heat and whisk constantly until the mixture begins to thicken and the whisk begins to leave tracks on the base of the pan. Remove the pan from the heat.

3 Whisk in the melted butter, drop by drop until the sauce begins to thicken, then pour it in a little more quickly, leaving behind the milky solids at the base of the pan. Whisk in the orange rind and 2–4 tablespoons of the orange juice. Season with salt and cayenne pepper and keep warm, stirring occasionally.

4 Cut off the tough ends from the asparagus spears and trim to the same length. If peeling, hold each spear gently by the tip, then using a vegetable peeler, strip off the peel and scales from just below the tip to the end. Rinse in cold water.

5 Fill a large deep frying pan or wok with 2 inches of water and bring to a boil over medium–high heat. Add the asparagus and bring back to a boil, then simmer for about 5 minutes, until just tender.

6 Carefully transfer the spears to a large colander to drain, then lay them on a paper towel and pat dry. Arrange on a large serving platter or individual plates and spoon over a little sauce. Scatter the orange zest over the sauce and serve at once.

COOK'S TIP

This sauce is a kind of hollandaise and needs gentle treatment. If the egg yolk mixture thickens too quickly, remove from the heat and plunge the base of the pan into cold water to prevent the sauce from curdling. The sauce should keep over hot water for 1 hour, but don't let it get too hot.

Stuffed Artichoke Bottoms

INGREDIENTS

Serves 4–6

8 ounces button mushrooms
1 tablespoon butter
2 shallots, finely chopped
2 ounces full- or medium-fat soft
   cheese
2 tablespoons chopped walnuts
3 tablespoons grated Swiss cheese
4 large or 6 small artichoke bottoms
   (from cooked artichokes, leaves and
   choke removed, or cooked frozen
   or canned artichoke bottoms)
salt and freshly ground black pepper
fresh parsley sprigs, to garnish

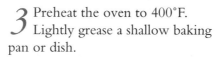

3 Preheat the oven to 400°F.
Lightly grease a shallow baking
pan or dish.

4 In a small bowl, combine the soft
cheese and mushrooms. Add the
walnuts and half the grated cheese.

5 Divide the mushroom mixture
among the artichoke bottoms
and arrange them in the baking pan
or dish. Sprinkle over the remaining
cheese and bake for 12–15 minutes,
or until bubbly and browned. Serve
hot, garnished with parsley sprigs.

1 Wipe or rinse the mushrooms
and pat dry. Put them in a food
processor fitted with a metal blade
and pulse until finely chopped.

2 Melt the butter in a non-stick
frying pan and cook the shallots
over medium heat for 2–3 minutes
until softened. Add the mushrooms,
raise the heat slightly, and cook for
5–7 minutes until they have rendered
and reabsorbed their liquid and are
almost dry, stirring frequently. Season
with salt and pepper.

Ratatouille

INGREDIENTS

Serves 6

2 medium eggplants (about 1 pound)
4–5 tablespoons olive oil
1 large onion, halved and sliced
2 or 3 garlic cloves, very finely chopped
1 large red or yellow bell pepper, seeded and cut into thin strips
2 large zucchini, sliced
1½ pounds ripe tomatoes, peeled, seeded and chopped, or 2 cups canned crushed tomatoes
1 teaspoon dried herbes de Provence
salt and freshly ground black pepper

1 Preheat the broiler. Cut the eggplants into ¾-inch slices, then brush with olive oil on both sides and broil until lightly browned, turning once. Cut the slices into cubes.

VARIATION

To remove the pepper skin and add flavor to the ratatouille, quarter the pepper and broil, skin-side up, until blackened. Enclose in a brown paper bag and set aside until cool. Peel off the skin, then remove the core and seeds and cut into strips. Add to the mixture with the cooked eggplant.

2 Heat 1 tablespoon of the olive oil in a large heavy saucepan or flameproof casserole and cook the onion over medium-low heat for about 10 minutes until lightly golden, stirring frequently. Add the garlic, pepper and zucchini and cook for 10 minutes more, stirring occasionally.

3 Add the tomatoes and eggplant cubes, dried herbs, salt and pepper and simmer gently, covered, over low heat for about 20 minutes, stirring occasionally. Uncover and continue cooking for 20–25 minutes more, stirring occasionally, until all the vegetables are tender and the cooking liquid has thickened slightly. Serve the ratatouille hot or at room temperature.

Potatoes Dauphinois

INGREDIENTS

Serves 6
2¼ pounds potatoes
3⅔ cups milk
pinch of ground nutmeg
1 bay leaf
1–2 tablespoons butter, softened
2 or 3 garlic cloves, finely chopped
3–4 tablespoons crème fraîche or
   heavy cream (optional)
salt and freshly ground black pepper

3 Generously butter a 14-inch oval gratin dish or an 8-cup shallow baking dish and sprinkle the garlic over the base.

4 Using a slotted spoon, transfer the potatoes to the gratin or baking dish. Season the milk, then pour over enough of the milk to come just to the surface of the potatoes, but not cover them. Spoon a layer of crème fraîche or heavy cream over the top, or, add more of the milk to cover.

5 Bake the potatoes for about 1 hour until the milk is absorbed and the top is a deep golden brown.

1 Preheat the oven to 350°F. Cut the potatoes into fairly thin slices.

2 Put the potatoes in a large saucepan and pour over the milk, adding more to cover if needed. Add the salt and pepper, nutmeg and the bay leaf. Bring slowly to a boil over medium heat and simmer for about 15 minutes until the potatoes just start to soften, but are not completely cooked, and the milk has thickened.

Individual Brioches

These buttery rolls with their distinctive little topknots are delicious with a spoonful or two of jam and a cup of *café au lait*.

INGREDIENTS

Serves 8
scant 1 tablespoon active dry yeast
1 tablespoon superfine sugar
2 tablespoons warm milk
2 eggs
1½ cups flour
½ teaspoon salt
6 tablespoons butter, softened
1 egg yolk beaten with water, for glazing

1 Lightly butter eight individual brioche pans or muffin cups. Put the yeast and sugar in a small bowl, add the milk and stir until dissolved. Let stand for about 5 minutes until foamy, then beat in the eggs.

2 Put the flour and salt into a food processor fitted with a metal blade, then with the machine running, slowly pour in the yeast mixture. Scrape down the sides and continue processing for 2–3 minutes, or until the dough forms a ball. Add the butter and pulse about 10 times, or until the butter is incorporated.

3 Transfer the dough to a lightly buttered bowl and cover with a cloth. Set aside to rise in a warm place for about 1 hour until doubled in size, then punch down.

4 Set aside a quarter of the dough. Shape the remaining dough into eight balls and put into the prepared pans. Shape the reserved dough into eight smaller balls, then make a depression in the top of each large ball and set a small ball into it.

5 Allow the brioches to rise in a warm place for about 30 minutes until doubled in size. Preheat the oven to 400°F.

6 Brush the brioches lightly with the egg glaze and bake them for 15–18 minutes until golden brown. Transfer to a wire rack and let cool before serving.

COOK'S TIP

The dough may also be baked in the characteristic large brioche pan with sloping fluted sides. Put about three-quarters of the dough into the pan and set the remainder in a depression in the top, cover and let rise for about 1 hour, then bake for 35–45 minutes.

Brittany Butter Cookies

These little cookies are similar to shortbread, but richer. Like most of the cakes and pastries from this province, they are made with the lightly salted butter, *beurre demi-sel*, from around Nantes.

INGREDIENTS

Serves 18–20
6 egg yolks, lightly beaten
1 tablespoon milk
2 cups flour
⅞ cup superfine sugar
⅞ cup lightly salted butter, at room temperature, cut into small pieces

1 Preheat the oven to 350°F. Lightly butter a large heavy baking sheet. Mix 1 tablespoon of the egg yolks with the milk to make a glaze and set aside.

2 Sift the flour into a large bowl and make a well in the center. Add the egg yolks, sugar and butter and, using your fingertips, work them together until smooth and creamy.

3 Gradually bring in a little flour at a time from the edge of the well, working it to form a sticky dough.

4 Pat out the dough to about ½-inch thick and cut out rounds using a cookie cutter. Transfer to a baking sheet, brush with egg glaze, then using the back of a knife, score with lines to create a lattice pattern.

5 Bake the cookies for 12 minutes, or until golden. Cool in the pan for 15 minutes, then let cool completely on a wire rack.

COOK'S TIP

To make one large Brittany Butter Cake, pat the dough with well floured hands into a 9-inch loose-based cake tin or springform pan. Brush with egg glaze and score the lattice pattern on top. Bake for 45 minutes–1 hour until firm to the touch and golden brown.

Lemon Tart

This tart has a refreshing tangy flavor. You can find it in bistros and pâtisseries all over France.

INGREDIENTS

Serves 8–10
12 ounces shortcrust or sweet
    shortcrust pastry
grated rind of 2 or 3 lemons
⅔ cup freshly squeezed lemon juice
½ cup superfine sugar
4 tablespoons crème fraîche or
    heavy cream
4 eggs, plus 3 egg yolks
confectioners' sugar, for dusting

1 Preheat the oven to 375°F. Roll out the pastry thinly and use to line a 9-inch pie pan. Prick the base of the pastry.

2 Line the pastry shell with foil and fill with baking beans. Bake for about 15 minutes until the edges are set and dry. Remove the foil and beans and continue baking for 5–7 minutes more until golden.

3 Place the lemon rind, juice and sugar in a bowl. Beat until combined and then gradually add the crème fraîche or heavy cream and beat until well blended.

4 Beat in the eggs, one at a time, then beat in the egg yolks and pour the filling into the pastry case. Bake for 15–20 minutes, until the filling is set. If the pastry begins to brown too much, cover the edges with foil. Let cool. Dust with confectioners' sugar before serving.

Apple Charlotte

This classic dessert takes its name from the straight-sided pan with heart-shaped handles in which it is baked. The buttery bread crust encases a sweet yet sharp apple purée.

INGREDIENTS

Serves 6

2½ pounds apples
2 tablespoons water
⅔ cup light brown sugar
½ teaspoon ground cinnamon
¼ teaspoon ground nutmeg
7 slices firm textured sliced white bread
5–6 tablespoons butter, melted
custard, to serve (optional)

COOK'S TIP

If preferred, microwave the apples without water in a large glass dish on High (100% power), tightly covered, for 15 minutes. Add the sugar and spices and microwave, uncovered, for about 15 minutes more until very thick, stirring once or twice.

2 Preheat the oven to 400°F. Trim the crusts from the bread and brush with melted butter on one side. Cut two slices into triangles and use as many as necessary to cover the base of a 6-cup charlotte pan or soufflé dish, placing the bread triangles buttered-sides down and fitting them tightly. Cut fingers of bread the same height as the pan or dish and use them to line the sides, overlapping them slightly.

3 Pour the apple purée into the pan or dish. Cover the top with bread slices, buttered-side up, cutting them as necessary to fit.

4 Bake the charlotte for about 20 minutes, then reduce the oven temperature to 350°F and bake for 25 minutes until well browned and firm. Let stand for 15 minutes. To turn out, place a serving plate over the pan or dish, hold tightly, and invert, then lift off the pan or dish. Serve with custard, if desired.

1 Peel, quarter and core the apples. Cut into thick slices and put in a large saucepan with the water. Cook, covered, over medium heat for 5 minutes, then uncover and cook for 10 minutes until the apples are soft. Add the sugar, cinnamon and nutmeg and continue cooking for 5 minutes, stirring frequently, until the apples are soft and thick.

Cream Puffs

INGREDIENTS

Serves 4–6
10 ounces plain chocolate
8 tablespoons warm water
3 cups vanilla ice cream

For the cream puffs
¾ cup plain flour
¼ teaspoon salt
pinch of ground nutmeg
¾ cup water
6 tablespoons unsalted butter, cut
   into 6 pieces
3 eggs

1 Preheat the oven to 400°F and lightly butter a baking sheet.

2 To make the cream puffs, sift the flour, salt and nutmeg together in a large mixing bowl. Bring the water and butter to a boil. Remove the saucepan from the heat and add the dry ingredients all at once. Beat with a wooden spoon for 1 minute until the ingredients are well blended and the mixture starts to pull away from the sides of the pan, then set the pan over low heat and cook the mixture for about 2 minutes more, beating constantly. Remove the pan from the heat.

3 Beat 1 egg in a small bowl and set aside. Add the remaining eggs, one at a time, to the flour mixture, beating well after each. Add the beaten egg by teaspoonfuls until the dough is smooth and shiny; it should pull away and fall slowly when dropped from a spoon.

4 Using a tablespoon, drop the dough onto the baking sheet in 12 mounds. Bake for 25–30 minutes until the pastry is well risen and browned. Turn off the oven and leave the puffs to cool with the oven door open.

5 To make the sauce, place the chocolate and water in a double-boiler or in a bowl placed over a pan of hot water and let melt, stirring occasionally. Keep the sauce warm until ready to serve, or reheat it over simmering water.

6 Split the cream puffs in half and put a small scoop of vanilla ice cream in each. Arrange on a serving platter or divide among individual plates. Pour the chocolate sauce over the top and serve at once.

Crème Caramel

Also called *crème renversée*, this is one of the most popular French desserts, and is wonderful when freshly made. This version is slightly lighter than the traditional recipe.

INGREDIENTS

Serves 6–8

1¼ cups granulated sugar

4 tablespoons water

1 vanilla bean or 2 teaspoons vanilla extract

1¾ cups milk

1 cup heavy cream

5 large eggs

2 egg yolks

1 Put ⅞-cup of the sugar in a small, heavy saucepan with the water to moisten. Bring to a boil over a high heat, swirling the pan to dissolve the sugar completely. Let boil, without stirring, until the syrup turns a dark caramel color. (This will take about 4–5 minutes.)

2 Pour the caramel into a soufflé dish. Swirl the dish to coat the base, then place in a roasting pan.

3 Preheat the oven to 325°F. With a small sharp knife, carefully split the vanilla bean lengthwise and scrape the black seeds into a saucepan. Add the milk and cream and bring just to a boil over medium-high heat, stirring frequently. Remove the pan from the heat, cover and set aside for about 15–20 minutes.

4 In a bowl, whisk the eggs and egg yolks with the remaining sugar for 2–3 minutes until smooth and creamy. Whisk in the hot milk and strain the mixture into the caramel-lined dish. Cover with foil.

5 Place the dish in a roasting pan and pour in enough boiling water to come halfway up the side of the dish. Bake the custard for 40–45 minutes until a knife inserted about 2-inches from the edge comes out clean. (The custard should be just set.) Remove from the roasting pan and cool for ½ hour. Chill overnight.

6 To turn out, carefully run a sharp knife around the edge of the dish to loosen the custard. Cover the dish with a serving plate and, holding them tightly, invert the dish and plate together. Lift one edge of the dish, allowing the caramel to run over the sides, then slowly lift off the dish.

Crêpes Suzette

This is one of the best-known French desserts and is easy to do at home. You can make the crepes in advance; you will be able to put the dish together quickly at the last minute.

INGREDIENTS

Serves 6
⅔ cup flour
¼ teaspoon salt
2 tablespoons superfine sugar
2 eggs, lightly beaten
1 cup milk
4 tablespoons water
2 tablespoons orange flower water or orange liqueur (optional)
2 tablespoons unsalted butter, melted

For the orange sauce
6 tablespoons unsalted butter
¼ cup superfine sugar
grated zest and juice of 1 large unwaxed orange
grated zest and juice of 1 lemon
⅔ cup fresh orange juice
4 tablespoons orange liqueur, plus more for flaming (optional)
brandy, for flaming (optional)
orange segments, to decorate

1 In a large mixing bowl, sift together the flour, salt and sugar. Make a well in the center and pour in the beaten eggs. Using an electric whisk, beat the eggs, bringing in the flour from the edge of the bowl a little at a time. Whisk in the milk and water to make a smooth batter.

2 Whisk the orange flower water or liqueur, if using. Strain the batter into a large pitcher and set aside for 20–30 minutes. If the batter thickens, add a little milk or water to thin.

3 Heat a 7–8-inch crêpe pan (preferably non-stick) over medium heat. Stir the melted butter into the crêpe batter. Brush the hot pan with a little extra melted butter and pour in about 2 tablespoons of the batter. Quickly tilt and rotate the pan to cover the base with a thin layer of batter. Cook for about 1 minute until the top is set and the base is golden. With a spatula, gently lift the edge to check the color, then carefully turn over the crêpe and cook for 20–30 seconds, just to set. Slide the crêpe out onto a plate.

4 Continue cooking the crêpes, layering them with plastic wrap to prevent sticking. (Crêpes can be prepared ahead to this point – wrap and chill until ready to use.)

5 To make the sauce, melt the butter in a large frying pan over medium-low heat, then stir in the sugar, orange and lemon zest and juice, the additional orange juice and the orange liqueur.

6 Place a crêpe in the pan browned-side down, swirling gently to coat with the sauce. Fold it in half, then in half again to form a triangle and push to the side of the pan. Continue heating and folding the crêpes until all are warm and covered with the sauce.

7 To flame the crêpes, heat 2 tablespoons of orange liqueur and brandy. Remove the pan from the heat, ignite the liquid, then gently pour over the crêpes. Serve at once.

NORTH
AMERICA

New England Clam Chowder

INGREDIENTS

Serves 8

4 dozen cherrystone or littleneck
  clams, scrubbed
6 cups water
¼ cup finely diced salt pork or bacon
1½ cups chopped onions
1 bay leaf
2½ cups diced peeled potatoes
2 cups milk, warmed
1 cup light cream
salt and freshly ground black pepper
chopped fresh parsley, for garnishing

1 Rinse the clams in cold water.
  Drain. Place them in a kettle with
the water and bring to a boil. Cover
and steam until the shells open, about
10 minutes. Remove from the heat.

2 When the clams have cooled
  slightly, remove them from their
shells. Discard any clams that have
not opened. Chop the clams coarsely.
Strain the cooking liquid through a
strainer lined with cheesecloth, and
reserve it.

3 In a large heavy saucepan, fry the
  salt pork or bacon until it renders
its fat and begins to brown. Add the
onions and cook over low heat until
softened, 8–10 minutes

4 Add the bay leaf, potatoes, and
  clam cooking liquid. Stir. Bring
to a boil and cook 5–10 minutes.

5 Stir in the chopped clams.
  Continue to cook until the
potatoes are tender, stirring
occasionally. Season with salt and
pepper.

6 Reduce the heat to low and stir
  in the warmed milk and cream.
Simmer very gently 5 minutes more.
Discard the bay leaf, taste and adjust
the seasoning before serving, sprinkled
with parsley.

COOK'S TIP

If clams have been dug, purging helps to
rid them of sand and stomach contents.
Put them in a bowl of cold water, sprinkle
with ½-cup cornmeal and some salt. Stir
lightly and let stand in a cool place for
about 3–4 hours.

Eggs Benedict

INGREDIENTS

Serves 4

1 teaspoon vinegar
4 eggs
2 English muffins or 4 rounds of bread
butter, for spreading
2 slices of cooked ham, ¼-inch thick,
  each cut in half crosswise
fresh chives, for garnishing

For the sauce

3 egg yolks
2 tablespoons fresh lemon juice
¼ teaspoon salt
½ cup (1 stick) butter
2 tablespoons light cream
freshly ground black pepper

4 Bring a shallow pan of water to a boil. Stir in the vinegar. Break each egg into a cup, then slide it carefully into the water. Delicately turn the white around the yolk with a slotted spoon. Cook until the egg is set to your taste, 3–4 minutes. Remove to paper towels to drain. Very gently cut any ragged edges off the eggs with a small knife or scissors.

5 While the eggs are poaching, split and toast the muffins or toast the bread slices. Butter while still warm.

6 Place a piece of ham, which you may brown in butter if you wish, on each muffin half or slice of toast. Trim the ham to fit neatly. Place an egg on each ham-topped muffin. Spoon the warm sauce over the eggs, garnish with chives and serve.

1 For the sauce, put the egg yolks, lemon juice, and salt in the container of a food processor or blender. Blend for 15 seconds.

2 Melt the butter in a small pan until it bubbles. (Do not let it brown.) With the motor running, pour the hot butter into the food processor or blender through the feed tube in a slow, steady stream. Turn off the machine as soon as all the butter has been added.

3 Scrape the sauce into the top of a double boiler, over simmering water. Stir until thickened, 2–3 minutes. (If the sauce curdles, whisk in 1 tablespoon of boiling water.) Stir in the cream and season with pepper. Keep warm over the hot water.

Oyster Stew

INGREDIENTS

Serves 6

2 cups milk
2 cups light cream
1 quart shucked oysters, drained, with
   their liquor reserved
⅛ teaspoon paprika
2 tablespoons butter
1 tablespoon chopped fresh parsley
salt and freshly ground black pepper

1 Combine the milk, cream, and oyster liquor in a heavy saucepan.

2 Heat the mixture over medium heat until small bubbles appear around the edge of the pan. Do not allow it to boil. Reduce the heat to low and add the oysters.

3 Cook, stirring occasionally, until the oysters plump up and their edges begin to curl. Add the paprika, and salt and pepper to taste.

4 Meanwhile, warm 6 soup plates or bowls. Cut the butter into 6 pieces and put one piece in each bowl.

5 Ladle in the oyster stew and sprinkle with parsley. Serve immediately, with soda crackers if desired.

Oysters Rockefeller

INGREDIENTS

Serves 6

1 pound fresh spinach leaves
½ cup chopped scallions
½ cup chopped celery
½ cup chopped fresh parsley
1 garlic clove
2 anchovy fillets
4 tablespoons butter or margarine
½ cup dry bread crumbs
1 teaspoon Worcestershire sauce
2 tablespoons anise-flavored liqueur
   (Pernod or Ricard)
½ teaspoon salt
hot pepper sauce
36 oysters in shell
fine strips of lemon rind, for garnishing

COOK'S TIP

To open an oyster push the point of an oyster knife about ½-inch into the "hinge" of the shell. Push down firmly. The lid should pop open.

1 Wash the spinach well. Drain, and place in a heavy saucepan. Cover and cook over low heat until just wilted. Remove from the heat. When the spinach is cool enough to handle, squeeze it to remove excess water.

2 Put the spinach, scallions, celery, parsley, garlic, and anchovy fillets in a food processor and process until finely chopped.

3 Heat the butter or margarine in a skillet. Add the spinach mixture, bread crumbs, Worcestershire sauce, liqueur, salt, and hot pepper sauce to taste. Cook 1–2 minutes. Let cool, and refrigerate until ready to use.

4 Preheat the oven to 450°F. Line a baking sheet with crumpled foil.

5 Open the oysters and remove the top shells. Arrange them, side by side, on the foil. (It will keep them upright.) Spoon the spinach mixture over the oysters, smoothing the tops with the back of the spoon.

6 Bake until piping hot, about 20 minutes. Serve immediately, garnished with lemon rind.

Cape Cod Fried Clams

INGREDIENTS

Serves 4

36 cherrystone clams, scrubbed
1 cup buttermilk
¼ teaspoon celery salt
¼ teaspoon cayenne pepper
oil, for deep-frying
1 cup dry bread crumbs
2 eggs, beaten with 2 tablespoons
    water
lemon wedges and tartar sauce or
    catsup, for serving

1 Rinse the clams well. Put them in a kettle with 2 cups of water and bring to a boil. Cover and steam until the shells open.

2 Remove the clams from their shells, and cut away the black skins from the necks. Discard any clams that have not opened. Strain the cooking liquid and reserve.

3 Place the buttermilk in a large bowl and stir in the celery salt and cayenne pepper. Add the clams and ½-cup of their cooking liquid. Mix well. Let stand for 1 hour

4 Heat the oil in a deep-fryer or large saucepan until it reaches 375°F (or when a cube of bread dropped in the oil turns golden brown in 40 seconds).

5 Drain the clams and roll them in the bread crumbs to coat all over. Dip them in the beaten eggs and then roll them in the bread crumbs again.

6 Fry the clams in the hot oil, a few at a time, stirring, until they are crisp and brown, about 2 minutes per batch. Remove with a slotted spoon and drain on paper towels.

7 Serve the fried clams hot, accompanied by lemon wedges and tartar sauce or catsup.

Maine Lobster Dinner

INGREDIENTS

Serves 4

4 live lobsters, 1½ pounds each
3 tablespoons chopped mixed fresh
  herbs, such as parsley, chives, and
  tarragon
1 cup (2 sticks) butter, melted and kept
  warm
8 ears of tender fresh corn, shucked
salt and freshly ground black pepper
lemon halves, for serving

1 Preheat the broiler. Kill each lobster quickly by inserting the tip of a large chef's knife between the eyes.

2 Turn the lobster over onto its back and cut it in half, from the head straight down to the tail. Remove and discard the hard sac near the head, and the intestinal vein that runs through the middle of the underside of the tail. All the rest of the lobster meat is edible.

3 Combine the chopped herbs with the melted butter.

4 Place the lobster halves, shell side up, in a foil-lined broiler pan or a large roasting pan. (You may have to do this in two batches.) Broil about 8 minutes. Turn the lobster halves over, brush generously with the herb butter, and broil 7–8 minutes more.

5 While the lobsters are cooking, drop the corn into a large pot of rapidly boiling water and cook until just tender, 4–7 minutes. Drain.

6 Serve the lobsters and corn hot, with salt, freshly ground black pepper, lemon halves and individual bowls of herb butter. Provide crackers for the claws, extra plates for cobs and shells, finger bowls and lots of napkins.

Lone Star Steak and Potato Dinner

INGREDIENTS

Serves 4

3 tablespoons olive oil
5 large garlic cloves, minced
1 teaspoon coarse black pepper
½ teaspoon ground allspice
1 teaspoon ground cumin
½ teaspoon chili powder
2 teaspoons dried oregano
1 tablespoon cider vinegar
4 boneless sirloin steaks, ¾ inch thick
salt
tomato salsa, for serving
freshly cooked corn-on-the-cob, for
   serving (optional)

For the potatoes

¼ cup vegetable oil
1 onion, chopped
1 teaspoon salt
2 pounds potatoes, boiled and diced
2–5 tablespoons chopped canned green
   chilies, to taste

3 Add the pepper, spices, oregano and vinegar to the garlic and stir to blend thoroughly. If necessary, add just enough water to obtain a moderately thick paste.

4 Add the steaks to the dish and turn to coat evenly on both sides with the spice mixture. Cover and let stand for 2 hours, or refrigerate the steaks overnight. (Bring them to room temperature before cooking.)

COOK'S TIP

The steaks can also be cooked on a charcoal grill. Prepare the fire, and when the coals are glowing red and covered with grey ash, spread them in a single layer. Cook the steaks in the center of an oiled grill rack set about 5-inches above the coals for 1 minute per side to sear them. Move them away from the center and cook 10–12 minutes longer for medium-rare, turning once.

5 For the potatoes, heat the oil in a large nonstick skillet. Add the onion and salt. Cook over medium heat until softened, about 5 minutes. Add the potatoes and chilies. Cook, stirring occasionally, until well browned, 15–20 minutes.

6 Season the steaks on both sides with salt to taste. Heat a ridged grill pan. When hot, add the steaks and cook, turning once, until done to your taste. Allow about 2 minutes on each side for medium-rare, and 3–4 minutes for well-done.

7 If necessary, briefly reheat the potatoes. Serve immediately, with the tomato salsa and corn, if using.

1 Heat the olive oil in a heavy skillet. When hot, add the garlic and cook, stirring often, until tender and just brown, about 3 minutes; do not let the garlic burn.

2 Transfer the garlic and oil to a shallow dish large enough to hold the steaks in one layer.

Idaho Beef Stew

INGREDIENTS

Serves 6

¼ cup vegetable oil
2 onions, chopped
4 large carrots, thickly sliced
3 pounds chuck steak, cubed
3 tablespoons flour
3 cups unsalted beef stock
1 cup strong black coffee
2 teaspoons dried oregano
1 bay leaf
1 cup shelled fresh or frozen peas
salt and freshly ground black pepper
mashed potatoes, for serving

1 Heat 2 tablespoons of the oil in a large flameproof casserole. Add the onions and carrots and cook over medium heat until lightly browned, about 8 minutes. Remove them with a slotted spoon, transfer to a plate or dish, and reserve.

2 Add another tablespoon of oil to the casserole and then add the beef cubes. Raise the heat to medium-high and cook until browned all over. (Work in batches if necessary.) Season with salt and pepper.

3 Return the vegetables to the casserole. Add the flour and the remaining tablespoon of oil. Cook, stirring constantly, 1 minute. Add the stock, coffee, oregano and bay leaf. Bring to a boil and cook, stirring often, until thickened. Reduce the heat to low, then cover the casserole and simmer gently until the beef is tender, about 1–1½ hours.

4 Add the peas and simmer 5–10 minutes more. Discard the bay leaf, and taste for seasoning. Serve hot, with mashed potatoes.

Red Flannel Hash with Corned Beef

INGREDIENTS

Serves 4

6 bacon slices
¾ cup chopped onion
2½ cups peeled, boiled, and diced
  potatoes
1½ cups chopped corned beef
1½ cups diced cooked beets (not in
  vinegar)
¼ cup light cream or half and half
¼ cup minced fresh parsley
salt and freshly ground black pepper

1 Cook the bacon until golden and crisp. Remove and drain on paper towels. Pour off all but 2 tablespoons of the fat, reserving the rest for later.

2 Cut the bacon into ½-inch pieces and place in a bowl. Cook the onion in the bacon fat over a low heat, until softened. Add the onion to the bacon.

3 Mix in the potatoes, corned beef, beets, cream and parsley. Season well. Heat 4 tablespoons of the reserved bacon fat, or other fat, in the skillet. Add the hash mixture, spreading it evenly in the skillet with a spatula. Cook over low heat until the base is brown, about 15 minutes. Flip the hash out onto a plate.

4 Gently slide the hash back into the skillet and cook on the other side until lightly browned. Serve the hash immediately.

Country Meat Loaf

INGREDIENTS

Serves 6

2 tablespoons butter or margarine
½ cup chopped onion
2 garlic cloves, minced
½ cup chopped celery
1 pound lean ground beef
½ pound ground veal
½ pound lean ground pork
2 eggs
1 cup fine fresh bread crumbs
½ cup chopped fresh parsley
2 tablespoons chopped fresh basil
½ teaspoon fresh or dried thyme leaves
½ teaspoon salt
½ teaspoon pepper
2 tablespoons Worcestershire sauce
¼ cup chili sauce or catsup
6 bacon slices

1 Preheat the oven to 350°F.

2 Melt the butter or margarine in a small skillet over low heat. Add the onion, garlic and celery, and cook until softened. Remove and let cool slightly.

3 In a large mixing bowl combine the onion, garlic and celery with all the other ingredients except the bacon. Mix together lightly, using a fork or your fingers. Do not overwork, or the meat loaf will be too compact.

4 Form the meat mixture into an oval loaf. Carefully transfer it to a shallow baking pan.

5 Lay the bacon slices across the meat loaf. Bake for 1¼ hours, basting occasionally with the juices and bacon fat in the pan.

6 Remove from the oven and drain off the fat. Let the meat loaf stand 10 minutes before serving.

San Antonio Tortilla

INGREDIENTS

Serves 4

1 tablespoon vegetable oil
½ onion, sliced
1 small green bell pepper, seeded and
  sliced
1 garlic clove, chopped
1 tomato, chopped
6 black olives, chopped
3 small potatoes (about 10 ounces
  total), cooked and sliced
2 ounces sliced chorizo, cut in strips
1 tablespoon chopped canned
  jalapeños, or to taste
½ cup shredded cheddar cheese
6 extra large eggs
3 tablespoons milk
½–¾ teaspoon salt
¼ teaspoon ground cumin
¼ teaspoon dried oregano
¼ teaspoon paprika
freshly ground black pepper

1 Preheat the oven to 375°F.

2 Heat the oil in a nonstick skillet. Add the onion, bell pepper and garlic and cook over medium heat until softened, 5–8 minutes.

3 Transfer the vegetables to a 9-inch round nonstick cake pan. Add the tomato, olives, potatoes, chorizo and jalapeños. Sprinkle with the shredded cheese and set aside.

4 In a bowl, combine the eggs and milk and whisk until frothy. Add the salt, cumin, oregano, paprika, and pepper to taste. Whisk to blend.

5 Pour the egg mixture into the vegetable mixture, tilting the pan to spread it evenly.

6 Bake until set and golden, about 30 minutes. Serve hot or cold.

Baked Pork Loin with Red Cabbage and Apples

INGREDIENTS

Serves 8

4½-pound boned loin of pork
½ teaspoon ground ginger
4 tablespoons butter, melted
about 1½ cups sweet apple cider or
   dry white wine
salt and freshly ground black pepper

For the Cabbage

3 tablespoons butter or margarine
1½ cups finely sliced onions
1 teaspoon caraway seeds
3 tart-sweet apples, quartered, cored,
   and sliced
1 tablespoon dark brown sugar
3½-pound head of red cabbage, cored
   and shredded
6 tablespoons cider vinegar, or ¼ cup
   wine vinegar and 2 tablespoons
   water
½ cup beef stock
½ cup sweet apple cider or white wine
1 teaspoon salt
¼ teaspoon fresh or dried thyme leaves

1 Preheat the oven to 350°F.

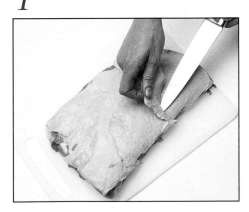

2 Trim any excess fat from the pork roast. Tie it into a neat shape, if necessary. Sprinkle with the ginger, salt and pepper.

3 Place the pork, fat side down, in a large Dutch oven. Cook over medium heat, turning frequently, until browned on all sides, about 15 minutes. Add a little of the melted butter if the roast starts to stick.

4 Cover, transfer to the oven and roast for 1 hour, basting frequently with the pan drippings, melted butter, and cider or wine.

5 Meanwhile, to prepare the cabbage, melt the butter or margarine in a large heavy skillet and add the onions and caraway seeds. Cook over low heat until softened, 8–10 minutes. Stir in the apple slices and brown sugar. Cover the pan and cook 4–5 minutes more.

6 Stir in the cabbage. Add the vinegar. Cover and cook about 10 minutes. Pour in the stock and cider or wine, add the salt and thyme leaves, and stir well. Cover again and cook over medium-low heat for 30 minutes.

7 After this time, remove the pot from the oven. Transfer the roast to a plate and keep hot. Tilt the pot and spoon off and discard all but 2 tablespoons of the fat.

8 Transfer the cabbage mixture from the skillet to the Dutch oven and stir well to mix thoroughly with the roasting juices.

9 Place the pork roast on top of the layer of cabbage. Cover and return to the oven. Cook another hour, basting occasionally with the cider or wine.

San Francisco Chicken Wings

INGREDIENTS

Serves 4

⅓ cup soy sauce
1 tablespoon light brown sugar
1 tablespoon rice vinegar
2 tablespoons dry sherry wine
juice of 1 orange
2-inch strip of orange peel
1 star anise
1 teaspoon cornstarch
¼ cup water
1 tablespoon chopped fresh ginger root
¼–1 teaspoon Oriental chili-garlic
    sauce, to taste
3½ pounds chicken wings (22–24), tips
    removed

1 Preheat the oven to 400°F.

2 Combine the soy sauce, brown sugar, vinegar, sherry, orange juice and peel, and star anise in a saucepan. Bring to a boil over medium heat.

4 Remove the soy sauce mixture from the heat and stir in the minced ginger and chili-garlic sauce.

3 Combine the cornstarch and water in a small bowl and stir until blended. Add to the boiling soy sauce mixture, stirring well. Boil 1 minute more, stirring constantly.

5 Arrange the chicken wings, in one layer, in a large baking dish. Pour over the soy sauce mixture and stir to coat the wings evenly.

6 Bake the chicken until tender and lightly browned, 30–40 minutes, basting occasionally. Serve the wings hot or warm.

Galveston Chicken

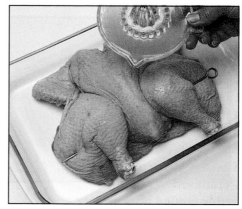

INGREDIENTS

Serves 4

3½-pound chicken
juice of 1 lemon
4 garlic cloves, chopped
1 tablespoon cayenne pepper
1 tablespoon paprika
1 tablespoon dried oregano
½ teaspoon coarse black pepper
2 teaspoons olive oil
1 teaspoon salt

———— COOK'S TIP ————

Roasting chicken in an oven that has not been preheated produces a particularly crispy skin.

1 With a sharp knife or poultry shears, remove the backbone from the chicken. Turn it breast side up. With the heel of your hand, press down to break the breastbone, and open the chicken flat like a book. Insert a skewer through the chicken, at the thighs, to keep it flat during cooking.

2 Place the chicken in a shallow dish and pour over the lemon juice.

3 In a small bowl, combine the garlic, cayenne, paprika, oregano, oil and pepper. Mix well. Rub evenly over the surface of the chicken.

4 Cover and let marinate for 2–3 hours at room temperature, or refrigerate overnight (and return to room temperature before roasting).

5 Season the chicken with salt on both sides. Transfer it to a shallow roasting pan.

6 Put the pan in a cold oven and set the temperature to 400°F. Roast until the chicken is done, about 1 hour, turning occasionally and basting with the pan juices. To test if the chicken is done, prick with a skewer: the juices that run out should be clear.

Coleslaw

INGREDIENTS

Serves 8

1 cup mayonnaise
½ cup white wine vinegar
1 tablespoon Dijon mustard
2 teaspoons sugar
1 tablespoon caraway seeds
8 cups finely sliced green cabbage,
   or a mixture of green and
   red cabbage
1 cup grated carrots
1 cup finely sliced yellow or
   red onions
salt and freshly ground black pepper

1 Combine the mayonnaise, vinegar, mustard, sugar and caraway seeds. Season to taste with salt and pepper.

2 Put the cabbage, carrots and onions in a large bowl.

3 Add the dressing to the vegetables and mix well. Taste for seasoning. Cover and refrigerate for 1–2 hours. The cabbage will become more tender the longer it marinates.

Pennsylvania Dutch Fried Tomatoes

INGREDIENTS

Serves 4

2–3 large green or very firm red
   tomatoes (about ½ pound)
⅓ cup flour
4 tablespoons butter or bacon fat
sugar, if needed
4 slices of hot buttered toast
¾ cup half and half
salt and freshly ground black pepper

1 Slice the tomatoes into ½-inch rounds. Coat lightly with flour.

2 Heat the butter or bacon fat in a skillet. When it is hot, add the tomato slices and cook until browned. Turn them once, and season generously with salt and pepper.

3 If the tomatoes are particularly green, sprinkle each slice with a little sugar. Cook until the other side is brown, 3–4 minutes more.

4 Divide the tomatoes among the slices of toast and keep hot.

5 Pour the half and half into the hot skillet and bring to a simmer. Cook 1–2 minutes, stirring to mix in the brown bits and cooking juices. Spoon the gravy over the tomatoes, and serve immediately.

VARIATION

For Fried Tomatoes with Ham, top the toast with ham slices before covering with the tomatoes.

Sweet Potato Biscuits

INGREDIENTS

Makes about 24

1¼ cups flour
4 teaspoons baking powder
1 teaspoon salt
1 tablespoon brown sugar
¾ cup mashed cooked sweet potatoes
⅔ cup milk
4 tablespoons butter or margarine, melted

1 Preheat the oven to 450°F.

2 Sift the flour, baking powder and salt into a bowl. Add the sugar and stir to mix.

3 In a separate bowl, combine the sweet potatoes with the milk and melted butter or margarine. Mix well until evenly blended.

4 Stir the dry ingredients into the sweet potato mixture to make a dough. Turn onto a floured surface and knead to mix for 2 minutes.

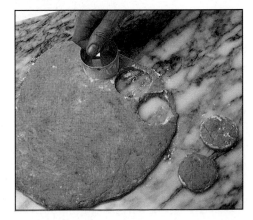

5 Roll or pat out the dough to ½-inch thickness. Cut out rounds with a 1½-inch cookie cutter.

6 Arrange the rounds on a greased cookie sheet. Bake until puffed and lightly golden, about 15 minutes. Serve the biscuits warm.

Boston Brown Bread

INGREDIENTS

Makes 2 small loaves

1 tablespoon butter or margarine, at
    room temperature
1 cup yellow cornmeal
1 cup graham or whole-wheat flour
1 cup rye flour
2 teaspoons baking soda
1 teaspoon salt
2 cups buttermilk, at room
    temperature
¾ cup molasses
1 cup chopped raisins
butter or cream cheese, for serving

1 Grease two 1-pound food cans, or
two 1-quart pudding molds, with
the soft butter or margarine.

2 Sift all the dry ingredients together
into a large bowl. Tip in any bran
from the whole-wheat flour. Stir well
to blend.

3 In a separate bowl, combine the
buttermilk, molasses, and raisins.
Add to the dry ingredients and mix.

4 Pour the batter into the prepared
molds, filling them about two-
thirds full. Cover the tops with
buttered foil, and tie or tape it
down so that the rising bread
cannot push off the foil lid.

5 Set the molds on a rack in a
large kettle with a tight-fitting lid.
Pour in enough warm water to come
halfway up the sides of the molds.
Cover the pan, bring to a boil, and
steam for 2½ hours. Check occasionally
that the water has not boiled away,
and add more if necessary.

6 Unmold the bread on a warmed
serving dish. Slice and serve with
butter or cream cheese for spreading.

Marbled Brownies

INGREDIENTS

Makes 24

8 ounces plain chocolate
3 ounces butter
4 eggs
10½ ounces sugar
5 ounces all-purpose flour
½ teaspoon salt
1 teaspoon baking powder
2 teaspoons vanilla extract
4 ounces walnuts, chopped

For the plain mixture

2 ounces butter, at room temperature
6 ounces cream cheese
3½ ounces sugar
2 eggs
1 ounce all-purpose flour
1 teaspoon vanilla extract

1 Preheat a 350°F oven. Line a 13 x 9-inch baking pan with waxed paper and grease.

2 Meanwhile, beat the eggs until light and fluffy. Gradually add the sugar and continue beating until blended. Sift over the flour, salt and baking powder and fold to combine.

3 Melt the chocolate and butter over very low heat, stirring constantly. Set aside to cool.

4 Stir in the cooled chocolate mixture. Add the vanilla and walnuts. Measure and set aside 16 fluid ounces of the chocolate mixture.

5 For the plain mixture, cream the butter and cream cheese with an electric mixer.

6 Add the sugar and continue beating until blended. Beat in the eggs, flour and vanilla extract.

7 Spread the unmeasured chocolate mixture in the tin. Pour over the plain mixture. Drop spoonfuls of the reserved chocolate mixture on top.

8 With a metal spatula, swirl the mixtures to marble. Do not blend completely. Bake until just set, 35–40 minutes. Turn out when cool and cut into squares for serving.

Apple and Cranberry Muffins

INGREDIENTS

Makes 12
4 tablespoons butter or margarine
1 egg
½ cup sugar
grated rind of 1 large orange
½ cup freshly squeezed orange juice
1cup flour
1 teaspoon baking powder
½ teaspoon bicarbonate of soda
1 teaspoon ground cinnamon
½ teaspoon grated nutmeg
½ teaspoon ground allspice
¼ teaspoon ground ginger
¼ teaspoon salt
1–2 apples
1 cup cranberries
½ cup walnuts, chopped
confectioners' sugar, for dusting
   (optional)

1 Preheat the oven to 350°F.
Meanwhile, grease a 12-cup
muffin pan or use paper liners.

2 Melt the butter or margarine over
gentle heat. Set aside to cool.

5 In a large bowl, sift together the
flour, baking powder, bicarbonate
of soda, cinnamon, nutmeg, allspice,
ginger and salt. Set aside.

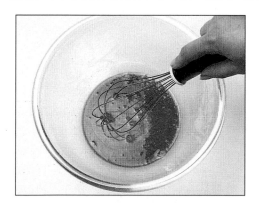

3 Place the egg in a mixing bowl
and whisk lightly. Add the melted
butter or margarine and whisk until
thoroughly combined.

4 Add the sugar, orange rind and
juice. Whisk to blend. Set aside.

6 Quarter, core and peel the apples.
With a sharp knife, dice the apples
to obtain 1¼ cups.

7 Make a well in the dry ingredients
and pour in the egg mixture.
With a spoon, stir until just blended.

8 Add the apples, cranberries and
walnuts and stir to blend.

9 Fill the cups three-quarters full
and bake until the tops spring
back when touched lightly, 25–30
minutes. Transfer to a rack to cool.
Dust with confectioners' sugar, if liked.

Shaker Summer Pudding

INGREDIENTS

Serves 6–8

1 loaf of white farmhouse-type bread,
   1–2 days old, sliced
1½ pounds fresh red currants
¼ cup plus 2 tablespoons sugar
¼ cup water
1½ pounds berries: raspberries,
   blueberries, and blackberries
juice of ½ lemon
whipped cream, for serving (optional)

1 Trim the crusts from the bread slices. Cut a round of bread to fit in the bottom of a 6-cup domed pudding mold or mixing bowl. Line the sides of the mold with bread slices, cutting them to fit and overlapping them slightly. Reserve enough bread slices to cover the top of the mold.

2 Combine the red currants with ¼ cup of the sugar and the water in a non-reactive saucepan. Heat gently, crushing the berries lightly to help the juices to flow. When the sugar has dissolved, remove from the heat.

3 Tip the currant mixture into a food processor and process until quite smooth. Press through a fine-mesh nylon strainer set in a bowl. Discard the fruit pulp left in the strainer.

4 Put the berries in a bowl with the remaining sugar and the lemon juice. Stir well.

5 One at a time, remove the cut bread pieces from the mold and dip in the red-currant purée. Replace to line the mold evenly.

6 Spoon the berries into the lined mold, pressing them down firmly and evenly. Top with the reserved cut bread slices, which have been dipped in the currant purée.

7 Cover the mold with plastic wrap. Set a small plate, just big enough to fit inside the rim of the mold, on top of the pudding. Weigh it down with cans of food. Refrigerate the pudding 8–24 hours.

8 To unmold, remove the weights, plate and plastic wrap. Run a knife between the mold and the pudding to loosen it. Turn out onto a serving plate. Serve in thick wedges, with whipped cream if desired.

Apple Maple Dumplings

INGREDIENTS

Serves 8
4½ cups flour
2 teaspoons salt
1½ cups shortening
¾–1 cup ice water
8 firm, tart-sweet apples
1 egg white
⅔ cup sugar
3 tablespoons whipping cream
½ teaspoon vanilla extract
1 cup maple syrup
whipped cream, for serving

1 Preheat the oven to 425°F.

2 Sift the flour and salt into a large bowl. Using a pastry blender or 2 knives, cut in the shortening until the mixture resembles coarse meal. Sprinkle with ¾–1 cup water and mix until the dough holds together. If it is too crumbly, add a little more water. Gather into a ball. Wrap in wax paper and refrigerate at least 20 minutes.

3 Peel the apples. Remove the cores, cutting from the stem end, without cutting through the base.

4 Roll out the dough thinly. Cut squares almost large enough to enclose the apples. Brush the squares with egg white. Set an apple in the center of each square of dough.

5 Combine the sugar, cream and vanilla in a small bowl. Spoon some into the hollow of each apple.

6 Pull the points of the dough squares up around the apples and moisten the edges where they overlap. Mold the dough around the apples, pleating the top. Do not cover the center hollows. Crimp the edges tightly to seal.

7 Set the apples in a large greased baking dish, at least ¾ inch apart. Bake 30 minutes. Lower the oven temperature to 350°F and continue baking until the pastry is golden brown and the apples are tender, about 20 minutes more.

8 Transfer the dumplings to a serving dish. Mix the maple syrup with the juices in the baking dish and drizzle over the dumplings.

9 Serve the dumplings hot with whipped cream.

Huckleberry Coffee Cake

INGREDIENTS

Serves 10

2 cups flour
1 tablespoon baking powder
1 teaspoon salt
⅓ cup butter or margarine, at room
    temperature
¾ cup granulated sugar
1 egg
1 cup milk
½ teaspoon grated lemon rind
2 cups fresh or frozen huckleberries,
    well drained
1 cup confectioners' sugar
2 tablespoons fresh lemon juice

1 Preheat the oven to 350°F.

2 Sift the flour with the baking
powder and salt.

3 In a large bowl, beat the butter
or margarine with the sugar until
light and fluffy. Beat in the egg and
milk. Fold in the flour mixture,
mixing well until evenly blended to
a batter. Mix in the lemon rind.

4 Spread half of the batter in a
greased 13 x 9 x 2-inch baking
pan. Sprinkle with 1 cup of the berries.
Top with the remaining batter and
sprinkle with the rest of the berries.
Bake until golden brown or until a
cake tester inserted in the center
comes out clean, 35–45 minutes.

5 Mix the confectioners' sugar
gradually into the lemon juice to
make a smooth glaze with a pourable
consistency. Drizzle the glaze over the
top of the warm coffee cake and allow
it to set before serving, still warm or at
room temperature.

Northwestern Brown Betty

INGREDIENTS

Serves 6

2¼ pounds pears (about 8)
¼ cup lemon juice
3 cups fresh bread crumbs, preferably
  from egg bread
6 tablespoons butter, melted
⅔ cup dried cherries
⅔ cup coarsely chopped hazelnuts
½ cup brown sugar, firmly packed
1–2 tablespoons butter, cut in small
  pieces
whipped cream, for serving

1 Preheat the oven to 375°F. Grease
  an 8-inch square cake pan.

2 Peel, core, and dice the pears.
  Sprinkle them with the lemon
juice to prevent discoloration.

3 Combine the bread crumbs and
  melted butter in a bowl. Spread a
scant one-third of the crumb mixture
on the bottom of the prepared dish.

4 Top with half of the pears.
  Sprinkle over half of the dried
cherries, half of the hazelnuts, and half
of the sugar. Repeat the layers, then
finish with a layer of crumbs.

5 Dot with the pieces of butter.
  Bake until golden, 30–35 minutes.
Serve hot, with whipped cream.

CAJUN & CREOLE

Corn and Crab Bisque

A Louisiana classic, and certainly luxurious enough for a dinner party, which makes it worth the trouble. The crab shells together with the corn cobs, from which the kernels are stripped, make a fine-flavored stock.

SERVES 8

INGREDIENTS
4 large ears of corn
2 bay leaves
salt, freshly ground black and white
 pepper, and cayenne
1 cooked crab weighing about 2¼ lb
2 tbsp butter
2 tbsp plain flour
1¼ cups whipping cream
6 scallions, finely chopped
hot French bread or Italian bread sticks
 to serve

1 Pull away the husks and silk from the ears of corn and strip off the kernels (see step 1 of Corn Cakes with Grilled Tomatoes for the method).

2 Keep the corn kernels to the side and put the stripped cobs into a deep saucepan or flameproof casserole. Cover with 12½ cups cold water, and add the bay leaves and 2 tsp salt. Bring to a boil and leave to simmer while you prepare the crab.

3 Pull away the two flaps between the big claws of the crab, stand it on its 'nose' where the flaps were and bang down firmly with the heel of your hand on the rounded end.

4 Separate the crab from its top shell, keeping the shell.

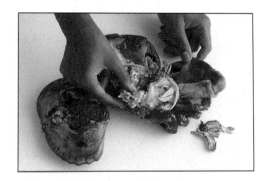

5 Push out the crab's mouth and its abdominal sac immediately below the mouth, and discard.

6 Pull away the feathery gills surrounding the central chamber and discard. Scrape out all the semi-liquid brown meat from the crab and keep it.

7 Crack the claws in as many places as necessary to extract all the white meat. Pick out the white meat from the fragile cavities in the central body of the crab. Set aside all the crabmeat, brown and white. Put the spidery legs, back shell and all the other pieces of shell into the pan with the corn cobs. Simmer for a further 15 minutes, then strain the stock into a clean pan and boil hard to reduce to 9 cups.

8 Meanwhile melt the butter in a small pan and sprinkle in the flour. Stir constantly over a low heat until the roux is the color of rich cream.

9 Remove from the heat, and slowly stir in 1 cup of the stock. Return to the heat and whisk until it thickens, then whisk this thickened mixture into the pot of strained stock.

10 Add the corn kernels, return to a boil and simmer for 5 minutes.

11 Add the crabmeat, cream and scallions and season with salt, black or white pepper (or a bit of both) and cayenne. Return to a boil and simmer for a further 2 minutes. Serve with hot French bread or Italian bread sticks.

COOK'S TIP

You can, if you prefer, ask your fish-monger to remove all the inedible bits of the crab — the mouth, stomach sac and gills.

Corn Cakes with Grilled Tomatoes

SERVES 4

INGREDIENTS

1 large ear of corn
¾ cup plain flour
1 egg
a little milk
salt and freshly ground black pepper
2 large firm tomatoes
1 garlic clove
1 tsp dried oregano
2–3 tbsp oil, plus extra for frying
8 cupped leaves iceberg lettuce
shredded fresh basil leaves to garnish

1 ▲ Pull the husks and silk away from the corn, then hold the ear upright on a board and cut downwards with a heavy knife to strip off the kernels. Put them into a pan of boiling water and cook for 3 minutes after the water has returned to the boil, then drain and rinse under cold water to cool quickly.

2 Put the flour into a bowl and break the egg into a well in the middle, then start stirring in the flour with a fork, adding a little milk to make a soft dropping consistency. Stir in the drained corn and season.

3 ▲ Preheat the broiler. Halve the tomatoes horizontally and make 2 or 3 criss-cross slashes across the cut side of each half. Crush the garlic and rub it, the oregano and some salt and pepper over the cut surface of each half, then drizzle with oil and broil until lightly browned.

4 ▲ While the tomatoes broil, heat a little of the oil in a wide frying pan and drop a tablespoon of batter into the center. Cook, one at a time, over a low heat and turn as soon as the top is set. Drain on paper towel and keep warm while cooking remaining cakes. The mixture should make at least 8 cakes.

5 Put 2 corn cakes onto lettuce leaves, garnish with basil and serve with a grilled tomato half.

Muffuletta Sandwich

In New Orleans you buy your Muffuletta sandwich ready-made from one of the grocery stores on Chartres Street that are famous for it, and where they also make up the olive pickle (an essential ingredient) by the barrel-load. There it comes in a special 10 in diameter soft loaf, like an extra large hamburger bun, served in quarters. You can make it in a French loaf.

SERVES 4

INGREDIENTS
For the olive pickle
1 celery stalk, finely chopped
1 garlic clove, crushed
1 canned sweet red pepper, drained and finely chopped
²⁄₃ cup pitted green olives, finely chopped
2 tbsp pickled cocktail onions, drained and coarsely chopped
2 tsp capers, drained and halved
3 tbsp olive oil
2 tsp red wine vinegar

For the sandwich
1 large French loaf
4 thin slices prosciutto
2 oz Provolone or Emmenthal cheese, thinly sliced
black pepper
2 oz Italian salami, rinded and thinly sliced

2   To make the sandwich, halve the loaf and cut it lengthways. Line the base with prosciutto. Lay the cheese on top and grind on some black pepper, then overlay with slices of salami.

3   Finally spoon the olive pickle on top of the salami and press the sandwich shut.

1   Mix all the vegetable and pickled ingredients for the olive pickle, then stir in the oil and vinegar and refrigerate.

Creole Omelette

SERVES 3–4

INGREDIENTS

1 large Spanish onion, finely chopped
2 tbsp butter
1 garlic clove, crushed
2 tbsp soft white breadcrumbs
4 large tomatoes, skinned and chopped
½ cup lean cooked ham, finely
*   chopped*
salt, freshly ground black pepper and
*   cayenne*
6 eggs, lightly beaten
chopped fresh parsley to garnish

1 Soften the onion in the butter in a heavy frying pan, stirring regularly over a low heat for about 10 minutes.

2   Add the garlic and breadcrumbs and continue to stir over the heat until the breadcrumbs begin to crisp.

3   Add the tomatoes and cook for 10–15 minutes until they have broken down. Stir in the ham and season the mixture quite highly to compensate for the eggs.

4   Preheat the broiler. Stir the beaten eggs through the mixture and continue to stir over the heat, breaking up the base as it sets to allow the uncooked mixture through.

5 When the omelette begins to set, leave it over a low heat until it is almost completely set.

6 Finish the omelette under the broiler to cook the top. Serve either turned out on to a warm serving plate or straight from the pan, cut in wedges. Garnish with chopped parsley.

COOK'S TIP

You can leave out the ham to make the omelette suitable for vegetarians. Or, you can replace the ham with cut-up spicy sausages.

Creole Cheese Potato Puffs

It's worth boiling extra potatoes just to have some left over to mash for this heartening starter.

SERVES 4–6

INGREDIENTS
3 tbsp milk
2 tbsp butter
2¹/₂ cups cold mashed potatoes
¹/₂ cup grated Cheddar cheese
4 scallions, chopped
salt, freshly ground black pepper and grated nutmeg
2 eggs, separated
watercress and cherry tomatoes to garnish

3   Whisk the egg whites to soft peaks. Mix a tablespoon or two of the whites thoroughly into the potato mixture to loosen it, then fold the rest of the whites through the potato as lightly as you can.

4   Spoon the mixture into the muffin pan and bake in the oven for about 15 minutes, until the puffs have risen and are tinged golden brown. Serve immediately, garnished with watercress and cherry tomatoes.

1   Preheat the oven to 425°F and generously butter a 12-hole non-stick muffin pan, buttering the sections between the indents as well.

2   Warm the milk and butter to just below boiling point in a small pan, then mix thoroughly into the mashed potatoes with the cheese, scallions and seasoning. Mix in the egg yolks and beat thoroughly.

COOK'S TIP

Garnished elegantly, these puffs make a pretty starter, but on a more homely occasion they are just as good served with sausages and tomato ketchup.

Eggs Sardou

Restaurants don't come and go much in New Orleans: Antoine's, where this dish was created in 1908, is still there, right in the heart of jazzland. The dish's popularity has spread and it now crops up on brunch menus as well as being a favorite starter.

SERVES 4

INGREDIENTS
4 large artichokes
1¼ lb raw spinach
4 tbsp butter
2 tbsp plain flour
¾ cup milk
4 canned anchovy fillets, drained and
    mashed
freshly ground black pepper, grated
    nutmeg, Tabasco sauce and salt
4 eggs

For the Hollandaise sauce
2 tbsp white wine vinegar
4 black peppercorns
1 bay leaf
2 egg yolks, at room temperature
½ cup butter, at warm room temperature,
    cubed
salt and freshly ground black pepper

I   With a sharp knife, cut the stems from the artichokes, then cut off the top half of each artichoke and scoop out the prickly center. Set aside.

2   Wash the spinach thoroughly, trimming off any discolored bits and the coarser stems. Put the spinach into a deep pan with just the water that clings to it. Cover and cook until it wilts right down. Turn out into a colander and, when it's cool enough to handle, squeeze out much of the moisture. Slice across the ball of spinach both ways to chop it.

3   To make the Hollandaise sauce, boil the vinegar with 2 tsp water, the peppercorns and bay leaf in a small pan until the liquid is reduced to 1 tbsp. Leave to cool.

4   Cream the egg yolks with one cube of soft butter and a pinch of salt in a heatproof bowl, then strain in the vinegar, set the bowl over a pan of boiling water and turn off the heat.

5   Whisk in the remaining butter one cube at a time, adding each cube as the one before melts into the sauce. Continue whisking until the sauce is shiny and thick. Season with salt and pepper. Leave over the pan of water to keep warm.

6   Bring a wide pan full of salted water to a boil. Add the artichokes, cover and cook for 30 minutes or until tender. Lift them with a slotted spoon onto warmed serving plates and keep warm.

7   Meanwhile, to finish the spinach, melt the butter in a wide pan, mix in the flour and stir for 1 minute over the heat until the roux froths and bubbles. Take off the heat and pour in the milk gradually, stirring constantly. When the sauce loosens, return it to the heat and continue stirring in the milk.

8   When the sauce starts to simmer, stir in the mashed anchovies and leave to simmer for about 5 minutes. Then add the chopped spinach, return to a simmer, season with black pepper, nutmeg, Tabasco sauce and salt if it needs it, and keep warm.

9   Poach the eggs 2 at a time in the pan of artichoke cooking water.

10   To assemble the dish, spoon some spinach into each artichoke, allowing it to spill over the edges. Set a poached egg on the plate and spoon Hollandaise sauce over.

Poussins with Dirty Rice

This rice is called dirty not because of the bits in it (though the roux and chicken livers do 'muss' it up a bit) but because jazz was called 'dirty music', and the rice here is certainly jazzed up.

SERVES 4

INGREDIENTS
For the rice
4 tbsp cooking oil
¼ cup plain flour
4 tbsp butter
1 large onion, chopped
2 celery stalks, chopped
1 sweet green pepper, seeded and diced
2 garlic cloves, crushed
7 oz ground pork
*8 oz chicken livers, trimmed
    and sliced*
*salt, freshly ground black pepper and
    Tabasco sauce*
1¼ cups chicken stock
4 scallions, chopped
3 tbsp chopped fresh parsley
*generous 1 cup American unconverted
    long-grain white rice, cooked*

For the birds
4 poussins
2 bay leaves, halved
2 tbsp butter
salt and freshly ground black pepper
1 lemon

1 In a small heavy saucepan, make a roux with 2 tbsp of the oil and the flour. When it is a chestnut-brown color, remove the pan from the heat and place it immediately on a cold surface.

2 Heat the remaining 2 tbsp oil with the butter in a frying pan and stir-fry the onion, celery and sweet pepper for about 5 minutes.

3 Add the garlic and pork and stir-fry for 5 minutes, breaking up the pork and stirring to cook it all over.

4 Add the chicken livers and fry for 2–3 minutes until they have changed color all over. Season with salt, pepper and a dash of Tabasco sauce.

5 Stir the roux into the stir-fried mixture, then gradually add in the stock. When it begins to bubble, cover and cook for 30 minutes, stirring occasionally. Then uncover and cook for a further 15 minutes, stirring frequently.

6 Preheat the oven to 400°F. Mix the scallions and parsley into the meat mixture and stir it all into the cooked rice.

7 Put ½ bay leaf and 1 tbsp rice into each poussin. Rub the outside with the butter and season with salt and pepper.

8 Put the birds on a rack in a roasting pan, squeeze the juice from the lemon over them and roast in the oven for 35–40 minutes, basting twice with the pan juices.

9 Put the remaining rice into a shallow ovenproof dish, cover it and place on a low shelf in the oven for the last 15–20 minutes of the birds' cooking time.

10 Serve the birds on a bed of dirty rice with the roasting pan juices (drained of fat) poured over.

COOK'S TIP

You can substitute quails for the poussins, in which case offer 2 per person and stuff each little bird with 2 tsp of the dirty rice before roasting for about 20 minutes.

Chicken and Shrimp Jambalaya

The mixture of chicken, seafood and rice suggests a close relationship to the Spanish paella, but the name is more probably derived from 'jambon' (the French for ham), 'à la ya' (Creole for rice). Jambalayas are a colorful mixture of highly flavored ingredients, and are always made in large quantities for big family or celebration meals.

SERVES 10

INGREDIENTS

2 × 3 lb chicken
salt and freshly ground black pepper
1 lb piece raw smoked ham
4 tbsp lard or bacon fat
1/2 cup plain flour
3 medium onions, finely sliced
2 sweet green peppers, seeded and sliced
11/2 lb fresh ripe tomatoes, skinned and chopped
2–3 garlic cloves, crushed
2 tsp chopped fresh thyme or 1 tsp dried thyme
24 medium-sized shrimp, de-headed and peeled
3 cups unconverted white long-grain rice
2–3 dashes Tabasco sauce
1 bunch scallions, finely chopped
3 tbsp chopped fresh parsley

2   Dice the ham coarsely, discarding the rind and fat.

3   In a large heavy-based pan or flameproof casserole, melt the lard or bacon fat and brown the chicken pieces all over, lifting them out with a slotted spoon and setting them aside as they are done.

4 ▲ Turn the heat down, sprinkle the flour onto the fat in the pan and stir continuously until the roux turns light golden-brown.

5   Return the chicken pieces to the pan, add the diced ham, onions, green peppers, tomatoes, garlic and thyme and cook, stirring regularly, for 10 minutes, then stir in the shrimp.

6 Stir the rice into the pan with four one-and-a-half cups of cold water. Season with salt, pepper and Tabasco sauce. Bring to a boil and cook over a gentle heat until the rice is tender and the liquid is fully absorbed. Add a little extra boiling water if the rice looks as though it is drying out before it is completely cooked.

7 Mix the scallions and parsley into the finished dish, reserving a little of the mixture to scatter over the jambalaya. Serve hot.

COOK'S TIP

The roux thickening is a vital part of Cajun cooking, particularly essential to jambalaya. Cook the roux over a low heat, watching like a hawk to see it doesn't develop dark flecks, which indicate burning. Don't stop stirring for an instant.

I   Cut each chicken into 10 pieces and season with salt and pepper.

Louisiana Seafood Gumbo

Gumbo is a soup, but is served over rice as a main course. This recipe is based on a gumbo that chef John Folse, of the renowned Louisiana restaurant Lafitte's Landing, served on a visit to London. In his neck of the bayous, where they are cheap and prolific, oysters are an important ingredient. However, his suggestion to substitute mussels for oysters works very well too.

SERVES 6

INGREDIENTS
1 lb mussels
1 lb shrimp
1 cooked crab weighing about 2¹/₄ lb
salt
1 small bunch of parsley, leaves chopped and stems reserved
²/₃ cup cooking oil
1 cup plain flour
1 sweet green pepper, seeded and chopped
1 large onion, chopped
2 celery stalks, sliced
3 garlic cloves, finely chopped
3 oz smoked spiced sausage, skinned and sliced
6 scallions, chopped
cayenne and Tabasco sauce
boiled unconverted white long-grain rice to serve

1 Wash the mussels in several changes of cold water, scrubbing away any barnacles and pulling off the black 'beards' that protrude between the shells. Discard any mussels that are broken or any open ones that don't close when you tap them firmly.

2 Heat 1 cup water in a deep saucepan and, when it boils, add the mussels, cover tightly and cook over a high heat, shaking regularly, for 3 minutes. As the mussels open, lift them out with tongs into a sieve set over a bowl. Discard any that refuse to open after a further 1 minute's cooking.

3 Shell the mussels, discarding the shells. Return the liquor from the bowl to the pan and make the quantity up to 9 cups with water.

4 Shell the shrimp and put the shells and heads into the saucepan.

5 Remove all the meat from the crab (see the Corn and Crab Bisque recipe), separating the brown and white meat. Add all the pieces of shell to the saucepan with 2 tsp salt.

6 Bring the shellfish stock to the boil, skimming regularly to remove the froth that rises as boiling point approaches.

7 When no more froth rises from the shellfish stock, add the parsley stalks and simmer for 15 minutes. Cool the stock, then strain off the liquor, discarding all the solids. Make up to 9 cups with water.

8 Make a roux with the oil and flour. Stir constantly over the heat with a wooden spoon or whisk until it reaches a golden-brown color. It is vital to stir constantly to darken the roux without burning. Should black specks occur at any stage of cooking, discard the roux and start again.

9 As soon as the roux is the right color, add the pepper, onion, celery and garlic and continue cooking until they are soft – about 3 minutes. Then add the sausage. Reheat the stock.

10 Stir the brown crabmeat into the roux, then ladle in the hot stock a little at a time, stirring constantly until it is all smoothly incorporated. Bring to a low boil and simmer the soup for 30 minutes, partially covered.

11 Add the shrimp, mussels, white crabmeat and scallions. Return to a boil, season with salt if necessary, cayenne and a dash or two of Tabasco sauce, and simmer for a further minute.

12 Add the chopped parsley leaves and serve immediately, ladling the soup over the hot rice in soup plates.

COOK'S TIP

It's important to have the onion, green pepper and celery prepared and ready to add to the roux the minute it reaches the correct golden-brown stage, as this arrests its darkening.

Fried Fish with Tartar Sauce and Hush Puppies

The story goes that fishermen frying their catch used to drop pieces of stiffened batter into the fat to fry. They would then throw the fried batter to their dogs to hush their hungry howlings — hence the name of hush puppies, a traditional Southern food.

SERVES 4

INGREDIENTS
For the tartar sauce
²/₃ cup mayonnaise
1 tbsp chopped dill pickles
5 pitted green olives, chopped
2 scallions, finely chopped
1 tbsp lemon juice
1–2 dashes Tabasco sauce

For the hush puppies
1 cup cornmeal
¹/₂ cup plain flour
1¹/₂ tsp baking powder
1 garlic clove, crushed with 1 tsp salt
2 scallions, finely chopped
1 egg, lightly beaten
about 5 tbsp milk
2 tbsp butter

For the fish coating
¹/₄ cup plain flour
¹/₄ cup cornstarch
¹/₂ cup cornmeal
¹/₂ tsp dried oregano
¹/₂ tsp dried thyme
1 tsp salt
1 tsp cayenne
1 tsp paprika
2 tsp dry mustard powder
1 egg
about ¹/₂ cup milk

For the fish fillets
oil for deep-frying
4 skinned flounder fillets, thawed if frozen
lemon slices and fresh parsley sprigs to
garnish

I   Mix all the ingredients for the tartar sauce and set aside.

2   Next make the hush puppy batter. Mix the cornmeal, flour and baking powder and stir in the crushed garlic and scallions. Fork in the egg.

3   Heat 5 tbsp milk and the butter together slowly until the butter melts, then raise the heat and, when it boils, stir thoroughly into the dry ingredients, adding a little more milk if necessary to make a stiff dough. Leave to cool.

4   To make the fish coating, mix the flours and all the herbs and seasonings for the fish coating in a shallow dish. Beat the egg and milk together lightly in another shallow dish.

5   Scoop out pieces of hush puppy batter no bigger than a walnut and roll into balls between wetted hands.

6   Heat the oil for deep-frying. Fry the hush puppies in batches, turning them until they are deep golden brown

all over. They will swell in cooking, and it's important that they are cooked right to the middle, so don't have the oil fiercely hot to start with. It should sizzle and froth up round them as you drop them in, but not brown them immediately. Lift them out with a slotted spoon and drain on paper towels as they are done. Keep warm.

7   Coat the fish fillets, first in the egg mixture and then in the cornmeal mixture.

8   Fry the fillets 2 at a time for 2–3 minutes on each side, until crisp and golden brown. Drain on kitchen paper and serve with the hush puppies, garnished with lemon slices and sprigs of parsley.

COOK'S TIP

Louisiana cooks use a specially fine ground cornmeal in their coating mixture. The nearest I've found to it is masa harina, from which Mexican cooks make tortillas. You can find it in shops specializing in Mexican and Southwestern ingredients but also in supermarkets with Spanish food sections.

Maque Choux

A Cajun classic, good with ham and chicken. Some cooks add a little sugar to heighten the sweetness, but for most the natural sweetness of the corn is enough.

SERVES 4–6

INGREDIENTS
4 tbsp butter
1 large onion, finely chopped
1 sweet green pepper, seeded and diced
2 large tomatoes, skinned and chopped
4 cups frozen corn kernels, thawed
½ cup milk
salt, freshly ground black pepper and cayenne

I Melt half the butter in a large pan and soften the onion in it, stirring regularly over a low heat for about 10 minutes until it begins to turn pale gold. Add the sweet pepper and stir over the heat for a further minute, then add the tomatoes and leave to cook gently while you prepare the corn.

2 Put the corn kernels and milk into a food processor or blender and process in brief bursts to break up the kernels to a chunky but fluid consistency.

3 Stir the corn mixture thoroughly into the pan and cook, partially covered, over a low heat for 20 minutes. Stir regularly, making sure that it does not stick to the bottom. If the mixture threatens to become too dry, add a little more milk. Should it still be rather wet in the latter stages, uncover, raise the heat a little and stir constantly for the last 5 minutes.

4 Stir in the rest of the butter and season quite highly with salt, black pepper and cayenne. Serve hot.

COOK'S TIP

You are aiming at a consistency rather like that of scrambled eggs and, like scrambled eggs, Maque Choux is also good with bacon and fried bread for breakfast.

Baked Sweet Potatoes

Sweet potatoes go well with the favorite Cajun seasonings: plenty of salt, white pepper as well as black and cayenne, and lavish quantities of butter. Serve half a potato per person as an accompaniment to meat, sausages or fish, or a whole one as a supper dish, perhaps topped with crisped and crumbled bacon and accompanied by a green side salad peppered with watercress.

SERVES 3—6

INGREDIENTS
3 pink-skinned sweet potatoes, each weighing about 1 lb
salt
6 tbsp butter, sliced
black and white pepper and cayenne

2　The potatoes can either be served in halves or whole. For halves, split each one lengthwise and make close diagonal cuts in the flesh of each half. Then spread with slices of butter, and work the butter and seasonings roughly into the cuts with a knife point.

3　Alternatively, make an incision along the length of each potato if they are to be served whole. Open them slightly and put in butter slices along the length, seasoning with salt and the peppers.

1　Wash the potatoes, leaving the skins wet. Rub salt into the skins, prick them all over with a fork, and place on the middle shelf of the oven. Turn on the oven at 400°F and bake the potatoes for about an hour, until the flesh yields and feels soft when pressed.

COOK'S TIP

Sweet potatoes cook more quickly than ordinary ones, and there is no need to preheat the oven.

Beignets

In New Orleans where a night on the town really can last all night, revellers are glad of a pit-stop at the Café du Monde, which serves its favorite treats of 'café au lait' and sugary beignets 24 hours a day. Chef John Folse of Lafitte's Landing restaurant, who is deeply interested in Louisiana history, says the recipe was brought to Louisiana in 1727 by Ursuline nuns. This is his version of their recipe.

MAKES 20

INGREDIENTS
1 packet dried yeast
3½ cups plain flour
1 tsp salt
¼ cup sugar
1¼ cups milk
3 eggs, beaten
2 tbsp butter, melted
oil for deep-frying
1 cup confectioners' sugar

1 Dissolve the yeast in 4 tbsp warm water and set aside.

2 In a large mixing bowl, combine the flour, salt and sugar and mix well. Fold in the dissolved yeast, milk, eggs and melted butter.

3 Continue to mix until a smooth dough is formed.

4 Knead the dough until smooth and elastic. Cover the dough with a towel and leave to rise in a warm place for 1 hour.

5 Roll out the dough to ¼ in thick on a well-floured surface. Cut into rectangular shapes about 2 × 3 in and put them in a lightly floured jelly roll tin.

6 Cover with a towel and leave to rise in a warm place for an hour or until they have doubled their size.

7 Put the confectioners' sugar into a deep dish or oven tin. Heat the oil for deep-frying and fry the beignets in batches, turning each, until golden brown on both sides. Drain well on paper towels.

8 As each batch of beignets is cooked, transfer with a slotted spoon to the confectioners' sugar and shake them about to coat liberally all round.

COOK'S TIP

The important thing with beignets, as with all doughnuts, is to have the oil at the right temperature to cook the dough right through to the middle before the outside is too dark brown.

Treat the first beignet or two as a test. Break them open and if they are still sticky in the middle lower the heat and allow the oil to cool down a bit before continuing with the next batch.

Eat the beignets soon after cooking, and certainly on the same day as they are made.

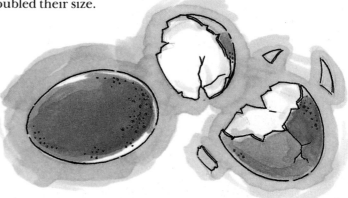

Pecan Pie

A favorite pie all over the southern states, where pecans flourish. Louisiana is no exception.

SERVES 6

INGREDIENTS

For the pastry
1¾ cups plain flour
pinch of salt
½ cup butter
dry beans or rice for baking pie crust

For the filling
3 eggs
good pinch of salt
1 tsp vanilla extract
¾ firmly packed cup dark brown sugar
4 tbsp light corn syrup
4 tbsp butter, melted
1 cup chopped pecan kernels, plus 12 pecan halves

To serve
whipped cream or vanilla ice cream

1   Mix the flour with a pinch of salt, then rub in the butter with your fingertips to a coarse sand consistency. Add iced water a little at a time, mixing first with a fork, then with your hand, until the mixture gathers into a dough. Be skimpy with the water.

2 Wrap the dough in plastic wrap and refrigerate for 30–40 minutes. Preheat the oven to 375°F for 20 minutes before you bake the pie crust.

3   Grease an 8–9 in loose-based pie pan. Roll out the pastry to line the pan, pressing it gently into place with your fingers.

4   Run the rolling pin over the top of the tin to sever the surplus pastry.

5   Prick the pie crust all over and line with foil. Fill it with dry beans or rice and bake for 15 minutes, then remove the foil and beans and bake for a further 5 minutes. Take the pie crust from the oven and lower the oven heat to 350°F.

6 Meanwhile, to make the filling, beat the eggs lightly with the salt and vanilla extract, then beat in the sugar, syrup and melted butter. Finally mix in the chopped pecans.

7   Spread the mixture in the half-baked pie crust and bake for 15 minutes, then take it from the oven and stud with the pecan halves in a circle.

8 Return to the oven and bake for a further 20–25 minutes until a thin metal skewer pushed gently into the center comes out clean, with no uncooked mixture attached.

9 Cool the pie for 10–15 minutes and serve it warm with whipped cream or a scoop of vanilla ice cream.

COOK'S TIP

For individual desserts you can serve Pecan Tartlets. Just divide the crust into six parts and follow the same instructions. Check the center of the tartlets after 20 minutes – as they are smaller they may cook more quickly.

CARIBBEAN

Spinach Pastries

INGREDIENTS

Makes 10–12
For the pastry
2 cups flour
½ cup butter or margarine, chilled and
    diced
1 egg yolk
milk, to glaze

For the filling
2 tablespoons butter or margarine
1 small onion, finely chopped
6–8 ounces fresh leaf
    spinach, chopped
½ teaspoon ground cumin
½ vegetable stock cube, crumbled
freshly ground black pepper

1 Preheat the oven to 400°F. Lightly
grease the hollows of a muffin pan.

2 First make the spinach filling.
Melt the butter or margarine in a
saucepan, add the onion and cook
gently until softened. Stir in the spinach,
then add the cumin, stock cube and
pepper and cook for 5 minutes or until
the spinach has wilted. Set aside to cool.

3 To make the pastry, put the flour
in a large bowl and rub in the
butter or margarine, until the mixture
resembles fine bread crumbs. Add the
egg yolk and 2–3 tablespoons cold
water and mix to a firm dough. Turn
out the pastry on to a floured surface.

4 Knead for a few seconds, divide the
dough in half and roll out one half to
a square or rectangle. Cut out 10–12
rounds using a 3½-inch pastry cutter.
Press into the hollows of the prepared
pan. Spoon about 1 tablespoon of the
spinach mixture into the pastry cases.

5 Roll out the remaining dough and
cut out slightly smaller rounds to
cover the pastries. Press the edges with
a fork, to seal. Prick the tops with the
fork. Brush with milk and bake for
15–20 minutes until golden brown.
Serve hot or cold.

Salt Cod Fritters (Stamp and Go)

These delicious fritters are also
known as Accras.

INGREDIENTS

Makes 15
1 cup self-rising flour
1 cup flour
½ teaspoon baking powder
6 ounces soaked salt cod, shredded
1 egg, beaten
1 tablespoon chopped scallion
1 garlic clove, crushed
½ teaspoon freshly ground black
    pepper
½ hot chili pepper, seeded and finely
    chopped
¼ teaspoon turmeric (optional)
3 tablespoons milk
vegetable oil, for shallow frying

1 Sift the flours and baking powder
together into a bowl, then add the
salt cod, egg, scallion, garlic, pepper,
hot pepper and turmeric, if using. Add
a little of the milk and mix well.

2 Gradually stir in the remaining
milk, adding just enough to make a
thick batter. Stir thoroughly so that all
ingredients are completely combined.

3 Heat a little oil in a large frying pan
until very hot. Add spoonfuls of
the mixture and fry for a few minutes
on each side until golden brown and
puffed. Lift out the fritters, drain on
paper towels and keep warm while
cooking the rest of the mixture in the
same way. Serve the fritters hot or
cold, as a snack, or hors d'oeuvres.

Peppered Steak in Sherry Cream Sauce

This dish would be perfect for supper, served on a bed of noodles or with boiled plantains.

INGREDIENTS

Serves 4
1½ pounds steak
1 teaspoon spice seasoning
2 tablespoons butter
6–8 shallots, sliced
2 garlic cloves, crushed
½ cup sherry
3 tablespoons water
5 tablespoons light cream
salt and freshly ground black pepper
cooked plantain, to serve
chopped fresh chives, to garnish

1 Cut the meat into thin strips, discarding any fat or gristle.

2 Season the meat with pepper and spice seasoning and let marinate in a cool place for 30 minutes.

3 Melt the butter in a large frying pan and sauté the meat for 4–5 minutes until browned on all sides. Transfer to a plate and set aside.

4 Add the shallots and garlic to the pan, fry gently for a few minutes, then add the sherry and water and simmer for 5 minutes. Stir in the single cream.

5 Reduce the heat and adjust the seasoning. Stir in the meat and heat until hot but not boiling. Serve with plantain and garnish with chives.

Oxtail and Lima Beans

This is a traditional Caribbean stew; old-fashioned, economical, and good and spicy. It requires long cooking and lots of oxtail, but is a treat well worth the patience. As with many stews, it is delicious the next day, so make plenty.

INGREDIENTS

Serves 4 or more

3 pounds oxtail, chopped into pieces
7½ cups water
1 onion, finely chopped
3 bay leaves
4 thyme sprigs
3 whole cloves
6 ounces dried lima beans, soaked overnight
2 garlic cloves, crushed
1 tablespoon tomato paste
14-ounce can chopped tomatoes
1 teaspoon ground allspice
1 hot chili pepper
salt and freshly ground black pepper

1 Place the oxtail pieces in a large heavy pan, add the onion, bay leaves, thyme and cloves and cover with water. Bring to a boil, then reduce the heat.

2 Cover the pan and simmer for at least 2½ hours or until the meat is very tender, adding water whenever necessary.

3 Meanwhile, drain the beans and cover with water. Bring to a boil and simmer for 1–1¼ hours. Drain and set aside.

4 When the oxtail is cooked and the stock is well reduced, add the garlic, tomato paste, tomatoes, allspice, hot pepper, salt and black pepper. Add the lima beans and simmer for another 20 minutes. The stew should be fairly thick, but if it looks dry add a little water. Adjust the seasoning and serve.

"Seasoned-up" Lamb in Spinach Sauce

Lamb, spinach and ginger go well together. Powdered ginger has a strong distinctive flavor and should be used sparingly – you could use grated fresh ginger, if you prefer.

INGREDIENTS

Serves 4

1½ pounds stewing lamb, cubed
½ teaspoon ground ginger
½ teaspoon dried thyme
2 tablespoons olive oil
1 onion, chopped
2 garlic cloves, crushed
1 tablespoon tomato paste
½ hot chili pepper chopped (optional)
2½ cups stock or water
4 ounces fresh spinach, finely chopped
salt and freshly ground black pepper

1 Place the lamb in a glass or china dish, season with the ginger, thyme and salt and pepper and let marinate in a cool place for at least 2 hours or overnight in the fridge.

2 Heat the olive oil in a large heavy saucepan, add the onion and garlic and fry gently for 5 minutes or until the onion is soft.

3 Add the lamb, together with the tomato paste and hot pepper, if using. Fry over a moderate heat for about 5 minutes, stirring frequently, then add the stock or water. Cover and simmer for about 30 minutes, until the lamb is tender. Stir in the spinach. Simmer for 8 minutes until the sauce is fairly thick. Serve hot with boiled rice or root vegetables.

Lamb Pilaf

This dish was brought by East Indians to the West Indies.

INGREDIENTS

Serves 4

1 pound stewing lamb
1 tablespoon curry powder
1 onion, chopped
2 garlic cloves, crushed
½ teaspoon dried thyme
½ teaspoon dried oregano
1 fresh or dried chili
2 tablespoons butter or margarine, plus
   more for serving
2½ cups beef or chicken stock or
   coconut milk
1 teaspoon freshly ground black pepper
2 tomatoes, chopped
2 teaspoons sugar
2 tablespoons chopped scallions
1 pound basmati rice
scallion strips, to garnish

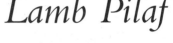

1 Cut the lamb into cubes and place in a shallow glass or china dish. Sprinkle with the curry powder, onion, garlic, herbs and chili and stir well. Cover loosely with plastic wrap and let marinate in a cool place for 1 hour.

2 Melt the butter or margarine in a saucepan and fry the lamb for 5–10 minutes on all sides. Add the stock or coconut milk, bring to a boil, then lower the heat and simmer for 35 minutes or until the meat is tender.

3 Add the black pepper, tomatoes, sugar, scallions and rice, stir well and reduce the heat. Make sure that the rice is covered by 1 inch of liquid and add a little water if necessary. Simmer the pilaf for 25 minutes or until the rice is cooked, then stir a little extra butter or margarine into the rice before serving. Garnish with scallion strips.

Barbecued Jerk Chicken

Jerk refers to the blend of herb and spice seasoning rubbed into meat, before it is roasted over charcoal sprinkled with pimiento berries. In Jamaica, jerk seasoning was originally used only for pork, but jerk chicken is equally good.

INGREDIENTS

Serves 4
8 chicken pieces

For the marinade
1 teaspoon ground allspice
1 teaspoon ground cinnamon
1 teaspoon dried thyme
¼ teaspoon freshly grated nutmeg
2 teaspoons raw sugar
2 garlic cloves, crushed
1 tablespoon finely chopped onion
1 tablespoon chopped scallion
1 tablespoon vinegar
2 tablespoons oil
1 tablespoon lime juice
1 hot chili pepper, chopped
salt and freshly ground black pepper
lettuce leaves, to serve

1 Combine all the marinade ingredients in a small bowl. Using a fork, mash them together well to make a thick paste.

2 Lay the chicken pieces on a plate or board and make several lengthwise slits in the flesh. Rub the seasoning all over the chicken and into the slits.

3 Place the chicken pieces in a dish, cover with plastic wrap and let marinate overnight in the fridge.

4 Shake off any excess seasoning from the chicken. Brush with oil and either place on a baking sheet or on a barbecue grill if barbecuing. Cook under a preheated broiler for 45 minutes, turning often. Or, if barbecuing, light the coals and when ready, cook over the coals for 30 minutes, turning often. Serve hot with lettuce leaves.

--- COOK'S TIP ---

The flavor is best if you marinate the chicken overnight. Sprinkle the charcoal with aromatic herbs such as bay leaves for even more flavor.

Thyme and Lime Chicken

INGREDIENTS

Serves 4

8 chicken thighs
2 tablespoons chopped scallion
1 teaspoon dried or chopped fresh thyme
2 garlic cloves, crushed
juice of 1 lime or lemon
6 tablespoons melted butter
salt and freshly ground black pepper
cooked rice, to serve
lime slices and cilantro sprigs,
   to garnish

1 Put the chicken thighs in an ovenproof dish or on a platter, skin-side down and, using a sharp knife, make a slit, lengthwise along the thigh bone of each thigh. Mix the scallion with a little salt and pepper and press the mixture into the slits.

2 Mix together the thyme, garlic, lime or lemon juice and all but 2 tablespoons of the butter in a small bowl and spoon over each chicken thigh.

3 Spoon the remaining butter over the top. Cover the chicken loosely with plastic wrap and let marinate in a cool place for several hours or overnight in the fridge.

4 Preheat the oven to 375°F. Remove the plastic wrap from the chicken and cover the dish with foil. Bake the chicken for 1 hour, then remove the foil and cook for a few more minutes to brown. Serve hot, with rice and garnish with lime slices and cilantro sprigs.

COOK'S TIP

You may need to use two limes, depending on their size and juiciness. Or, for a less sharp flavor, use lemons instead.

Salmon in Mango and Ginger Sauce

Mango and salmon complement each other, especially with the subtle flavor of tarragon.

INGREDIENTS

Serves 2

2 salmon steaks (about 10 ounces each)
a little lemon juice
1 or 2 garlic cloves, crushed
1 teaspoon dried tarragon, crushed
2 shallots, coarsely chopped
1 tomato, coarsely chopped
1 ripe mango (about 6 ounces of flesh), chopped
⅔ cup fish stock or water
1 tablespoon ginger syrup
2 tablespoons butter
salt and freshly ground black pepper

1 Place the salmon steaks in a shallow dish and season with the lemon juice, garlic, tarragon and salt and pepper. Set aside in the fridge to marinate for at least 1 hour.

2 Meanwhile, place the shallots, tomato and mango in a blender or food processor and blend until smooth. Add the fish stock or water and the ginger syrup, blend again and set aside.

3 Melt the butter in a frying pan and sauté the salmon steaks for about 5 minutes on each side.

4 Add the mango purée, cover and simmer until salmon is cooked.

5 Transfer the salmon to warmed serving plates. Heat the sauce through, adjust the seasoning and pour over the salmon. Serve hot.

Fried Snapper with Avocado

Caribbean fried fish is often eaten with Fried Dumplings or hard-dough bread, and, as in this recipe, is sometimes accompanied by avocado – it makes a delicious light supper or lunch.

INGREDIENTS

Serves 4

1 lemon
4 red snappers, about 8 ounces each, prepared
2 teaspoons spice seasoning
flour, for dusting
oil, for frying
2 avocados and sliced corn-on-the-cob, to serve
chopped fresh parsley and lime slices, to garnish

1 Squeeze the lemon juice both inside and outside the fish and sprinkle them all over with the spice seasoning. Set the fish aside in a shallow dish to marinate in a cool place for a few hours.

2 Lift the fish out of the dish and dust thoroughly with the flour, shaking off the excess.

3 Heat the oil in a nonstick pan over a moderate heat. Add the fish and fry for about 10 minutes on each side until browned and crisp.

4 Halve the avocados, remove the pits and cut in half again. Peel away the skin and cut the avocado flesh into thin strips.

5 Place the fish on warmed serving plates with the avocado and corn slices. Serve hot, garnished with parsley and lime slices.

Fillets of Trout in Wine Sauce with Plantains

Tropical fish would add a distinctive flavor to this dish, but any filleted white fish can be cooked in this way.

INGREDIENTS

Serves 4
4 trout fillets
spice seasoning, for dusting
2 tablespoons butter or margarine
1 or 2 garlic cloves
²/₃ cup white wine
²/₃ cup fish stock
2 teaspoons honey
1–2 tablespoons chopped fresh parsley
1 yellow plantain
salt and freshly ground black pepper
oil, for frying

1 Season the trout fillets with the spice seasoning and marinate for 1 hour.

———— COOK'S TIP ————

Plantains belong to the banana family and can be green, yellow, or brown, depending on ripeness. Unlike bananas, plantains must be cooked. Their subtle flavor works well in spicy dishes.

2 Melt the butter or margarine in a large frying pan and heat gently for 1 minute. Add the fillets and sauté for about 5 minutes, until cooked through, turning carefully once. Transfer to a plate and keep warm.

3 Add the wine, fish stock and honey to the pan, bring to a boil and simmer to reduce slightly. Return the fillets to the pan and spoon over the sauce. Sprinkle with parsley and simmer gently for a few minutes.

4 Meanwhile, peel the plantain, and cut into rounds. Heat a little oil in a frying pan and fry the plantain slices for a few minutes, until golden, turning once. Transfer the fish to serving plates, stir the sauce, adjust the seasoning and pour over the fish. Garnish with the fried plantain.

Ackee and Salt Cod

This is a classic of Jamaican cuisine, popular in the Caribbean, served with boiled green bananas.

INGREDIENTS

Serves 4

1 pound salt cod
2 tablespoons butter or margarine
2 tablespoons vegetable oil
1 onion, chopped
2 garlic cloves, crushed
8 ounces chopped fresh tomatoes
½ hot chili pepper, chopped (optional)
½ teaspoon freshly ground black pepper
½ teaspoon dried thyme
½ teaspoon ground allspice
2 tablespoons chopped scallions
1-pound 6-ounce can ackee, drained
Fried Dumplings, to serve

1 Place the salt cod in a bowl and cover with cold water. Leave it to soak for at least 12 hours, changing the water two or three times. Discard the water and rinse in fresh cold water.

2 Put the salt cod in a large saucepan of cold water, bring to a boil, then remove the fish and allow to cool on a plate. Remove and discard the skin and bones, then flake the fish and set aside.

3 Heat the butter or margarine and oil in a large heavy frying pan over a moderate heat. Add the onion and garlic and sauté for 5 minutes. Add the tomatoes and hot chili pepper, if using, and cook gently for another 5 minutes.

4 Add the salt cod, black pepper, thyme, allspice and scallions, stir to mix, then stir in the ackee, taking care not to crush them. If you prefer a moister dish, add a little water or stock. Serve hot with Fried Dumplings.

Spinach Plantain Rounds

This delectable way of serving plantains is a little fussy to make, but well worth it! The plantains must be ripe, but still firm.

INGREDIENTS

Serves 4
2 large ripe plantains
oil, for frying
2 tablespoons butter or margarine
2 tablespoons finely chopped onion
2 garlic cloves, crushed
1 pound fresh spinach, chopped
pinch of freshly grated nutmeg
1 egg, beaten
whole wheat flour, for dusting
salt and freshly ground black pepper

1 Using a small sharp knife, carefully cut each plantain lengthwise into four slices.

2 Heat a little oil in a large frying pan and fry the plantain slices on both sides until light golden brown but not fully cooked. Drain on paper towels and reserve the oil.

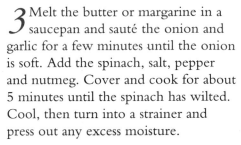

3 Melt the butter or margarine in a saucepan and sauté the onion and garlic for a few minutes until the onion is soft. Add the spinach, salt, pepper and nutmeg. Cover and cook for about 5 minutes until the spinach has wilted. Cool, then turn into a strainer and press out any excess moisture.

4 Curl the plantain slices into rings and secure each ring with half a wooden toothpick. Pack each ring with a little of the spinach mixture.

5 Place the egg and flour in two separate shallow dishes. Add a little more oil to the frying pan if necessary and heat until moderately hot. Dip the plantain rings in the egg and then in the flour and fry on both sides for 1–2 minutes until golden brown. Drain on paper towels and serve hot or cold with a salad, or as part of a dinner.

COOK'S TIP

If fresh spinach is not available, use frozen spinach, thawed and drained. The plantain rings can be small or large, and if preferred ground meat, fish or beans can be used instead of spinach for the filling.

Fried Dumplings

Fried Dumplings or "dumplins" are easy to make and the "sister" to Bakes, as they are also known in the Caribbean and Guyana. They are usually served with salt cod or fried fish, but they can be eaten quite simply with butter and jam or cheese. Children love them!

INGREDIENTS

Makes about 10
4 cups self-rising flour
2 teaspoons sugar
½ teaspoon salt
1¼ cups milk
oil, for frying

1 Sift the dry ingredients together into a large bowl, add the milk and mix and knead until smooth.

2 Divide the dough into ten balls, kneading each ball with floured hands. Press the balls gently to flatten into 3–inch rounds.

3 Heat a little oil in a nonstick frying pan until moderately hot. Place half the dumplings in the pan, reduce the heat to low and fry for about 15 minutes until they are golden brown, turning once.

4 Stand them on their sides for a few minutes to brown the edges, before removing them and draining on paper towels. Serve warm.

Spicy Potato Salad

This tasty salad is quick to prepare, and makes a satisfying accompaniment to grilled or barbecued meat or fish.

INGREDIENTS

Serves 6

2 pounds potatoes, peeled
2 red bell peppers
2 celery stalks
1 shallot
2 or 3 scallions
1 green chili, finely chopped
1 garlic clove, crushed
2 teaspoons finely chopped
    fresh chives
2 teaspoons finely chopped
    fresh basil
1 tablespoon finely chopped fresh
    parsley
1 tablespoon light cream
3 tablespoons mayonnaise
1 teaspoon mild mustard
½ tablespoon sugar
chopped fresh chives, to garnish

1 Boil the potatoes until tender but still firm. Drain and cool, then cut into 1-inch cubes and place in a large salad bowl.

2 Halve the peppers, cut away and discard the core and seeds and cut into small pieces. Finely chop the celery, shallot, and scallions and slice the chili very thinly, discarding the seeds. Add the vegetables to the cubed potatoes together with the garlic and chopped herbs.

3 Blend together the cream, mayonnaise, mustard and sugar in a small bowl, stirring until the mixture is well combined.

4 Pour the dressing over the potato and vegetable salad and stir gently to coat evenly. Serve, garnished with the chopped chives.

Rice and Peas

This very popular dish also known as Peas and Rice on the islands in the Eastern Caribbean is far more interesting and tasty than its name suggests.

INGREDIENTS

Serves 6

6 ounces red kidney beans
2 fresh thyme sprigs
¼ cup coconut cream
2 bay leaves
1 onion, finely chopped
2 garlic cloves, crushed
½ teaspoon ground allspice
4 ounces chopped, red or green bell pepper
2 cups long grain rice
salt and freshly ground black pepper

1 Place the red kidney beans in a large bowl. Cover with water and let soak overnight.

2 Drain the beans, place in a large pan and add enough water to cover the beans by about 1 inch. Bring to a boil and boil over a high heat for 10 minutes, then reduce the heat and simmer for about 1½ hours or until the beans are tender.

3 Add the thyme, coconut cream, bay leaves, onion, garlic, allspice, red or green bell pepper and seasoning and stir in 2½ cups water.

4 Bring to a boil and add the rice. Stir well, reduce the heat and simmer, covered, for 25–30 minutes, until all the liquid is absorbed. Serve as an accompaniment to fish, meat or vegetarian dishes.

Dhal Puri

Otherwise known as roti, these thin fried breads can also be made with white flour. They are delicious served with meat, fish or vegetable dishes.

INGREDIENTS

Makes about 15

4 cups self-rising flour
1 cup whole wheat flour
1½ cups cold water
2 tablespoons oil, plus extra for frying
salt, to taste

For the filling

12 ounces yellow split peas
1 tablespoon ground cumin
2 garlic cloves, crushed

1 Sift together the dry ingredients into a bowl, then add the water a little at a time gradually kneading the mixture to make a soft dough. Knead for a short while until supple.

2 Add the oil to the dough and continue to knead until completely smooth. Put the dough in a plastic bag or wrap in plastic wrap and let stand in a cool place or in the fridge for at least 30 minutes, or overnight.

3 To make the filling, put the peas in a saucepan, cover with water and cook until the peas are half cooked – they should be tender on the outside, but still firm in the middle. Allow the water to evaporate during cooking, until the pan is dry, but watch carefully and add a little extra water to prevent burning, if necessary.

4 Spread the peas out onto a tray to cool, then grind to a paste and mix with the cumin and garlic.

5 Divide the dough into about 15 balls. Slightly flatten each ball of dough, put about 1 tablespoon of mixture into the center and fold over the edges to enclose the mixture.

6 Dust a rolling pin and a board with flour and roll out the dhal puri, taking care not to overstretch, until they are about 7 inches in diameter.

7 Heat a little oil on a tawa (roti pan) or in a heavy or cast-iron frying pan, swirling the oil to cover the base. Cook the dhal puris for about 3 minutes on each side, until light brown. Fold them into a clean dish towel, to keep warm. Serve warm.

Fried Yellow Plantains

When plantains are yellow, they are ripe and ready to enhance most meat, fish or vegetarian dishes. The riper the plantain, the darker and sweeter they are.

INGREDIENTS

Serves 4
2 yellow plantains
oil, for shallow frying
finely chopped chives, to garnish

1 Using a small sharp knife, remove the ends of the plantains, and cut in half.

2 Slit the skin only, along the natural ridges of each plantain.

3 Ease up the edge of the skin and run the tip of your thumb along the plantains, lifting the skin.

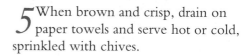

5 When brown and crisp, drain on paper towels and serve hot or cold, sprinkled with chives.

4 Peel away the skin and slice the plantains lengthwise. Heat a little oil in a large frying pan and fry the plantain slices for 2–3 minutes on each side until golden brown.

Buttered Spinach and Rice

The spinach, usually mixed in with the rice but once forgotten, was then added as a topping and became a favorite.

Ingredients

Serves 4

3 tablespoons butter or margarine
1 onion, finely chopped
2 fresh tomatoes, chopped
1 pound basmati rice, washed
2 garlic cloves, crushed
2½ cups stock or water
12 ounces fresh spinach, shredded
salt and freshly ground black pepper
2 tomatoes, sliced, to garnish

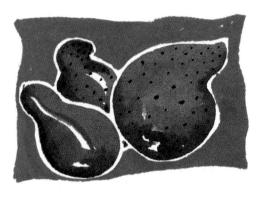

1 Melt 2 tablespoons of the butter or margarine in a large heavy saucepan and fry the onion for a few minutes until soft. Add the chopped tomatoes and stir well.

2 Add the rice and garlic, cook for 5 minutes, then gradually add the stock, stirring all the time. Season well.

3 Cover and simmer gently for 10–15 minutes or until the rice is almost cooked, then reduce the heat to low.

4 Spread the spinach in a thick layer over the rice. Cover the pan and cook over a low heat for 5–8 minutes until the spinach has wilted. Dot the remaining butter over the top and then serve, garnished with sliced tomatoes.

--- Cook's Tip ---

If fresh spinach is not available, you can use frozen leaf spinach instead. Thaw and drain 8 ounces frozen spinach and cook as in the recipe for about 3–5 minutes. Finely shredded collard greens can also be used.

Mashed Sweet Potatoes

White sweet potatoes are best for this recipe, rather than orange sweet potatoes. White yams make a good substitute, especially poona (Ghanaian) yam.

Ingredients

Serves 4

2 pounds sweet potatoes
4 tablespoons butter
3 tablespoons light cream
freshly grated nutmeg
1 tablespoon chopped fresh chives
salt and freshly ground black pepper

1 Peel the sweet potatoes under cold running water and place in a bowl of salted water. Cut or slice them and place in a large saucepan and cover with cold water. Cook, covered for about 30 minutes.

2 When the potatoes are cooked, drain and add the butter, cream, nutmeg, chives and seasoning. Mash with a potato masher and then fluff up with a fork. Serve warm as an accompaniment to a curry or stew.

Bread and Butter Custard

This dessert is a delicious family favorite. A richer version can be made with fresh cream instead of evaporated milk. It can also be made using other dried fruit – mango is particularly good.

INGREDIENTS

Serves 4
1 tablespoon softened butter
3 thin slices of bread, crusts removed
14-ounce can evaporated milk
²/₃ cup fresh milk
½ teaspoon ground cinnamon
3 tablespoons raw sugar
2 eggs, whisked
½ cup golden raisins
freshly grated nutmeg
a little confectioner's sugar, for dusting

1 Preheat the oven to 350°F and lightly butter an ovenproof dish. Butter the bread and cut into small pieces.

2 Lay the buttered bread in several layers in the prepared dish.

3 Whisk together the evaporated milk and the fresh milk, mixed spice, sugar and eggs in a large bowl. Pour the mixture over the bread and butter. Sprinkle over the raisins and let stand for 30 minutes.

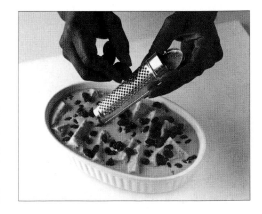

4 Grate a little nutmeg over the top and bake for 30–40 minutes until the custard is just set and golden. Serve sprinkled with confectioner's sugar.

Duckanoo

This tasty pudding originated in west Africa.

INGREDIENTS

Serves 4–6

1 pound/3 cups fine cornmeal
12 ounces fresh coconut, chopped
2½ cups fresh milk
¾ cup raisins
4 tablespoons butter or margarine, melted
½ cup raw sugar
4 tablespoons water
¼ teaspoon freshly grated nutmeg
½ teaspoon ground cinnamon
1 teaspoon vanilla extract

1 Place the cornmeal in a large bowl. Blend the coconut and the milk in a blender or food processor until smooth. Stir the coconut mixture into the cornmeal, then add all the remaining ingredients and stir well.

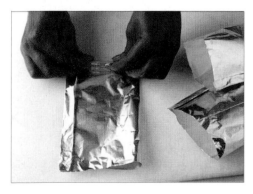

2 Take six pieces of foil and fold into 5- x 6-inch pockets leaving an opening on one short side. Fold the edges of the remaining sides tightly to make sure that they are well sealed.

3 Put one or two spoonfuls of the mixture into each pocket and fold over the edge of the foil to seal.

4 Place the foil pockets in a large saucepan of boiling water. Cover and simmer for about 45–60 minutes. Lift out the pockets from the water and remove the foil. Serve the duckanoo by themselves or with fresh cream.

Fruits of the Tropics Salad

INGREDIENTS

Serves 4–6

1 medium pineapple
14-ounce can guava halves in syrup
2 medium bananas, sliced
1 large mango, peeled, pitted and diced
4 ounces preserved ginger and
  2 tablespoons of the syrup
4 tablespoons thick coconut milk
2 teaspoons sugar
½ teaspoon freshly grated nutmeg
½ teaspoon ground cinnamon
strips of coconut, to decorate

1 Peel, core and cube the pineapple, and place in a serving bowl. Drain the guavas, reserve the syrup and chop. Add the guavas to the bowl with one of the bananas and the mango.

2 Chop the preserved ginger and add to the pineapple mixture.

3 Pour 2 tablespoons of the ginger syrup, and the reserved guava syrup into a blender or food processor and add the other banana, the coconut milk and the sugar. Blend to make a smooth creamy purée.

4 Pour the banana and coconut mixture over the fruit, add a little grated nutmeg and a sprinkling of cinnamon. Serve chilled, decorated with strips of coconut.

Avocado Salad in Ginger and Orange Sauce

This is an unusual fruit salad since avocado is more often treated as a vegetable. However, in the Caribbean it is used as a fruit, which of course it is!

INGREDIENTS

Serves 4
2 firm ripe avocados
3 firm ripe bananas, chopped
12 fresh cherries or strawberries
juice of 1 large orange
shredded fresh ginger root (optional)

For the ginger syrup
2 ounces fresh ginger root, chopped
3³/4 cups water
1 cup raw sugar
2 cloves

1 First make the ginger syrup; place the ginger, water, sugar and cloves in a saucepan and bring to a boil. Reduce the heat and simmer for about 1 hour, until well reduced and syrupy.

2 Remove the ginger and discard and set aside to cool. Store in a covered container in the fridge.

3 Peel the avocados, cut into cubes and place in a bowl with the bananas and cherries or strawberries.

4 Pour the orange juice over the fruits. Add 4 tablespoons of the ginger syrup and mix gently, using a metal spoon. Chill for 30 minutes and add a little shredded ginger, if using.

MEXICO

Tlalpeño-style Soup

For a hearty version of this simple soup, add some cooked chick-peas or rice.

INGREDIENTS

Serves 6
6 cups chicken stock
2 cooked chicken breasts, boned,
  skinned and cut into large strips
1 drained canned *chipotle* or
  jalapeño pepper, rinsed
1 avocado

> ——— COOK'S TIP ———
>
> When using canned chilies, it is important to rinse them very thoroughly before adding them to the pan, to remove the flavor of any pickling liquid.

1 Heat the stock in a large saucepan and add the chicken and chili. Simmer over very low heat for 5 minutes to heat the chicken and release the flavor from the chili.

2 Cut the avocado in half, remove the pit and peel off the skin. Slice the avocado flesh neatly.

3 Remove the chili from the stock, using a slotted spoon, and then discard it. Pour the soup into heated serving bowls, distributing the chicken evenly among them.

4 Carefully add a few avocado slices to each bowl and serve.

Avocado Soup

INGREDIENTS

Serves 4
2 large ripe avocados
4 cups chicken stock
1 cup light cream
salt and freshly ground white pepper
1 tablespoon finely chopped cilantro,
  to garnish (optional)

> ——— COOK'S TIP ———
>
> The easiest way to mash the avocados is to hold each seeded half in the palm of one hand and mash the flesh in the shell with a fork, before scooping it into the bowl. This keeps the avocado from slipping around when it is being mashed.

1 Cut the avocados in half, remove the pits and mash the flesh (see Cook's Tip). Put the flesh into a sieve and, using a wooden spoon, press it through into a warm soup bowl.

2 Heat the chicken stock with the cream in a saucepan. When the mixture is hot, but not boiling, whisk it into the puréed avocado.

3 Season to taste with salt and pepper. Serve immediately, sprinkled with the cilantro, if using. The soup may be served chilled, if desired.

Mixed Tostadas

Like little edible plates, these golden crisp-fried tortillas can support any toppings that are not too juicy.

INGREDIENTS

Makes 14
oil, for shallow frying
14 freshly prepared unbaked
   corn tortillas
1 cup mashed red kidney or pinto
   beans
1 head iceberg lettuce, shredded
oil and vinegar dressing (optional)
2 cooked chicken breasts, skinned and
   thinly sliced
1 cup Guacamole (see Index)
1 cup coarsely grated Cheddar cheese
pickled *jalapeño* peppers, seeded and
   sliced, to taste

1 Heat the oil in a frying pan and fry the tortillas until golden brown on both sides and crisp but not hard.

2 Spread each tortilla with a layer of beans. Put a layer of shredded lettuce (which can be left plain or lightly tossed with a little dressing) over the beans.

3 Arrange pieces of chicken in a layer on top of the lettuce. Carefully spread over a layer of the guacamole and finally sprinkle over a layer of the grated cheese.

4 Arrange the mixed tostadas on a large platter. Serve on individual plates, but eat using your hands.

Quesadillas

These delicious filled and deep-fried tortilla turnovers make a popular snack, and smaller versions make excellent canapés.

INGREDIENTS

Makes 14
14 freshly prepared tortillas

For the filling
1 cup finely chopped or grated
   Cheddar cheese
3 *jalapeño* peppers, seeded and cut
   into strips
oil, for frying
salt

1 Have the tortillas ready, covered with a clean cloth. Combine the grated cheese and chili strips in a bowl. Season with salt. Set aside.

2 Heat the oil in a frying pan. Then, holding an unbaked tortilla on your palm, put a spoonful of filling along the center, avoiding the edges.

> ——— COOK'S TIP ———
>
> For other stuffings, try leftover beans with chilies or chopped chorizo sausage fried with a little chopped onion.

3 Fold the tortilla and seal the edges by pressing or crimping together. Fry in hot oil, on both sides, until golden brown and crisp.

4 Using a spatula, lift out the quesadilla and drain it on paper towels. Transfer to a plate and keep warm while frying the remaining quesadillas. Serve hot.

Chimichangas

INGREDIENTS

Makes 14
½ quantity Picadillo
14 freshly prepared unbaked
   flour tortillas
oil, for frying
whole radishes with leaves, to garnish

COOK'S TIP

Chimichangas originally came from the state of Sonora and are made with the large plate-sized tortillas that are a speciality of the region. Any size that suits the cook will do just as well.

1 Spoon 4 tablespoons of Picadillo down the center of each tortilla. Fold in the sides, then the top and bottom, envelope-fashion, or simply roll up and secure with a toothpick.

2 Pour the corn oil into a frying pan to a depth of about 1 inch. Set the pan over medium heat. Fry the chimichangas, a few at a time, for 1–2 minutes, or until golden.

3 Drain on paper towels and keep warm. Serve the chimichangas garnished with whole radishes.

Tacos

The taco, a Mexican sandwich, makes a great quick snack. All you need is a supply of tortillas or taco shells, and a selection of fillings. See the Index for recipes.

INGREDIENTS

Makes as many as you like
freshly prepared corn tortillas or
   prepared taco shells

For the fillings
Picadillo topped with Guacamole
chopped chorizo fried and mixed with
   chopped Cheddar cheese and chilies
Frijoles Refritos with sliced *jalapeño*
   peppers, Guacamole, and cubed
   cheese
leftover Mole Poblano de Guajolote
   with Guacamole
cooked shredded pork or chicken with
   salsa and shredded lettuce

1 To make tacos, all you need is a supply of fresh corn tortillas, and as many of the suggested fillings as you can muster. The idea is to use your imagination, and cooks often vie with one another to see who can produce the most interesting combination of flavors. Chilies and guacamole are always welcome, in the taco or served as an extra on the side.

2 To make traditional soft tacos, simply spoon the filling onto the tortilla, wrap the tortilla around the filling – and eat.

3 To make hard tacos, secure the rolled up and filled tortilla with a toothpick, then briefly fry until crisp and golden.

4 Prepared U-shaped taco shells are not Mexican, but make a very fast version of this snack. Hold one taco shell at a time in one hand, and fill with the fillings of your choice.

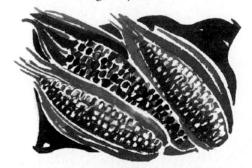

Tortilla Flutes

Flutes, or *flautas,* look as good as they taste.

INGREDIENTS

Makes about 12
24 freshly prepared unbaked
  flour tortillas
2 tomatoes, peeled, seeded
  and chopped
1 small onion, chopped
1 garlic clove, chopped
2–3 tablespoons corn oil
2 freshly cooked chicken breasts,
  skinned and shredded
salt

To garnish
sliced radishes
stuffed green olives

1 Place the unbaked flour tortillas in pairs on a work surface, with the right-hand tortilla overlapping its partner by about 2 inches.

2 Put the tomatoes, onion, and garlic into a food processor and process to a purée. Season with salt to taste.

3 Heat 1 tablespoon of the oil in a frying pan and cook the tomato purée for a few minutes, stirring to blend the flavors. Remove from the heat and stir in the shredded chicken, mixing well.

4 Spread about 2 tablespoons of the chicken mixture on each pair of tortillas, roll them up into flutes and secure with a toothpick.

5 Heat a little oil in a frying pan large enough to hold the flutes comfortably. Cook more than one at a time if possible, but don't overcrowd the pan. Fry the flutes until light brown all over. Add more oil if needed.

6 Drain the cooked flutes on paper towels and keep hot. When ready to serve, transfer to a platter and garnish with radishes and olives.

COOK'S TIP

If the flour tortillas are too hard to roll up easily, fry them for just a few seconds in hot oil, then quickly stuff and roll tnem.

Chilaquiles

INGREDIENTS

Serves 4

corn or peanut oil, for frying
6 leftover corn tortillas, cut or torn into
  ¹/₂-inch strips
10-ounce can tomatillos (Mexican
  green tomatoes)
1 onion, finely chopped
2–3 drained canned *jalapeño* peppers,
  rinsed, seeded and chopped
2 tablespoons chopped fresh cilantro
1 cup grated Cheddar cheese
³/₄ cup chicken stock
salt and freshly ground black pepper

To garnish
chopped scallion
stuffed green olives
chopped cilantro

1 Heat 3 tablespoons of the oil in a large frying pan. Fry the tortilla strips, a few at a time, on both sides, without browning. Add more oil if needed. Drain on paper towels.

2 Place the tomatillos and juice in a food processor. Add the onion, *jalapeños* and cilantro; purée.

3 Season the tomatillo purée with salt and pepper. Heat 1 tablespoon oil in the clean frying pan, add the tomatillo mixture and cook gently for 2–3 minutes, stirring frequently.

4 Pour a layer of the sauce into the bottom of a flameproof casserole or shallow baking dish and top with a layer of tortilla strips and a layer of grated cheese. Continue until all the ingredients have been used, reserving some cheese for sprinkling on top.

5 Pour the chicken stock over the dish and sprinkle with the reserved cheese. If using a flameproof casserole, cover and cook over medium heat until all the liquid has been absorbed and the chilaquiles are heated through. Or bake the chilaquiles, uncovered, in a preheated 350°F oven for 30 minutes, or until heated through.

6 Serve directly from the casserole, garnished with chopped scallions, olives and cilantro.

Seviche

This makes an excellent appetizer. With the addition of sliced avocado, it could make a light summer lunch for four.

INGREDIENTS

Serves 6
1 pound mackerel fillets, cut into
   ½-inch pieces
1½ cups freshly squeezed lime or
   lemon juice
8 ounces tomatoes, chopped
1 small onion, very finely chopped
2 drained canned *jalapeño* peppers or
   4 *serrano* chilies, rinsed and chopped
4 tablespoons olive oil
½ teaspoon dried oregano
2 tablespoons chopped fresh cilantro
salt and freshly ground black pepper
lemon wedges and fresh cilantro,
   to garnish
stuffed olives, to serve

1 Put the fish into a glass dish and top with the lime juice, making sure that the fish is completely covered. Cover and chill for 6 hours, turning once. The fish will be opaque, "cooked" by the juice.

--- COOK'S TIP ---

For a more delicately flavored Seviche, use a white fish such as sole.

2 When the fish is opaque, lift it out of the juice and set it aside.

3 Combine the tomatoes, onion, peppers or chilies, olive oil, oregano and cilantro in a bowl. Add salt and pepper to taste, then pour in the reserved juice from the mackerel. Mix well and pour over the fish.

4 Cover the dish and return the seviche to the fridge for about an hour to allow the flavors to blend. Seviche should not be served too cold. Allow it to stand at room temperature for 15 minutes before serving. Garnish with lemon wedges and cilantro sprigs, and serve with stuffed olives sprinkled with chopped cilantro.

Red Snapper, Veracruz-style

This is Mexico's best-known fish dish. In Veracruz, red snapper is always used but fillets of any firm-fleshed white fish can be substituted successfully.

INGREDIENTS

Serves 4

4 large red snapper fillets
2 tablespoons freshly squeezed lime or lemon juice
½ cup olive oil
1 onion, finely chopped
2 garlic cloves, chopped
1½ pounds tomatoes, peeled and chopped
1 bay leaf, plus a few sprigs for garnish
¼ teaspoon dried oregano
2 tablespoons large capers, plus extra to serve (optional)
16 pitted green olives, halved
2 drained canned *jalapeño* peppers, seeded and cut into strips
butter, for frying
3 slices firm white bread, cut into triangles
salt and freshly ground black pepper

1 Arrange the fish fillets in a single layer in a shallow dish. Season with salt and pepper, drizzle with the lime juice and set aside.

2 Heat the oil in a large frying pan and sauté the onion and garlic until the onion is soft. Add the tomatoes and cook for about 10 minutes until the mixture is thick and flavorful. Stir the mixture from time to time.

3 Stir in the bay leaf, oregano, capers, olives and chilies. Add the fish and cook over very low heat for about 10 minutes or until tender.

COOK'S TIP

This dish can also be made with a whole red snapper, weighing about 3–3½ pounds. Bake together with the sauce, in a preheated oven at 325°F. Allow 10 minutes cooking time for every 1 inch of the fish's thickness .

4 While the fish is cooking, heat the butter in a small frying pan and sauté the bread triangles until they are golden brown on both sides.

5 Transfer the fish to a heated platter, pour over the sauce and surround with the fried bread triangles. Garnish with bay leaves and serve with extra capers, if you like.

Striped Bass in Sauce

This is a typical Mayan dish.

INGREDIENTS

Serves 6

3–3½ pounds striped bass or any non-
    oily white fish, cut into 6 steaks
½ cup corn oil
1 large onion, thinly sliced
2 garlic cloves, chopped
12 ounces tomatoes, sliced
2 drained canned *jalapeño* peppers,
    rinsed and sliced
flat-leaf parsley, to garnish

For the marinade

4 garlic cloves, crushed
1 teaspoon black peppercorns
1 teaspoon dried oregano
½ teaspoon ground cumin
1 teaspoon ground *achiote* (annatto)
½ teaspoon ground cinnamon
½ cup mild white vinegar
salt

1 Arrange the fish steaks in a single
layer in a shallow dish. Make the
marinade. Using a pestle, grind the
garlic and black peppercorns in a
mortar. Add the dried oregano, cumin,
achiote (annatto) and cinnamon and mix
to a paste with the vinegar. Add salt to
taste and spread the marinade on both
sides of each of the fish steaks. Cover
and let sit in a cool place for 1 hour.

2 Select a flameproof dish large
enough to hold the fish in a single
layer, and pour in enough of the oil to
coat the bottom. Arrange the fish in
the dish with any remaining marinade.

3 Top the fish with the onion, garlic,
tomatoes and chilies and pour the
rest of the oil over the top.

4 Cover the dish and cook over low
heat on top of the stove for 15–20
minutes, or until the fish is no longer
translucent. Serve at once garnished
with flat leaf parsley.

Salt Cod in Mild Chili Sauce

INGREDIENTS

Serves 6
2 pounds dried salt cod
1 onion, chopped
2 garlic cloves, chopped
1 fresh green chili, sliced, to garnish

For the sauce
6 dried *ancho* chilies
1 onion, chopped
½ teaspoon dried oregano
½ teaspoon ground coriander
1 *serrano* chili, seeded and chopped
3 tablespoons corn oil
3 cups fish or chicken stock
salt

--- COOK'S TIP ---

Dried salt cod is a great favorite in Spain and Portugal and throughout Latin America. Look for it in Spanish and Portuguese markets.

1 Soak the cod in cold water for several hours, depending on how hard and salty it is. Change the water once or twice during soaking.

2 Drain the fish and transfer it to a saucepan. Pour in water to cover. Bring to a gentle simmer and cook for about 15 minutes, until the fish is tender. Drain, reserving the stock. Remove any skin or bones from the fish and cut it into 1½-inch pieces.

3 Make the sauce. Remove the stems and shake out the seeds from the *ancho* chilies. Tear the pods into pieces, put in a bowl of warm water and soak until they are soft.

4 Drain the soaked chilies and put them into a food processor with the onion, oregano, coriander and *serrano* chili. Process to a purée.

5 Heat the oil in a frying pan and cook the purée, stirring, for about 5 minutes. Stir in the fish or chicken stock and simmer for 3–4 minutes.

6 Add the prepared cod and simmer for a few minutes longer to heat the fish through and blend the flavors. Serve garnished with the sliced chili.

Crab with Green Rice

INGREDIENTS

Serves 4

225g/8oz/1 cup long grain rice
60ml/4 tbsp olive oil
2 x 275g/10oz cans tomatillos
  (Mexican green tomatoes)
1 onion, chopped
2 garlic cloves, chopped
30ml/2 tbsp chopped fresh coriander
about 350ml/12fl oz/1½ cups
  chicken stock
450g/1lb crab meat, thawed if frozen,
  broken into chunks
salt
chopped fresh coriander, to garnish
lettuce leaves, to serve

1 Soak the rice in enough hot water to cover for 15 minutes, then drain thoroughly. Heat the oil in a frying pan and sauté the rice over a moderate heat, stirring until the rice is golden and the oil has been absorbed.

2 Drain the tomatillos, reserving the juice, and put them into a food processor. Add the onion, garlic and coriander, and process to a purée. Pour into a measuring jug and add the tomatillo juice. Pour in enough stock to make the quantity up to 475ml/ 16fl oz/2 cups. Season to taste.

3 Place the rice, tomato mixture and crab meat in a shallow pan. Cover and cook over a very low heat for about 30 minutes or until the liquid has been absorbed and the rice is tender. Serve on lettuce leaves, garnished with chopped fresh coriander.

COOK'S TIP

Mexican cooks always soak rice in water before cooking it. This seems to pay off, as their rice is always delicious, with every grain separate.

Prawns with Pumpkin Seed Sauce

INGREDIENTS

Serves 4

175g/6oz/1 generous cup *pepitas*
  (Mexican pumpkin seeds)
450g/1lb raw prawns, thawed if frozen,
  peeled and deveined
1 onion, chopped
1 garlic clove, chopped
30ml/2 tbsp chopped fresh coriander
225g/8oz tomatoes, peeled
  and chopped
1 drained canned *jalapeño* chilli, rinsed,
  seeded and chopped
1 red pepper, seeded and chopped
30ml/2 tbsp corn oil
salt
whole cooked prawns, lemon slices and
  fresh coriander sprigs, to garnish
rice, to serve

1 Grind the pumpkin seeds finely and shake through a sieve into a bowl and set to one side.

2 Cook the prawns in boiling salted water. As soon as they turn pink, remove with a slotted spoon and set them aside. Reserve the cooking water.

3 Purée the onion, garlic, coriander, tomatoes, chilli, red pepper and pumpkin seeds in a food processor. Heat the oil in a pan, stir and cook the mixture for 5 minutes. Season. Add prawn water to thin the mixture to a sauce consistency. Heat gently, add the prawns. Garnish and serve with rice.

Smoked Beef Tongue with Tomatillos

Tomatillos have a delicious, distinctive flavor and color.

INGREDIENTS

Serves 6 – 8

1 smoked beef tongue, about 5 pounds
3 tablespoons corn oil
2 onions, finely chopped
2 garlic cloves, chopped
3 or 4 drained pickled *serrano* or *jalapeño* peppers, seeded and chopped
2 tablespoons chopped fresh cilantro
2 x 10-ounce cans tomatillos (Mexican green tomatoes)
salt and freshly ground pepper
fresh cilantro, to garnish
small new potatoes, to serve

1 Thoroughly wash the tongue and put it into a large saucepan. Cover with cold water and bring to a boil. Remove any scum that rises to the surface. Lower the heat and simmer, covered, for 3 – 4 hours, until tender. Allow the tongue to cool in the stock.

2 Lift out the tongue when it is cool enough to handle, reserving the stock. Peel the skin from the tongue and trim the root end and discard. Cut the tongue into fairly thick slices and place these in a flameproof casserole.

3 Heat the oil in a large frying pan and sauté the onions and garlic with the chilies until the onion is tender. Add the cilantro, the tomatillos (with the can juices) and salt and pepper to taste. Stir to mix and pour over the tongue, adding a little reserved stock if the mixture is thick.

4 Cover the pan with foil or a lid and cook over a moderate heat for about 15 minutes, until hot. Serve at once, garnished with cilantro sprigs and accompanied by new potatoes sprinkled with chopped cilantro.

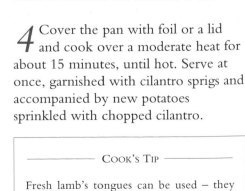

COOK'S TIP

Fresh lamb's tongues can be used – they only need to be cooked for 45 – 60 minutes.

Pork with Pineapple

INGREDIENTS

Serves 6

2 tablespoons corn oil
2 pounds boneless pork shoulder
  or loin, cut into 2-inch cubes
1 onion, finely chopped
1 large red bell pepper, seeded
  and finely chopped
1 or more *jalapeño* peppers, seeded and
  finely chopped
1 pound fresh pineapple chunks
8 fresh mint leaves, chopped
1 cup chicken stock
salt and freshly ground black pepper
fresh mint sprig, to garnish
rice, to serve

1 Heat the oil in a large frying pan
and sauté the pork cubes in batches
until lightly browned. Transfer the
pork to a flameproof casserole, leaving
the oil behind in the pan.

2 Add the onion, red pepper and the
jalapeño to the oil remaining in the
pan. Sauté until the onion is tender,
then add to the casserole with the
pineapple. Stir to combine.

3 Add the mint, then cover and
simmer gently for about 2 hours,
or until the pork is tender. Garnish
with fresh mint and serve with rice.

COOK'S TIP

If fresh pineapple is not available, use
pineapple canned in its own juice.

Veal in Nut Sauce

INGREDIENTS

Serves 6

3 – 3½ pounds boneless veal, cut into 2-inch cubes
2 onions, finely chopped
1 garlic clove, crushed
½ teaspoon dried thyme
½ teaspoon dried oregano
1½ cups chicken stock
¾ cup very finely ground almonds, pecans or peanuts
¾ cup sour cream
fresh oregano, to garnish
rice, to serve

COOK'S TIP

Choose domestically raised red veal if you can. It is naturally raised and widely thought to have the best flavor.

1 Put the cubes of veal, finely chopped onions, crushed garlic, thyme, oregano and chicken stock into a large flameproof casserole. Bring to a gentle boil. Cover tightly and simmer over low heat for about 2 hours or until the veal is cooked and tender.

2 Put the ground nuts in a food processor. Add ½ cup of the veal sauce and process for a few seconds until smooth. Press through a sieve into the casserole.

3 Stir in the sour cream and heat through gently, without boiling. Serve at once with rice, if desired.

Picadillo

Serve as a main dish with rice, or use to stuff peppers or fill tacos.

INGREDIENTS

Serves 6

2 tablespoons olive or corn oil
2 pounds ground beef
1 onion, finely chopped
2 garlic cloves, chopped
2 apples
1 pound tomatoes, peeled, seeded and chopped
2 or 3 drained pickled *jalapeño* peppers, seeded and chopped
scant ½ cup raisins
¼ teaspoon ground cinnamon
¼ teaspoon ground cumin
salt and freshly ground black pepper
tortilla chips, to serve

To garnish
1 tablespoon butter
¼ cup slivered almonds

1 Heat the oil in a large frying pan, add the beef, onion and garlic and fry, stirring occasionally, until the beef is brown and the onion is tender.

2 Peel, core and chop the apples. Add them to the pan with all the remaining ingredients, except the almonds. Cook, uncovered, for 20 – 25 minutes, stirring occasionally.

3 Just before serving, make the garnish by melting the butter in a small frying pan and sautéing the almonds until golden brown. Serve the Picadillo topped with the almonds and accompanied by the tortilla chips.

Mole Poblano de Guajolote

Mole Poblano de Guajolote is *the* great festive dish of Mexico. It is served at any special occasion, be it a birthday, wedding, or family get-together. Rice, beans, tortillas and guacamole are the traditional accompaniments.

INGREDIENTS

Serves 6–8

6–8 pounds turkey, cut into
  serving pieces
1 onion, chopped
1 garlic clove, chopped
salt
6 tablespoons lard or corn oil
fresh cilantro and 2 tablespoons toasted
  sesame seeds, to garnish

For the sauce

6 dried *ancho* chilies
4 dried *pasilla* chilies
4 dried *mulato* chilies
1 drained canned *chipotle* chili, seeded
  and chopped (optional)
2 onions, chopped
2 garlic cloves, chopped
1 pound tomatoes, peeled
  and chopped
1 stale tortilla, torn into pieces
⅓ cup raisins
1 cup ground almonds
3 tablespoons sesame seeds, ground
½ tsp coriander seeds, ground
1 teaspoon ground cinnamon
½ teaspoon ground anise
¼ teaspoon ground black peppercorns
4 tablespoons lard or corn oil
1½ ounces unsweetened chocolate,
  broken into squares
1 tablespoon sugar
salt and freshly ground pepper

— COOK'S TIP —

Roasting the dried chilies lightly, taking care not to burn them, brings out the flavor and is worth the extra effort.

---

1 Put the turkey pieces into a saucepan or flameproof casserole large enough to hold them in one layer comfortably. Add the onion and garlic, and enough cold water to cover. Season with salt, bring to a gentle simmer, cover and cook for about 1 hour or until the turkey is tender.

2 Meanwhile, put the *ancho, pasilla* and *mulato* chilies in a dry frying pan over gentle heat and roast them for a few minutes, shaking the pan frequently. Remove the stems and shake out the seeds. Tear the pods into pieces and put these into a small bowl. Add sufficient warm water to just cover and soak, turning from time to time, for 30 minutes, or until soft.

3 Lift out the turkey pieces and pat dry with paper towels. Reserve the stock in a measuring jug. Heat the lard in a large heavy frying pan and sauté the turkey pieces until lightly browned all over. Transfer to a plate and set aside. Reserve any oil left in the frying pan.

4 Transfer the chilies, along with the water in which they have been soaked, into a food processor. Add the *chipotle* chili, if using, with the onions, garlic, tomatoes, tortilla, raisins, ground almonds and spices. Process to a purée. Do this in batches, if necessary.

5 Add the lard to the fat remaining in the frying pan used for sautéing the turkey. Heat the mixture, then add the chili and spice paste. Cook, stirring, for 5 minutes.

6 Transfer the mixture to the pan or casserole in which the turkey was originally cooked. Stir in 2 cups of the turkey stock (make up the difference with water if necessary). Add the chocolate and season with salt and pepper. Cook over low heat until the chocolate has melted. Stir in the sugar. Add the turkey and more stock if needed. Cover the pan and simmer very gently for 30 minutes. Serve, garnished with fresh cilantro and sprinkled with the sesame seeds.

Frijoles

INGREDIENTS

Serves 6−8

1¼−1½ cups dried red kidney, pinto or black beans, rinsed and picked over

2 onions, finely chopped

2 garlic cloves, chopped

1 bay leaf

1 or more *serrano* chilies (small fresh hot green chilies)

2 tablespoons corn oil

2 tomatoes, peeled, seeded and chopped

salt

sprigs of fresh bay leaves, to garnish

— COOK'S TIP —

In the Yucatán, black haricot beans are cooked with the Mexican herb *epazote*.

---

1 Put the beans into a pan and add cold water to cover by 1 inch.

2 Add half the onion, half the garlic, the bay leaf and the chili(es). Bring to a boil and boil vigorously for about 10 minutes. Put the beans and liquid into a large saucepan, cover and cook over low heat for 30 minutes. Add boiling water if the beans start to become dry.

3 When the beans begin to wrinkle, add 1 tablespoon of the corn oil and cook for another 30 minutes or until the beans are tender. Add salt to taste and cook for 30 minutes more, but do not add any more water.

4 Remove the beans from the heat. Heat the remaining oil in a small frying pan and sauté the remaining onion and garlic until the onion is soft. Add the tomatoes and cook for a few minutes more.

5 Spoon 3 tablespoons of the beans out of the pot or pan and add them to the tomato mixture. Mash to a paste. Stir this into the beans to thicken the liquid. Cook for just long enough to heat through, if necessary. Serve the beans in small bowls and garnish with sprigs of fresh bay leaves.

Peppers Stuffed with Beans

Stuffed peppers are a popular Mexican dish. A special version – *Chiles en Nogada* – is served every year on August 28 to celebrate Independence Day. The green peppers are served with a sauce of fresh walnuts and a garnish of pomegranate seeds to represent the colors of the Mexican flag.

INGREDIENTS

Serves 6
6 large green bell peppers
1 recipe Frijoles Refritos (Refried Beans)
2 eggs, separated
½ teaspoon salt
corn oil, for frying
all-purpose flour, for dusting
½ cup whipping cream
1 cup grated Cheddar cheese
fresh cilantro sprigs, to garnish

1 Roast the peppers over a gas flame or under the broiler, turning occasionally, until the skins have blackened and blistered. Transfer the peppers to a plastic bag, secure the top and let sit for 15 minutes.

2 Preheat the oven to 350°F. Remove the peppers from the bag. Hold each pepper in turn under cold running water and gently rub off the skins. Slit the peppers down one side and remove the seeds and ribs, taking care not to break the pepper shells. Stuff with the Refried Beans.

3 Beat the egg whites in a large bowl until they stand in firm peaks. In another bowl, beat the yolks lightly together with the salt. Fold the yolks gently into the whites.

4 Pour the corn oil into a large frying pan to a depth of about 1 inch and heat. Spread out the flour in a shallow bowl or dish.

5 Dip the filled peppers in the flour and then in the egg mixture. Fry in batches in the hot oil until golden brown all over. Arrange the peppers in an ovenproof dish. Pour on the cream and sprinkle with the cheese. Bake in the oven for 30 minutes or until the topping is golden brown and the peppers are heated through. Serve at once, garnished with cilantro.

Chopped Zucchini

Calabacitas is an extremely easy recipe to make. If the cooking time seems unduly long, this is because the acid present in the tomatoes slows down the cooking of the zucchini. Use young tender zucchini.

INGREDIENTS

Serves 4
2 tablespoons corn oil
1 pound young zucchini, sliced
1 onion, finely chopped
2 garlic cloves, chopped
1 pound tomatoes, peeled, seeded and chopped
2 drained canned *jalapeño* peppers, rinsed, seeded and chopped
1 tablespoon chopped fresh cilantro
salt
fresh cilantro, to garnish

1 Heat the oil in a flameproof casserole and add all the remaining ingredients, except the salt.

2 Bring to simmering point, cover and cook over low heat for about 30 minutes until the zucchini are tender, checking from time to time that the dish is not drying out. If it is, add a little tomato juice, stock or water.

3 Season with salt and serve the Mexican way as a separate course. Alternatively, serve accompanied by any plainly cooked meat or poultry. Garnish with cilantro.

Refried Beans (Frijoles Refritos)

There is much disagreement about the translation of the term *refrito*. It means, literally, twice fried. Some cooks say this implies that the beans must be really well fried, others that it means twice cooked. However named, *Frijoles Refritos* are delicious.

INGREDIENTS

Serves 6–8
6–8 tablespoons lard or corn oil
1 onion, finely chopped
1 recipe Frijoles (cooked beans)

To garnish
freshly grated Parmesan cheese or crumbled farmer cheese
crisp-fried corn tortillas, cut into quarters

1 Heat 2 tablespoons of the lard in a large heavy frying pan and sauté the onion until it is soft and starting to turn translucent. Add about 1 cup of the Frijoles (cooked beans).

--- COOK'S TIP ---

Lard is the traditional (and best-tasting) fat for the beans, but many people prefer to use corn oil. Avoid using olive oil, which is too strongly flavored and distinctive.

2 Mash the beans with the back of a wooden spoon or potato masher, adding more beans and melted lard or oil until all the ingredients are used up and the beans have formed a heavy paste. Use extra lard if necessary.

3 Transfer to a warmed platter, piling the mixture up in a roll. Garnish with the cheese. Spike with the tortilla triangles, placing them at intervals along the length of the roll. Serve as a side dish.

Pumpkin in Brown Sugar

INGREDIENTS

Serves 4

2 pounds pumpkin,
   cut into wedges
2 cups dark brown sugar
½ cup water

1 Scrape the seeds out of the pumpkin wedges. Pack the wedges firmly together in a heavy flameproof casserole.

2 Divide the sugar among the pumpkin pieces, packing it into the hollows that contained the seeds.

3 Pour the water carefully into the the casserole to cover the bottom and prevent the pumpkin from burning. Take care not to dislodge the sugar when pouring in the water.

— COOK'S TIP —

The best pumpkin for this recipe is the classic orange-fleshed variety used for jack-o'-lanterns. Choose one that will fit neatly into your casserole when cut.

4 Cover and cook over low heat, checking the water level frequently, until the pumpkin is tender and the sugar has dissolved in the liquid to form a sauce.

5 Using a slotted spoon, transfer the pumpkin to a serving dish. Pour the sugary liquid from the pan over the pumpkin and serve at once with plain yogurt, sweetened with a little brown sugar, if desired.

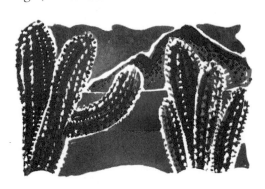

Buñuelos

INGREDIENTS

Serves 6
2 cups all-purpose flour
1 teaspoon baking powder
½ teaspoon salt
1 tablespoon granulated sugar
1 large egg, beaten
½ cup milk
2 tablespoons unsalted butter,
  melted
oil, for frying
granulated sugar, for dusting

For the syrup
1⅓ cups light brown sugar
3 cups water
1-inch cinnamon stick
1 clove

1 Make the syrup. Combine all the ingredients in a saucepan. Heat, stirring, until the sugar has dissolved, then simmer until the mixture is reduced to a light syrup. Remove and discard the spices. Keep the syrup warm while you make the *buñuelos*.

2 Sift the flour, baking powder and salt into a bowl. Stir in the sugar. In a mixing bowl, whisk the egg and the milk well together. Gradually stir in the dry mixture, then beat in the melted butter to make a soft dough.

3 Turn the dough onto a lightly floured board and knead until it is smooth and elastic. Divide the dough into 18 even-size pieces. Shape into balls. With your hands, flatten the balls to disks about 2 inches thick.

4 Use the floured handle of a wooden spoon to poke a hole through the center of each *buñuelo*. Pour oil into a deep frying pan to a depth of 2 inches. Alternatively, use a deep-fryer. Heat the oil to 375°F, or until a cube of day-old bread added to the oil browns in 30–60 seconds.

5 Fry the fritters in batches, taking care not to overcrowd the pan, until they are puffy and golden brown on both sides. Lift out with a slotted spoon and drain on paper towels.

6 Dust the *buñuelos* with sugar and serve with the syrup.

COOK'S TIP

Make the syrup ahead of time if you prefer, and chill it until ready to use, when it can be warmed through quickly.

Churros

INGREDIENTS

Makes about 24

1 cup water
1 tablespoon granulated sugar,
   plus extra for dusting
½ teaspoon salt
1½ cups all-purpose flour
1 large egg
½ lime or lemon
oil for frying

— COOK'S TIP —

You can use a funnel to shape the churros.
Close the end with a finger, add the batter,
then release into the oil in small columns.

1 Bring the water, sugar and salt to a
boil. Remove from the heat and
beat in the flour until smooth.

2 Beat in the egg, using a wooden
spoon, until the mixture is smooth
and satiny. Set the batter aside.

3 Pour the oil into a deep-frying pan
to a depth of about 2 inches. Add
the lime half, then heat the oil to
375°F. Test the oil by dropping in a
cube of day-old bread; it should brown
in 30–60 seconds.

4 Pour the batter into a pastry bag
fitted with a fluted nozzle. Pipe
3-inch strips of batter and add to the
oil, a few at a time. Fry for 3–4
minutes, or until golden brown.

5 Using a slotted spoon, remove the
churros from the pan and drain on
paper towels. Roll the hot churros in
granulated sugar before serving.

Sopaipillas

INGREDIENTS

Makes about 30

2 cups all-purpose flour, sifted
1 tablespoon baking powder
1 teaspoon salt
2 tablespoons lard or margarine
¾ cup water
corn oil, for deep frying
syrup or honey, to serve

— COOK'S TIP —

Use your imagination when deciding what
to serve with the puffs. Sprinkle them with
cinnamon and sugar, or syrup flavored with
rum. The fat little pillows could even be
served plain, as they taste delicious.

---

1 Put the flour, baking powder and
salt into a large bowl. Lightly rub
in the lard or margarine, using your
fingertips, until the mixture resembles
coarse breadcrumbs.

2 Gradually stir in the water, using a
fork, until the mixture clumps
together to form a soft dough.

3 Shape the dough into a ball, then
turn out onto a lightly floured
surface and knead very gently until
smooth. Roll out thinly to a rectangle
measuring about 15 x 18 inches. Using
a sharp knife, carefully cut into about
thirty 3-inch squares. For a decorative
edge, you could use a pastry wheel to
cut out the squares.

4 Heat the oil to 375°F, or until a
cube of day-old bread browns in
30–60 seconds.

5 Fry the puffs, a few at a time, in
the oil. As they brown and puff
up, turn over to cook the other side.
Remove with a slotted spoon and drain
on paper towels. It is important that
the temperature of the oil remains
constant during the cooking process.
Serve warm, with syrup or any sauce
of your choice.

Index

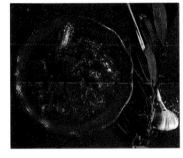

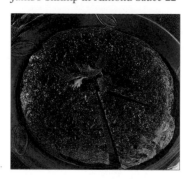